AUTUMNS

OF OUR JOY

AUTUMNS
OF OUR JOY

A MEMOIR OF ROMANCE, STEM CELLS, AND REBIRTH

For Ruth
Whose courage
and loving guidance
helped us and many
others through difficult
and frightening times—

Judith K. White 9/20/2015

JUDITH K. WHITE
WITH ALLEN L. WHITE

J. L. White

Thank you Ruth!

JUDITH K. WHITE
BROOKLINE, MASSACHUSETTS

To order: Amazon.com, createspace eStore
http:www.createspace.com/5544972 (soft cover)
http://www.amazon.com/dp/B0125RC242 (e-book)
Or contact: judithklinewhite@gmail.com

ISBN 978-1-514-239377
Typeface Minion Pro
Printed by Create Space

DEDICATION

To the medical professionals who dedicate their lives to researching and treating cancer and to loved ones we have lost to the disease: Yale White, Thomas Towler Kline, Christopher Kline, Alexander Kline, Hollis Kline, Carrie Levenson-Wahl, Dr. Paul Epstein

Part I

Life Together
1966–1998

OCTOBER 1966
My Favorite Day

If you meet someone in a bar, how long does it take to discover that you care about the same things? That you want to live your life according to a certain set of values? That you might share those values? Too long, I figured. I avoided bars. If you meet someone at a party? Perhaps less time. If you're introduced by a mutual friend? That time might shrink somewhat. But the setting in which I met Allen White for the first time told me a great deal about our mutually shared values before we ever exchanged a word.

October 1966. The idealistic sixties in full force. In an abandoned two-bedroom, Washington D.C., inner-city basement apartment, four people were earnestly scraping away at a stove that was caked with layer upon layer of blackened, burned food and fat. One person was dedicated to a single burner. Another to the stove top. Another to an oven rack. The last, with her hair pulled back tight from her face, was buried up to her shoulders in the oven itself, her right hand clutching a Brillo pad, vigorously moving in and out, up and down, back and forth. Another group was in the bathroom. I didn't stick around there long enough to see what horrors those brave folks were attacking.

I noticed the floor of a sort of living room was littered with crunchy little turds—from mice or rats, I couldn't say. I had been tutoring one of the nine children of the family destined to move into this apartment within a few days. I knew the place needed work, but I had never encountered such filth and decay.

After the organizer stuck a broom in my hand and I had made a few tentative sweeps, a young man stepped into the room. Tall, slender, dark hair, brown eyes magnified by thick glasses. He stood. Looked the situation over. Said nothing. Showed no emotion. At least he didn't turn and run, as I was tempted to do when I arrived. Whereas many of the volunteers were in their thirties and forties, this guy looked like an undergrad. Still holding that broom, I smiled at him and asked in my chirpy Midwestern way, "Are you with the G.W. group?"

He looked down at me, stared with something resembling disdain and finally answered, "Yeh." Not the most charming guy perhaps, but there he was on a cold autumn Sunday afternoon. He too had showed up in order to make this place livable for a destitute family with nine children. That was enough to intrigue me.

ROMANCE AMONG THE ROACHES. The leader set up the young man with paint and a roller and we became a two-person team. I swept a wall from top to bottom, leaving a narrow vertical column temporarily roach-free. My silent companion rolled on the paint quickly while the roaches climbed rapidly back up again. Some of the determined bugs made it back up to the top of the wall. Others became mired in the white, sticky stuff. Once that vertical section was cleared, we moved on to the next.

After five minutes, a wall beginning to gleam and at least some of the roaches drowned, we started to chat. Yes, he was a George Washington University student—a junior. He had transferred to G.W. after a year at Clark University in Worcester, Massachusetts—his hometown. He was majoring in geography. He was also interested in politics and liked living in this political city.

Of course, as I learned later, he had first impressions of me too. He thought the plum-colored imitation suede jeans I was wearing were ridiculous. Did he think I would wear my high school prom dress to this event for heaven's sake? For some odd reason, he had me pegged as a student at Montgomery Maryland Junior College. But no, I had graduated from Oberlin College the previous year and moved to Washington, D.C. almost immediately. A French major, I was working as a bi-lingual secretary at the World Bank —in the Law Department for a French Swiss lawyer, Jean-David Roulet, who was under my strict orders to speak nothing but his native language with me. Except for a few months when I was an infant and my father was stationed at Fort Leonard Wood in Missouri, and nine weeks with a college summer program in France, this was the first time I had lived outside of my home state—Ohio.

I had gone out with one of the volunteers a couple of times. Although at 38 Julian seemed ancient to me and I wasn't interested in dating him, before Al arrived I had accepted Julian's offer of a ride home. When Julian overheard Al ask if *he* could take me home after the cleanup, I glanced at Julian who graciously, unforgettably, momentously, nodded and bowed out. I climbed into what I later learned was Al's first car, purchased with his *Bar Mitzvah* money— his green 1963 four-door clunky Chevrolet sedan.

Badly in need of a turpentine wash-up, we headed for Dupont Circle and parked. As we approached People's Drugstore on foot, I experienced a brief but clear certainty that I would be walking beside this young man for many years in many countries and settings. I wondered, if that came true, would I continue to feel as if I were floating three inches off the ground?

I adored the first-floor, two-room apartment I shared with my roommate, Alice, in a brownstone tucked in between 21st and Florida Streets, just north of Dupont Circle. One of my happiest memories is the aroma of cinnamon toast—baked slowly in the oven my first morning there—and the strong association of that smell with my sense of independence, of no longer being a student, of having become a working woman with her own kitchen. My half of the rent was $75 a month.

Alice and I had arranged a dining area facing a large window overlooking the street. As Al and I approached the front door, I pointed out the window's oval shape—unique on that street. "For future reference," I hinted none too subtly.

After a few minutes of conversation, Al made a show of propping up one foot with its worn, dirty clodhopper right on my coffee table. He seemed to be doing so in a defiant way, as if he were saying without words, "I've got huge feet. Impressive aren't they? And if they're too big for you, too bad. Repulsed by their filth, clean little Ohio gal? Well, that's too bad too." I felt compelled to comment and asked about their size. Then came another vision: me tripping over loafers, boots, slippers, and sneakers for the rest of my life—all size 14.

After an hour of getting to know each other, Al spontaneously burst out with a suggestion. "Let's go into the Peace Corps together." It was something I had always thought about doing, but I knew I wouldn't do it alone. Peace Corps would be the perfect crossroads of all the mutual interests we had quickly discovered—travel, culture, languages, service. With remarkably little hesitation to a life-changing offer from someone I had known for barely three hours, I said, "Yes."

What came next appeared to contradict what had seemed to be a spontaneous and genuine Peace Corps invitation. Al said somewhat mysteriously that he had to leave because, he implied, a dinner date awaited.

As Al was walking out the door, he turned and asked me, "How do you spell Klein?" When I told him—K.L.I.N.E.—there was that blank non-reaction I'd already seen several times that afternoon, those long moments when he said nothing. Then came his dramatic final words of the day, "Well, that ends that." It was the first example of a long pattern of relating with one step forward and two steps (with those huge feet) backwards, a tempo that would take two years to undo. Later I learned that dinner was at the home of an aunt and uncle. No date, at least not of the usual sort, as he apparently was hoping I would assume.

AL'S IMPRESSIONS OF THAT DAY:

A woman of great delicacy and femininity who captured my interest. I also thought, 'This is not a woman from my part of the world. She's not from the Northeast. She may be from the Midwest.' I was impressed by her readiness to chat, her friendliness, and a smile that would instantly become etched in my psyche and, soon, in my heart. That she was there on a project of that nature was an instant bond. Other people in the room seemed more like the kind of people who would do social projects, whereas Judith looked as if she had to go out and buy used jeans in order to be appropriately dressed for this grubby occasion. She had class, not in the rich and fancy sense, but in the sense of intelligence, dedication, and quiet passion.

Our first date was shopping for turpentine. An unusual first encounter for a relationship that has lasted forty-six years. People's Drug Store. Kind of fun. All these decades later, a drugstore remains on the corner. Sweet, charming, adorable apartment conveniently, I thought, within walking distance from where I live. We talked about the Peace Corps. How about Afghanistan? I thought it was the most exotic place I could suggest. I was also testing her knowledge of geography. She knew of Afghanistan, but I doubt she could have found it quickly on a map.

I left feeling I wanted to see her again. I was continually impressed throughout that day with how womanly she was—how finely contoured—with her sweet smile and her funny, decidedly un-Semitic nose.

NOVEMBER 1966–NOVEMBER 1968
Together, Apart–Apart, Together

The following week we had our first date. At the end of my workday, I watched as Al approached the entrance to the World Bank. He looked anxious and tense and he was chewing on his tongue. Whereas I had been wearing those unsightly jeans when we met, I was now wearing a skirt—a fashionably short one. Much later Al told me that he took one look at my legs that evening and decided he could definitely live with them for the rest of his life.

We went out for dinner. Unlike later dinners which were more contentious, this one was polite and smooth. Standing in the hallway outside my apartment door, Al asked if he could kiss me good night.

Although his tall, dark, nerdy looks appealed to me greatly, what I felt for Al after this second meeting was not a powerful, irresistible attraction. It was a near certainty that we were meant to be together. I wanted to protect both of us, though. I didn't want to become overwhelmed. I didn't want to rush the physical. I was looking for emotional connection and intellectual engagement. I knew how quickly affection could escalate. I wanted to keep physical intimacy at bay for now. So, to that question—"May I kiss you good night?"—I prudishly answered, "Let's wait 'til next time."

We explored the city together. Al was my escort to the World Bank's Christmas ball. We attended live concerts at the Phillips Collection nearby, walked among the hills above my apartment, admired the mansions, watched movies at the Janus Theater. We also enjoyed outings together with lively, fun, Greg, the 10-year-old Al was tutoring. Sharing a parenting role, albeit for a short period, led to discussions of offspring. We agreed that if we ever raised children together, we would adopt some, including transracially. We both wanted a son like Greg. Such talk after a short time? Was this moving too fast? Was I idealizing this still infant relationship? I didn't think so. It felt natural to me.

I had always been "Judy" or "Jutz" to my immediate family. Very early in our relationship, Al insisted on calling me by my baptized name—Judith. He thought Judy sounded flighty whereas Judith projected dignity and uniqueness. He also liked its Old Testament connection. It seemed prematurely possessive to insist that other people make the switch, but I agreed with him. Judith sounded more befitting for the mature wife and mother I hoped to become. It was difficult for some of my friends to make the change, but both Al and I corrected them if they forgot. Now the only people who call me Judy are my high school friends, and even some of them have "gotten with the program."

We continued to enjoy dinners together. I loved cooking for Al and exploring inexpensive restaurants with him. However, the tension created by our mutual attraction and the twin challenges of a three-year age difference plus Al's concerns about our relationship hurting his father sometimes literally spilled over into our good times.

One evening I was so irritated with a since forgotten alienating comment Al had just made that I picked up an entire pitcher of ice water and emptied it upside down on our café table. Other times, I wouldn't even realize that he had found something I'd said obnoxious until I looked across the table and saw him dribbling apple sauce out his mouth and down his chin or discovered he was spitting peas at me. Such adolescent behavior was a reminder of how much growing-up lay ahead for my young love. Perhaps for me too.

WHEELS. Al borrowed a motorcycle and took me on a trip through Rock Creek Park. It was exhilarating feeling the swish of air, seeing the city from that vantage point. It occurred to me how vulnerable we were, but I didn't care. I was experiencing heaven on earth with my arms around him, my face against his back. In full romantic mode, I thought that if we died that day, at least we'd die together. It was, however, the last time I ever rode a motorcycle. Possibly in connection with that experience and that line of thinking, it occurred to me that if he were injured and confined to a wheelchair for the rest of his life, I would happily push him around. Forty-four years would go by before I did see him in a wheelchair and I was not the one pushing it. That was the responsibility of a hospital attendant.

As we confirmed our shared values and interests, our emotional connection slowly proceeded. During his exam week, he said he couldn't see me. He needed to study. Instead he called every night—sometimes, I later learned, as he sat in the dark with Johnny Mathis singing romantic tunes in the background. With no other distractions, especially from each other's physical presence and just words to rely on, we deepened our connection in ways that somehow had not been possible face-to-face. I thought, "If I ever marry this guy, I'll install phones on either side of the bed, so we can communicate."

A major breakthrough emerged when Al shared something painful from his past. He told me that he had either quit or been dismissed from three low-paying jobs—all of them the previous summer on Martha's Vineyard—an island he loved off the coast of Massachusetts. I could see how difficult it was for him to say it. It upset him to remember and to talk about it, but it seemed important to him to share it. It felt like a confession and perhaps also a test.

I had a sense he might be feeling, 'Will you still be interested in me after I tell you this story of a hapless employee who failed at three menial jobs?' On the contrary, I felt flattered and encouraged that he trusted me enough to share something so personal and embarrassing. It never occurred to me to regard that unsuccessful summer as a pattern I should be wary of. And with reason— every job he's held in the four decades since that troubled summer has been one success after another.

SPRINGFIELD, OHIO. AL MEETS THE FOLKS. When I was eight, my parents searched for an available plot on which to build a home. When they found a space on Old Mill Road with a narrow patch of land that ended at a high drop-off, my mother said, "Design us a house here. On this cliff." This request/ demand would produce one of the most treasured aspects of my teenage years and beyond—living in a house designed by my architect father, an apostle of Frank Lloyd Wright.

Two years later, with my mother pregnant with their fifth child (and first boy) and with the school year beginning soon, we moved into our new house where an exposed cliff ran along the entire length of the vaulted-ceilinged living room. Continuing the drama, three glass walls brought a natural envelope to the entire structure, a kind of tree-house with views of the forest, and a gorge and a gurgling stream our constant companions. Outdoors, we loved swinging out from the cliff tops over the brook on U-shaped grapevines.

The word had spread quickly. Rumors abounded: "Have you heard about that house that has a tree growing in it?" (Not true. The house surrounded a courtyard with a tree, but the tree was outside.) "Let's go see that house with the waterfall." (OK, that was getting close to the truth. My dad laid a thin pipe with holes at the top of the cliff wall. He controlled the flow of water that trickled down the cliff by turning on a switch. The drops ended in an interior pond.) I sometimes woke up to find people peeking into the as yet curtainless structure. One Sunday a neighbor counted 300 staring strangers wandering about the property. The front door was locked, but people reached into the vertical, not-yet-enclosed window space next to the door, turned the door handle from the inside, and walked in, their families in tow. My dad had to shoo them out.

I had told Al about the house, but it's difficult to imagine. I warned my family that they should be prepared. He would walk in, I told them, and say absolutely nothing for five minutes. That's exactly what he did. We all just sat quietly while he looked around and out the windows, absorbing a home the likes of which he (and for that matter, most everybody else) had never beheld. Its artistry and experimentalism challenged his self-image as the more sophisticated in our still young relationship.

AL ON FIRST VISIT TO MY FAMILY HOME:
I was misbelieving. Totally eye opening. One and only time I felt less experienced, less sophisticated than Judith. I guess because she was from Ohio and I was from Massachusetts, I felt vastly superior to her. The house was complex and so original. I had never been exposed to anything like it.

WORCESTER, MASSACHUSETTS. MY TURN TO MEET THE PARENTS. Al's father sent word that I should choose a restaurant where the four of us could meet for dinner for the first time. Because Yale was fluent in French, having studied clarinet in his teens at the Conservatory of Paris, I chose a French restaurant. I hoped that our mutual love of the language and perhaps the chance to speak it with waiters and each other might be a bond. The dinner went well, I thought, and I enjoyed both of Al's parents.

All the Worcester neighbors and relatives knew that Al had a girlfriend. There was only one non-Jewish family living on Wamsutta Avenue where Al grew up—a large Catholic family, the Toomeys. When the neighbors asked what I, the girlfriend, looked like, Al's mother, Sarah, answered, "A Toomey." She also said I was "plain." Although my looks may have required some adjust-

ment for this couple, just as they did for Al initially (that pug nose), I really
don't think she meant "plain" in the sense of "homely." I prefer to think she was
describing my Midwestern down-to-earthness, my lack of airs, my scant use of
makeup and jewelry.

In any case, when I first visited Worcester a month later, Al took me to meet
all the neighbors, aunts, and uncles. Sarah was one of eight children. I loved
feeling Al was sharing me and showing me off. After the "Toomey" and "plain"
comments, expectations were quite low, apparently. It was mid-winter. I wore
a wrap-around gold wool coat with a fox-fur collar that extended all the way
down the front. As every neighbor opened the door to welcome us, I heard
the same refrain spoken in a surprised tone and heavy Worcester ("Wuhsta")
accent: "Why yuh budifah." Translation: "Why, you're BEAUTIFUL!"

However, after five months the relationship was moving too slowly for me.
I began dating just before my thirteenth birthday and had been in several long-
term relationships. I was then twenty-three. Al, at twenty, had had girlfriends,
but none serious. His closed, secretive, sometimes sarcastic nature was wearing on me. I announced that I had accepted a job offer in Canada at Expo '67,
the World's Fair, and would be away from D.C. for seven months.

I left for Montreal knowing I would miss him, but fearing that if I stayed in
D.C., his youthfulness and inexperience combined with my impatience would
push us into a permanent breakup. I wanted our story to be lifelong—and
shared. I urged him to socialize, to date other women while I was away—in
other words, to grow up. But this was not to be. Instead he took a summer job
in Canada too, in the remote Northwest Country, at an isolated base camp and
nearby glacier in the St. Elias Mountains. His title was Research Meteorologist.
A team of about fifteen researchers populated the glacier in rotating shifts. He
didn't seem interested in any of the four female researchers.

At the beginning of the summer, before his cross-Canada bus trip to the
Yukon, Al visited me in Montreal. We had often visited museums in Washington, D.C. While we shared a love of fine art, we also shared the pain of several
emotional breakups followed by relieved tenuous reunions in the company
of some of the world's great artists. While we were visiting the Expo '67 art
museum, I wandered ahead, apparently too far for Al's taste. When he caught
up to me, he gave me this stern order: "NEVER leave my side in a museum." I
found that to be an amusing command from a young man whose claim on my
love and commitment was, at best, tenuous. People are attracted to different
art works, wanting to linger over some and dismiss others. I doubted that even
the most long-term couple moved in sync from one work of art to another. But

I did like the implication of that remark. It seemed to me (or was I just looking for clues?) that it implied a long-term relationship during which we would visit museums in many places for many years to come.

I can't recall when Al first shared his black-bound journal with me, but it is still in our possession forty-six years later. There are some loose pages that chronicle the transcontinental trip that began in Washington, D.C., crossed the Midwest, North Dakota, and Saskatchewan and, finally, traversed the pack-gravel Alaska Highway through British Columbia into the Yukon Territory. The first official entry is dated July 4, 1967, two days after Al's twenty-first birthday:

DIVIDE CAMP:

I'm not sure what gave me the inspiration to begin writing today. I suppose two wonderful letters from Judith. The incredible thing about writing like this is that in fact I am writing partially for myself and partially for Judith. What I say is what I feel, but what I feel is inseparably entwined with what Judith wants me to feel. Knowing Judith will read these thoughts enhances their value to me.

July 4 and this is the day of independence. Well, I certainly feel in step with the festivities. Each step outside is a new journey into independence for me. Free and clear and rejuvenated is how I feel. Untouchable. If there were a war of the nuclear variety, I feel I would be the last to die. Maybe I would never die. I'd be the one to begin things again. Yes . . .

I ask—do I sound twenty-one? Since meeting Judith, there has been in me a strong drive to act and sound at least that age. This is new for me. I'm not used to acting. I don't like it. The worry of this nonsense is that the very times I most actively endeavor to appear older, I act most immaturely. To act is to not accept oneself, to strive for what one is not, and to ignore what one is.

I thought today of these husbands leaving their wives for the summer. And I considered my apartness from my loved one. What does this mean? I will be apart now and not in the years to come? Or will I always require solitude for at least a short period of time? I would say the former. Much of the solitude during my life has been not of my own choosing. And aloneness is especially difficult to imagine when one has found the joy of being together. Oh for Chrissake, I love Judith's company. C'est tout.

I enjoy the feeling of being so damn far away from everyone. I still have not adjusted to my attraction, GW, Worcester, the world's problems; and, in a rather different sense, Judith seems so distant. But I'm enjoying it and have no regrets about coming here.

JULY 7, 1967

Oh God, at this moment—2:20 a.m.—do I miss Judith. I miss the vitality she instills in me, the feeling of total, productive functioning that I feel when I'm with her. Reading Schlesinger, with his fluent writing technique, sends me into a kind of fluent thought (words, where art thou?) movement. And when, I ask, do I think most fluently? With Judith and with myself. My God! If some day I unite the two, what a clear and wonderful mind I will have.

The time is not far off when a decision must be made. The situation is of the uncompromising type. It will hurt, miserably hurt, Father. But how miserably will it hurt me? If I can establish the degree of the latter, my conscience will lead me. I really do foresee a showdown. I'm upset and worried. I shiver with love for Judith and shiver at the thought of crushing Dad . . . and then there is one-third plus of the world starving. Jesus. Jesus, Jesus.

JULY 10, 1967

Schlesinger is magnificent. We are probably reading the same pages—no, she is ahead. But the same book and that is a good feeling. 2:30 a.m. at 8,600 feet. What the hell am I doing here? Is life one moment of lonesomeness after another? Does it only stop when all else stops? What will my life be like? I have lived less than one-third of it (hopefully). In the next years, what will be my calling? Will I, can I, be happy with her for, say fifty years? Fifty years? Fifty years. Fifty years. To write such a figure on paper enhances its significance. Will our petty feuds continue to be petty? Will I be proud to say, "This is my wife"? Will we be content? Talking to Betty recently I said, "I am seriously thinking of getting married."

Each day at 4:30 a.m. I shiver with desire for her. Her idiotic "escape" at the art museum. My constant feeling of, as she so precisely put it, rightness when I'm near her, or completeness, or functioning at peak performance (sounds like a good line for an ad)—love, but not complete commitment or sureness.

JULY 28, 1967: 2:30 A.M.

It's been quite a while. All my energies have been devoted to Judith. She must have a collection of my thoughts that rivals these notes in frankness. But there is just that extra bit which I have not revealed. Does one tell one's love every thought, every emotion? Is it best to do so? I have my doubts. I think that withholding can nurse a relationship. Complete exposure can ruin it. Yes, I think that is correct. The physical aspect continues to haunt me. Is it overly physical? 75 percent of my thoughts are in that realm.

WEDNESDAY, AUGUST 16, 1967

I'm dying to see Judith. Can I believe I feel so in love after seeing this young lady only six days out of four months? What does it mean? Do I want her always, so this is what this endurance signifies? Or is it a matter of love because of no real chance to explore others? Whatever it is, I feel I have become more serious about marriage. I have seen before the kind of marriage I don't want. Hasn't this summer been useful if not in an academic respect? I knew it would be. Solitude is a thought stimulant.

SATURDAY, AUGUST 26, 1967

You know, book, several times these past few days I've wanted to write, but the hectic pace has prohibited it. Here I sit on the ship Malaspina, gazing at the forested islands as we proceed through the Alaskan Inland Passage. It's been rainy as I had envisioned, and hoped.

So how do I feel about my past two months and my next ten days? The summer has been the most unusual, most informative, I've ever spent. A different place and different people evoke new feelings. New feelings helped me understand myself. The explanations often hurt badly, particularly when they arrive suddenly. The slower kind, the gradual enlightenment, is easier to absorb.

How do I feel about Montreal? Frankly, and as usual, my excitement wanes as the time nears. Why? Because at these times I again look at my situation especially closely. What I have experienced during this time apart sheds a new and not always bright light onto our relationship.

There was no phone on the glacier. In order to place a call, Al had to fly to a base camp twenty-five minutes from the glacier by ski plane. The group was dependent on that same plane to bring food and mail. Once he wrote that, because of weather conditions, the plane had not been able to land on the glacier. Food was getting scarce and he could barely look at another can of spam. Then no letters for a month. I was getting frantic, worrying that he might be starving, abandoned, maybe freezing to death. Finally, six letters arrived all at once. Later, he assured me he was speaking in general terms. Yes the weather had prevented the plane from landing, but there was never any danger of exhausting the food supply. Spam, at least, was always at the ready.

Two photos from that period encapsulate our different lives that summer, separated by 3,000 miles within Canadian territory. I'm at the center of a party, dressed up in a white wool shift that hits above my knees, my hair coiffed, holding a paper cup containing Grand Marnier. Some of my fellow Expo '67 hostesses mingle about. A fellow who probably worked for the U.S. Information Agency that organized the U.S. exhibits is there. Another guy, seated, was among the U.S. Marines who were assigned to work in the pavilion as a reward for service in Vietnam. Cosmopolitan Montreal was alive, full of visitors to Expo '67, twenty-somethings, parties, and nightclubs. My job as a hostess was pretty easy except when people who had waited in line for long periods became impatient and pushed through. I enjoyed using my French. I shared an apartment in the inner suburb of Westmount with four young women. At the nearby public library, I relished choosing my own reading material without the tyranny of required college reading.

Contrast this to Al's daily activities. In base camp, communicating with the fellow researchers on the glacier to ensure the meteorological research proceeded on track. Exploring the shores of Lake Kluane while meeting the eccentrics who lived nearby. On the glacier, regularly checking weather stations and recording data for the research project. Entertaining occasional hikers, mostly from Europe, who would appear as specks on the horizon and gradually come to life as they approached the camp after trudging through the wilderness as part of the Canadian centennial celebration. And short exploratory walks to nearby mountains, roped to colleagues as security against a misstep that could land one at the bottom of a deep crevice hidden to the eye by a blanket of snow.

ENGAGED. "Engaged" was probably a stretch. No down-on-the-knees proposal. No ring. No real "I love you. I'll love you forever. Will you marry me?" One evening after we had both returned from Canada to Washington, D.C., and were again seeing each other regularly, we were having dinner in a café with Al's favorite professor, Mory, and his wife, Virginia. We were seated in a booth side by side. Once Al laughed and I watched as crow's feet appeared in the outside corners of his eyes, then totally disappeared when he stopped laughing. Suddenly, I knew for certain that I would know him when the taut young skin was gone, when he was so old that those wrinkles would be deep and permanent. It was a certainty that comforted me decades later after the assault of dysfunctional cells threatened his life. By then he did have wrinkles elsewhere, but the eye area remained smooth. I kept checking.

That same early April evening in 1968, Al spoke the "M" word. We would apply to the Peace Corps as an engaged couple, get married in late June after his graduation, and enter the Peace Corps together as soon as we had an assignment. This was exactly what we had talked about the very first day we met. It seemed so right to me and I was cautiously thrilled. The next day he left to spend spring vacation in Worcester and give his family the news.

I understood that telling his father would be difficult, that the possibility of hurting his father by marrying a *shiksa* had been part of his hesitancy all along. Not hearing from him all week made me nervous, doubly so because two days into his vacation, on April 4, just after 6:00 p.m., The Rev. Dr. Martin Luther King, Jr. was shot and killed in Memphis. Dr. King had been the speaker at my Oberlin College graduation in 1965. His topic was "Sleeping Through a Revolution." The speech attracted intense media coverage. Earlier, Al and I had responded separately to King's message. His words were part of the inspiration for our volunteering in the tutoring program—for showing up to fix up that apartment the day we met.

At the time of the King assassination, I had been working for seven months as a social worker in the Children's Department of Washington, D.C. Public Welfare. On April 5 at 1 p.m., the supervisors ran through the building yelling for everyone to stop working and leave immediately. "They're coming to burn down the Welfare Department," they told us. "Go home. Go home now."

As I drove through the African-American neighborhood on my way back to prosperous Georgetown where I shared a house with four other young women, I saw fire and smoke everywhere. After I had waited at a gas station in a line several blocks long, the attendant said rather menacingly, "What's everyone filling up for? To escape? Or so the cars will burn better?"

I considered leaving the city to stay with my former roommate, Alice, who was by then married with a child and living in a D.C. suburb. But I decided to remain in the city even though it seemed to be hurtling toward a massive racial confrontation. Every sound, every step on the front porch was unnerving. I didn't hear a word from Al.

AL DECADES LATER ON WHY HE DIDN'T CONTACT ME FROM WORCESTER THAT WEEK:

I was far enough away from the violence that I didn't realize how dire the situation in Washington was. I was also focused on delivering the news of our marriage decision to my parents and preoccupied by their possible reaction.

Later, in April 1968, with our Peace Corps applications submitted and Al preparing for his final undergraduate exams, we visited my home in Ohio. We applied for a marriage license and had blood tests. With our diverse backgrounds, we found it hysterical that we had to affirm in writing that we were not first cousins. Al defiantly called me "Sis" in front of the officials.

But who would marry us? What would our ceremony be like? We met with a rabbi who refused to conduct the ceremony unless I converted. Converted to what exactly? Al's family belonged to that large cohort of culturally-root-ed, secular Jews, deeply conscious of their lineage but, at most, casual participants in the religious life of their community. Al had no expectations of my "converting."

We considered asking my parents' pastor, but Al was fearful that his dad could not bear to see his son married by a Protestant minister. We settled on a Justice of the Peace with a simple ceremony in my home. Then it was MY father's turn to be horrified. He was a PK—a preacher's kid. Both his grandfather and his father were Congregational ministers. To prepare for the christening of my third sister, my mother sewed for all four of her daughters red dresses with pinafore sleeves and matching bonnets. The six of us piled into the station wagon and drove from Ohio to Nebraska so that Granddaddy could continue the tradition of personally baptizing each of his grandchildren.

Christmas was a huge ritualized event in our house, with presents made or purchased way in advance, carefully wrapped, opened one at a time and oohed and aahed over. It took hours. Every Easter my three sisters and I dressed up in new dresses and shiny patent-leather shoes. My two little brothers in suits and ties. Before church, before Easter-egg hunts and treats, we walked one by one down the stairs as Dad filmed us, beginning with me, the eldest of the six. There was no sound. Just our smiling faces as we each mouthed in turn the cheerful phrase, "Happy Easter!" My parents knew how in love with Al I was. They accepted my choice. But NOT the wedding plans. "I pronounce you man and wife in the name of the . . . the what? The damn state?" Dad protested. "Not in MY house."

I was not happy with such a secular beginning to my marriage either. By now (forty-six years later) I've attended dozens of beautiful Jewish weddings. Had I known, I would have wanted to incorporate some of the rituals into our ceremony. We could have stood under a *chuppah*. We could have danced the *horah*. But Al never mentioned these centuries-long customs. I'm not sure how much he even knew about them.

We met with my parents' minister who graciously agreed not to mention the words "Jesus" or "Christ" during the ceremony. If Jesus was a no-show, at least God would be involved. My Dad relented. We could get married in the house.

With the wedding more or less planned, the evening before we returned to Washington, D.C. I asked Al about some remaining detail. He sighed and told me to do whatever I wanted. I said, "You don't seem very excited." He answered, "I'm not excited." I asked, "Well, what is it you feel then?" He replied, "I'm mostly resigned." "Resigned?" I spat out. "Is that the best you can do?"

"Yes," he said. "I'm in love with you, so I have to marry you."

"Well 'resigned' is just not good enough. If you can't muster up some excitement, we're not getting married," I said and I punched him in the stomach. In uncharacteristic fashion, Al reacted quickly. He struck me a blow in the stomach too. I'd never been hit before. I had no idea it could hurt so much. We never hit each other again.

We also called a halt to the wedding. I think he would have gone through with it, but with no expressed joy on his part, I wouldn't continue with the plans. I had chosen a wedding dress. I was able to cancel the order. We had already received a few wedding gifts. I returned them. Wedding invitations had been printed. I picked them up and threw them away and Al sent me a check for half the cost. I had resigned from, but not yet left, my job. I stayed on.

UNCERTAINTY. Al graduated in June 1968. It was hurtful to think of his mother, father, and sisters—a family I had once thought I would be a part of—sharing that experience without me, not able to see him receive his diploma that read "Special Honors in Geography."

His older sister, Betty, and I met one morning while they were in town. In a small café in Dupont Circle, we sat in a booth sipping coffee while I cried. In view were the backs of several washed-out homeless men sitting at the counter, slumped, trying to find a reason to go on living. When Betty reached across the table to pat my arm and said in an earnest, but perhaps overly dramatic voice, "Oh, but Judy, you know he loves you," all the men slowly turned on their stools in unison, gave me a dazed glance, and without changing expression rolled listlessly back again. Even though I was distressed, the scene amused me. It felt as if we were all performing in a theatrical production. But my life was no play.

Al returned home to Worcester to work for the summer. He wrote me regularly—chatty warm letters. I read them, but did not respond to any of them. He never commented or asked me to write. He just kept sending those letters.

I thought I was doing fine. My work was rewarding. I had enough money to buy some new clothes—a real treat after four years at Oberlin where inside-out, baggy sweatshirts were the norm. I was dating and partying. But one day my parents visited. My mother took one look at me and said, "Don't lose any more weight." I was unaware of it, but apparently I wasn't eating. I reached my full height of five feet, eight inches at age fourteen and ever since I had weighed 125 pounds. During the summer of 1968, I was startled to step on a scale and see the number 117! To my concerned mother, I must have looked like a skeleton.

In early fall, Al called me at work. He was in town, flying out the next day to Puerto Rico to begin Peace Corps training for a Central American Regional Development Project whose purpose was to build capacity among small fishermen to enhance their livelihoods. Could I have lunch? he asked.

I said, "Yes." THEN I thought about it. By the time I decided it was a terrible idea, it was too late. It had been three months since we had seen each other or heard each other's voices. He arrived on a borrowed motorcycle wearing a brand-new beige linen two-piece suit. He would certainly not need such a getup in the Peace Corps, so it must have been for my benefit. He looked so adorable in that damn suit, I could hardly stand it. Before he even got off the motorcycle, I said, "You have a lot of nerve asking me to have lunch with you just before you leave for the Peace Corps. We were supposed to go together. I never want to see you again. Just go to hell," I yelled. He never said a word. Just turned the cycle around and took off. I watched him until he was a little speck and returned to my office.

At that point I thought the nearly-two-year pattern of breakups followed by emotional reunions was over. I moped and coped and sort of rebounded as I always had. I was attending a Unitarian church in Arlington, Virginia. One Sunday stands out in my memory. As a service on the topic of water came to a close, live music enticed the parishioners out of their seats. We marched around the sanctuary and followed the musicians outside to a patio where volunteers served us cups of cool water. The experience was simultaneously communal, freeing, exhilarating and life confirming—just what I needed. But I attended that service alone and I was struggling. Even with Al out of the country and me still in D.C and no communication between us, I still believed I'd never love anyone else as much.

A month later, Al called my apartment from Puerto Rico. The training was okay, but he wasn't well suited for a fishing program. While he credited the program with helping him overcome the aversion he had to water due to nearly drowning twice as a child, he was not comfortable with a program that focused on oceans and rivers. One of the requirements was to demonstrate "drown proofing" by spending an entire hour slumped with your face in the water, expending only the energy necessary to lift your head and take a breath from time to time. Basically, floating limp with near zero movement.

With such a simple singular activity designed to simulate being cast off a capsized boat, the experience became meditative. Perhaps he was thinking about me? In any case, during that month, he realized that the trainees he most enjoyed and identified with were the married couples. He felt he had little in common with the single trainees. He felt married. He had investigated alternative programs—programs that were accepting married couples. There was one in Nicaragua where women would work in health and nutrition and men with small farmers, helping them improve crop production and organize co-ops for marketing. Earlier, we had agreed that we wanted a Spanish-speaking country so that we would have an opportunity to become fluent in that important language.

He had spoken with Peace Corps staff. To leave the fishing program and apply for another, he must complete half of the twelve weeks of the current training program. Meanwhile, we could apply for the Nicaraguan program as an engaged couple. The current training was in an isolated spot, but he could take the weekend off. Al had arranged for us to stay at a hotel in San Juan. He wanted me to come to San Juan to plan a wedding so that we could enter the Nicaraguan program together. He sounded awfully damn sure of himself. I went. We planned.

AL ON FIRST ENTERING THE PEACE CORPS WITHOUT ME:

Ambivalent. Not sure I was making the right decision. But clarity arrived soon. Starting with the first day, once I met married couples I knew I was ready to move beyond singlehood. It was on my mind all day, every day. Peace Corps was right. But the personal arrangements were not. I called Judith after two-three weeks. I knew my switching programs would be complicated and unwelcomed by the Peace Corps. Program availability, timing of switch—any of these could have delayed or threatened my continuing in the P.C. Remarkably, all proceeded seamlessly, perhaps a vindication of the choice I had made. I had done the spade work before extending my invitation to come to San Juan. I knew she wasn't one to sit around. I feared she might be seeing someone else or just refuse to start up again.

When she arrived in San Juan, I was just so happy to see her. Seeing her instantly confirmed my decision. Not a speck of regret. All the ups and downs of our two-year courtship were instantly water under the bridge.

Six weeks later, we had a small wedding at a beautiful, modern Unitarian church in Arlington, Virginia. My mother, father, three sisters, two brothers, and grandmother all came.

Al grew up in a large extended family. Eventually his parents and all seven of his mother's siblings lived in Massachusetts with their spouses, six of them in Worcester. He had seven first cousins on his mother's side, seven on his father's side. Before moving to Worcester, one uncle and aunt lived in Washington, D.C. They were the first members of Al's family I met. Decades later Aunt Lee would become like a second mother to us. Al's mother, who had never travelled without her husband, flew to the wedding with her sister, Rose. Whereas Al's father's objections to our relationship had troubled Al terribly throughout our courtship, Sarah had quietly accepted me. She said she could see such a difference in Al since he had met me. He was more confident. I loved her for making that Worcester-to-Washington journey, bringing her humor, non-judgmental nature, and unqualified love to the event. I loved her always.

Al's sister, Betty, whose advice he sometimes sought during our courtship, also came. Al's father and younger sister, Lisa, did not attend. All-in-all only four people from Al's huge family were there. But another couple, who were treated as relatives by Al's mother and her seven Levenson siblings, did come from New Jersey. As a boy, Nat had visited the large Levenson clan every summer. Handsome and charming with an equally beautiful and dynamic wife, Nina, they were stand-ins for all those no-shows and have remained a cherished part of our lives ever since.

AL ON OUR WEDDING:

Put together in a matter of weeks. I was comfortable with the wedding arrangements. Very suitable with where we were in our spirituality and family circumstances. Comfortable with Unitarian church and the minister there. Did not want a big fancy affair. Did not want our families to spend a lot of money. Kept it simple. A Peace Corps wedding in the spirit of frugality and conservation. Sorry my dad did not make it, but I didn't want to see him squirming in his seat, unhappy. It would have subtracted from the day. I was very confident that he would recover. I understood that facing a church wedding would be too much for him, though. I thought Judith and my dad would be an easy match owing to their shared love of languages and musicianship.

Nothing but fond memories of our wedding, although I made a wrong turn on the way and was almost late. Fun having my college buddies there. One of my favorite wedding photos shows my mother and Judith's father joyfully bantering, both laughing in their shared, hearty style. They had just met, but seemed to be enjoying each other as do lifelong friends.

For our week-long honeymoon, Al introduced me to Martha's Vineyard island. We stayed at The Dunes, where we had a room with a kitchen alcove. I was in heaven cooking for my new husband in that tiny space. Except for the years we lived abroad, for decades we vacationed on the island. Eventually, in 2000, we purchased a cottage of our own, but then, with our attention drawn elsewhere, we sold it twelve years later.

Next stop was Worcester and spending time with Al's dad for the first time as a married couple. Always reserved, serious, and strongly paternal, Yale greeted me with, "How is my daughter-in-law?" I had the feeling he had pondered and settled on that opening line. It was just right. I felt acknowledged and accepted. Sarah and Yale gave a party for us. I had met the aunts and uncles and neighbors on previous visits, but this time they were warmly welcoming and, in the Jewish tradition, placed checks in Al's hand. A few months later, Yale met my parents on neutral ground—the Virgin Islands— where both sets of parents vacationed with us between our Peace Corps training and our two-year assignment. While we were abroad, our parents exchanged visits both in Ohio and in Massachusetts. We were far away, but they had become friends.

DECEMBER 1968–JULY 1971
Peace Corps Honeymoon

New country. New language. New culture. New jobs. First time either of us had lived with anyone. Suddenly lots of sex. Among all the people we met in training, two couples and one single guy became immediate and life-long friends. Kina and John had been married six months. That seemed like an eternity compared to our mere two weeks. I thought they must by then know everything about marriage, that they had it all down pat. I spent one depressed day in training after one staff member announced, "Among you seven couples, 50 percent will be divorced in two years. Those are the statistics." That staff member had divorced while a volunteer and was bitter. In fact, two years later as we headed back to the U.S., all seven marriages were intact, even thriving.

Two months training in Camp Radley, Puerto Rico on an isolated mountaintop in the rain forest. The seven married couples were housed in primitive cabins. Four rooms to a cabin. One room for each couple, separated by one thin wall of wooden planks that did not reach the ceiling. Our conversations were whispered. Our lovemaking subdued. Each night I ran a hair dryer over the clammy sheets before we jumped into bed. Once, when one of the single guys was visiting, Al motioned for me to stop the hair dryer maneuver. He felt it was too intimate and also unfair to our friend who would be sleeping alone in a cold, damp bed that night. There were no single women in the program. I was already seeing more of what I knew for certain all along. Al was not the sarcastic adolescent-like guy he had been posing as, but a sensitive, empathetic, and wise young man.

Once, after the men had been away for a day, a trainee came running up to me and said, "Your husband is the strongest man in this camp." They had all taken turns on one of those competitive carnival contraptions that measure strength and helps you let off steam at the same time. A blow with a heavy mallet sends a heavy disk rising. Among the 25 men, Al's blow sent the disk to the highest level.

"Strongest man in this camp?" That was a revelation. I had honestly not given a thought to Al's comparative physical strength. I loved him for his mind, his soul, his quick wit. I wasn't attracted by big muscles. He was skinny, but at twenty-two, almost 6' 3", 180 pounds, I guess he was strong. For me that was an unanticipated bonus.

Yet apparently physical strength was not enough to win him a spot in a spontaneous volleyball game. When one team leader invited Al to join, I could see he was excited and anxious to participate. Then the leader changed his mind at the last minute —"Sorry, Al" —and substituted someone else instead. As Al made his way back to sit beside me to watch the game instead of play it, I was hiding behind sunglasses my tears of anger toward the leader, and sympathy with Al's disappointment. "I really wanted to play," he said dejectedly. I thought, 'If I'm this upset about a volleyball game, how am I going to tolerate sharing his emotions for a lifetime?'

We left the rainforest of Puerto Rico behind for a third month of training, this time in Nicaragua's capital, Managua. The heat was so intense we women would rub our skin, our chests, and our backs with ice that melted on contact. We even put ice cubes in our bras. The stench of rotting garbage and sweating bodies filled the city, especially the large central area near the markets where we were housed in cheap hotels. Oh, those markets: blocks of stalls with women selling tomatoes, home-concocted drinks, dried beans, chickens, fabric, hard biscuits. Some kept scaly primordial creatures—iguanas— in cages. Some kept an infant or toddler in a cardboard box.

I complained to the Peace Corps staff about our bathroom situation in the hotel. We shared the toilet with several other hotel "guests"—all Nicaraguan men. The sewer system was not built to handle paper. All used toilet paper was placed in an open basket. Not only was it sickening, it was also frighteningly unsanitary. I was the only one of the women in that situation. We were all housed in different hotels and the rest all had a private bathroom. The Peace Corps staff was not sympathetic. "Well if you can't adjust to that, you're not adaptable enough to adjust to serving in the Peace Corps," they threatened.

I knew that wasn't true, since once I was in our site, we would have our own home. They finally found a better situation for us during the final week of training.

Our two Managuan Spanish teachers, Oscar and Roberto, were married lawyers, just a few years older than we were. We learned they had volunteered because they were curious about who we were and what we were doing in their country. In Peace Corps lexicon, we were "Nicaragua 1," the first ever volunteers in the country. This curiosity was common to everyone. In some ways it dominated our lives. We were often asked, "¿Cuál es su misión?" (What is your purpose here?) In general, we were accepted and welcomed, but there was sometimes suspicion too. Were we with the CIA? Or were we Evangelicals? Couldn't the blame for that low-yielding crop be traced to Americans putting a man on the moon?

Oscar and Roberto quickly surmised that we were just a bunch of naïve young people. Volunteer wives and husbands were placed in separate classes. Close friends, our Spanish instructor duo sometimes amused each other by having us girls repeat words we only occasionally grasped as profane or even filthy. Al and I enjoyed their company and socialized with them often, and we continued to be in contact for decades.

Oscar and Roberto were also surreptitiously anti-government at a time when the Somoza family had ruled and robbed for nearly forty years. A challenge to the dictatorship could lead to torture, imprisonment, death. During the bitter civil war in the late 1970s, some five years after we departed, Oscar delivered hidden guns to the Sandinistas. He was beaten, and grew a moustache to cover his scars. Once the Somozas were ousted he became a judge. Years later we saw Roberto's photo on the front page of the *New York Times*. He was one of the chief negotiators who helped bring peace to that tormented land.

During our first week in our assigned village, La Trinidad, population 3,000, we were invited to a welcoming ceremony arranged by the town mayor assisted by a committee of prominent residents—store owners, an outspoken female doctor, the school principal, and Agricultural Department officials. There was a lot of pomp. There were dramatic speeches. Expectations seemed high. Although I considered myself an equal in terms of the importance of my work, these were pre-feminist times. I sat demurely and smiled. Al and I still quote the doctor, who, referred to me as "Y ella, su dulce compañera." (And, she, his sweet companion.)

Then they stopped speaking and waited for a response. Al rose to address the assembly. He had not said anything to me beforehand, but apparently he had been preparing remarks in his head. Poised, sincere, warm, he matched their flowery tones in this new language, addressing each official and then the group, telling them how much it meant for us to be there, how willingly we were dedicating two years of our lives to live and work among them. Since the specifics of our work were still vague, he spoke in generalities, but he asked for their support and friendship as we embarked on this important venture together.

That was the first of dozens and dozens of speeches I would eventually see Al deliver all over the world. With grace and calm, my twenty-two-year-old husband solidly in the spotlight, in the hot seat, speaking in newly acquired Spanish—an entire town depending on him to improve their lives, made a positive impression on the gathered officials. Years later, I realized that what I was seeing was the *Bar Mitzvah* boy. If he could successfully handle speaking to his whole extended family, his neighbors, his parents' friends, and his own friends plus sing in Hebrew, at age thirteen, perhaps that spontaneous speech in La Trinidad did not seem so daunting. I was certainly impressed.

Finally, our own place. The town had been prepared. The mayor and other leaders understood why we were there. They located us in one of the best houses. Unlike most of the homes, it had a tiled floor and a water closet with a flush toilet in the back of the central patio. It had electricity. There was a large living room, a bedroom, a kitchen. But the back of the house was dark. The only windows were along the front. We needed those windows for light and air. There was no glass. There were no screens. Throughout our 2-1/2 years as residents of La Trinidad, we were objects of tremendous curiosity. Among the 3,000 townspeople, few had seen anyone as tall as we both were, as fair skinned, as just plain American. Whether riding our horses, shopping for vegetables at the market, or strolling through town, we attracted attention.

Beginning early morning and lasting until we closed the shutters at night, children and usually several adults jostled for space at the windows, poking their heads in. They didn't try to engage us in conversation. They just stared and stared. Apparently we were more entertaining—and certainly cheaper—than the one local movie theater.

We asked the authorities to keep an eye out for a more isolated place for us. They found a house on the very edge of town. It had three acres of land with mango, orange and lemon trees and bordered *La Trinidad* River. It was separated from the two-lane Pan Am Highway by a dirt road that ran parallel to the highway. The kitchen had a large window overlooking that road. There were windows on all four sides, back and front doors. It was more primitive but also less claustrophobic than the first house.

Town officials ran an electric line from the corner which, happily, meant that the four houses between that corner and us all got electricity for the first time too. Few outlets, but an electric light bulb overhead in each of the three rooms. They poured loose, reddish concrete over the dirt floors. They installed running water. One faucet in the kitchen sink. One shower. Both cold-water only. And again our neighbors benefitted. Al braved the cold shower every day. I heated water and took sponge baths in the kitchen.

We equipped the kitchen with a concrete sink, a two-burner octane hot plate, and a small used fridge. The oven was a black tin box heated by placement over one of the burners. It all worked fine for two people, but when we sat down to a Christmas dinner with my visiting family (mother, father, two sisters, two brothers), the chicken I had been cooking for hours in that box was still raw and I was in tears.

No more flush toilet either. A latrine about ten feet from the back door. Plus the curiosity did not let up. Every morning on my first visit to the outhouse, the crowds were there along the fence. During that Christmas visit from my Ohio family, my sisters insisted my father accompany them to the outhouse to frighten away the occasional rat.

We had plenty of space for horses and eventually owned three: *Ligero* ("Light-foot," for her swift, gentle steps); *Fuego* ("Fire," for his temperament and orange color); and *Ganador* ("Winner," which was a sarcastic name because he was actually an irritatingly slow loser). Chickens too, and a rooster, although they kept disappearing. People had so little. Even as volunteers, we had so much.

AL ON HIS PEACE CORPS WORK:

I was trained as an agricultural extension agent with two purposes: 1) improve basic grain production through use of fertilizer, pesticides, and cropping techniques; 2) develop crop marketing systems that would eliminate the middle men and capture a greater percentage of the profits for the farmers. #1 was the Peace Corps goal for the program. #2 was my own invention as I learned about the economies of small-grain production and witnessed the small share of profits flowing out of the hands of farmers and into the hands of middlemen. The sponsor was the Programa Credito Rural del Banco Nacional de Nicaragua. My immediate supervisor was the head of the program office in La Trinidad, Antonio Castillo.

The work was totally outside my experience and skills. I had never farmed nor lived in an agricultural area. It was a challenge to acquire the skills that would bring value to my clients, but it was also stimulating as it deepened my understanding of an economy on which the poor depend in developing nations. I faced a steep learning curve, but at each step, enrichment, awakening, and reward.

Working hand in hand, shoulder to shoulder with small farmers who owned or shared with family members 5-10 acres of land, I learned how they see the world, how they evaluate risks and opportunities, how they interact with markets.

The initial challenge was to establish my credibility. I was North American. We were the first Peace Corps group to ever work in Nicaragua. Small-town and rural "Nicas" were accustomed to interacting with two types of Americans—missionaries, or American intelligence officers. "LA CIA" was a term heard often among suspicious friends and clients. Always cordial, they were still not trusting of what exactly I was there for. All this was coupled with difficult logistics to reach farmers via dirt roads prone to seasonal washout.

I had some success in improving crop yields and pest control. I worked with about twenty farmers. My view was that success with a few would have a powerful demonstration effect, transforming isolated progress into broader base change.

Learning was two-way. Farmers with above-average resources, education, and drive inspired me with their readiness to take risks. The notion of cooperative farming, even of basic information sharing, was not well developed. The paramount concern of the family was survival.

I struggled to introduce the principles of cooperative enterprise. It was a long, difficult path that spanned my two years of service.

One season I experimented with a crop new to these farmers—mani (peanuts). I wanted to run the experiment close to home so I could monitor it frequently. I chose a plot of land which was part of the land we rented. Unfortunately, it was on the edge of Rio La Trinidad. I was warned about flooding. Indeed, the entire town learned with some amusement that the river had washed away the gringo's plantings.

JUDITH'S WORK. DANGERS AND DELIGHTS. My tasks were to educate about better health and nutrition practices. Although we had received methods training and materials, we were pretty much on our own. I arranged with the town's Centro de Salud to give a series of charlas (show-and-tell talks) to pregnant women. But first I had to get them to show up. I set out going door to door. Standing in open doorways, I introduced myself and delivered my verbal invitation. Most of the women just stared at me. At my third stop, the woman said, "Yo no entendí ni una palabra de lo que Usted me dijo." (I did not understand a single word you said.) Probably none of the previous women had understood me either.

Eventually, though, ten to twelve women began attending with their small children. The country's dismal child mortality statistics became shockingly real as the women introduced themselves. "My name is Consuela. I have four children. Three living and one dead." "My name is Maria del Carmen. I have six children. Four living. Two dead." When one woman in the group said, "My name is Luisa. I have five children," and stopped speaking, the women asked her, "Well, how many living? How many have died?" When Luisa answered, "They're all living. None has died," the group was stunned. Most had never met anyone who had not lost a child. Luisa seemed mildly apologetic. Obviously, there was a lot of work to do.

Yet, with each child driving them further into poverty, with children weakened by malnutrition and vulnerable to disease, what all the women wanted most was to stop having children. The main challenge was that they could not discuss the issue with their husbands whose manliness expressed itself in producing more and more barefoot children. The center disbursed free birth-control pills, but these mothers said that if their husbands found the pills, they would be furious. In addition to many superstitions and much mistrust around the issue, there was the Catholic church directly across the street—the best kept building in town—whose doctrine forbade birth control. The priest—a well- educated, sophisticated Belgian—became a friend with whom we socialized. I discussed with him my health and nutrition teaching. I'm sure he also knew about the birth-control advice I dispensed. I believe he may have intellectually supported it. In any case, he did not protest.

Our most satisfying work turned out to be in the rural areas. We rode our horses up into the hills, visiting several villages in one day. Once a week on our behalf our friend, *Chepa*, turned her primitive kitchen filled with hanging vines of fresh garlic into a luncheonette and served us a delicious lunch of rice, beans, tortillas, chicken, and her home-made cheese, *cuajada*. We stayed overnight with Martin and Alicia Montenegro, a childless couple in their fifties who reminded us of Iowa farmers from the early 1900s. It was a little like going home to visit parents who quietly went about their many farm tasks and took care of us too, providing food, a cot, a blanket, and a place to wash up. Evenings they gave us their best chairs—wooden with high backs. We chatted quietly, while the couple occasionally roused themselves to drive an aggressive piglet or two out the open front door.

In a photo taken in front of a one-room school—really just a shack—I stand with an entire village of kindergarten-through-third-graders and their excellent teacher whose head barely reaches my shoulder. I grew to love the preparation and sharing of visuals, characters, and activities to reinforce my simple messages: *Maria Manos Sucias* (Mary Dirty Hands) to teach frequent hand washing; *Simon Zapatos* (Simon Shoes) to encourage keeping feet covered in order to avoid the energy-zapping worms that too often took over the children's bodies; *Señor Huevo* (Mr. Egg) to illustrate the importance of protein—the latter lesson delivered in competition with a hen who spent a laborious fifteen minutes laying an egg in the school's rafters, cackling in full *voce*.

The children had little control over these decisions, of course, but I was delivering the same messages to their mothers in somewhat more sophisticated ways—and never in written form. Most of them had barely completed third grade. Thanks to a donation from Caritas, the women showed up for my once-a-week visits to receive rations of oil, rice, and oats. Before they walked away with their filled containers, I gathered them around and demonstrated the best ways to keep their children healthy.

The challenges to effect change were many. Two of many elaborate myths involved both the concepts of "hot" and "cold" foods and the use of water which was brought by bucket to the home. These hot and cold divisions were difficult for us to grasp and had nothing to do with temperature. Water was used for cooking, rarely for bathing.

While I would encourage consumption of the fairly abundant and Vitamin-C-rich oranges as a remedy for a runny nose and cough, oranges were considered "cold," and were avoided precisely when children were ill, which was often.

I also alienated at least one family. Several women complained that the family I had asked to guard the supplies in between my visits was instead depleting them, using their special status to dole out the oil, oats, and rice to their far-flung relatives. I moved the supplies to a more trusted village leader, but in so doing, I humiliated the woman of the first household who, I heard, made angry threats against me. She never again attended one of my *charlas*.

The filthy babies were especially worrying for me—their fingernails and the wrinkles in their little necks caked with dirt. The need to search for firewood combined with minding the smoking clay stove all day was tedious. Adding the task of walking to a stream with children in tow to collect and haul water could seem overwhelming to these women. But beyond the inconvenience—or because of it?—the villagers believed that bathing a baby before its first birthday could be dangerous, even cause its death.

Nevertheless, I demonstrated how to wash a baby. I chose the healthiest, chubbiest four-month-old I could find and, of course, asked the young mother's permission. I instructed the hostess to boil water and let it cool to near room temperature—which was probably around 75 degrees. Then as the women gasped and the mother sat looking terrified, I lowered the naked baby into the water. There was a moment of surprise on her face, but she quickly relaxed into her first bath, smiled, and gurgled as I, who was not yet a mother myself, with one arm around her to support her, slowly washed her ears, her tiny mouth, in between her grimy little fingers and toes. All the while, I chatted and smiled in an attempt to lower the tension in my "audience." I lifted the infant out of the metal tub, wrapped her in a cloth, and handed the cheerful, fresh-smelling, clean baby back to her relieved mother. Then, for a week, it was my turn to be nervous. If the baby had become ill or died, my bath would have been blamed. I might have been run out of town, out of the country—or worse. She was fine.

In fact, although nearly everyone was warm, welcoming, and accepting of our presence, there was always an underlying fear of violence. At that time Nicaragua had the highest homicide rate of any country in the world. Macho culture prevailed. Their children might be ragged, walking around on dusty bare feet, with distended bellies and wasted limbs, but every man owned a handgun. They also drank. We often heard gunfire at night. We knew young widows who had lost husbands to those shots.

Given our naiveté and general lack of cultural savvy, we could have set off any number of negative reactions at any time. We innocently gave our beloved German Shepherd pup, *Nica*, a name which we later learned our hosts might find offensive. Once when we were walking around town with our fellow volunteer, Jim, who as the son of a diplomat had lived in several foreign countries and was much better attuned to cultural differences than either Al or I, we called out to our straying pet, "*Nica! Nica! Ven.*" Usually quite composed, Jim got a little nervous. *Nica* is a nickname, short for *Nicaraguense* which means Nicaraguan. Our hosts might find our naming a dog after them insulting, he explained.

We learned early while still in training that threats to our health and safety might come from many sources, when a Peace Corps nurse casually gave us instructions on how to treat snake bite. No statistics on how prevalent snakes were or how often this knowledge was required. Like the children on whose health we focused, we too were prone to parasites. We were given iodine tablets to purify water with which to wash raw fresh vegetables such as lettuce and tomatoes. We boiled all our drinking water. At the end of two years, only two volunteers out of twenty had not been treated for worms. I was one of the two, which was fortunate since by then I was pregnant.

Once I was cooking and *Nica* ran into the kitchen, trembling violently. Usually so delighted and eager to see us if we'd been apart for a few minutes or longer, she didn't even greet me. She headed straight behind the refrigerator and hid there—something I had never seen her do. Al arrived a few minutes later and explained. A farmer had given us permission to keep one of our horses across the road, in a field with his cows. Al had retrieved the horse from there several times with no problem. When he brought Nica with him, however, the nursing cows became alarmed. They ganged up on Nica and chased her. They began to encircle Al too, apparently to prevent his escape. Nica fled. Fast, fleet, and small, she scrambled under the barbed-wire fence. Al was an easier target. As the circle closed in, he grabbed a fence post, said a split-second prayer that he wouldn't rip off his hands on the sharp wire hooks, and propelled himself over. He miraculously avoided gashing his palms.

Twice Al was late arriving home. The first time, as it got darker and darker, I became more and more panicked. Without phones, I just had to wait it out. When I could no longer sit and worry (no TV to distract me either), I took Nica with me and started walking through the village.

As Nica and I moved through the streets that night, the first person I encountered on my anxiety walk was a man I knew vaguely. When I told him my dilemma, he sneered, "Oh I see. Is he often away at night?" Although I knew that Al was not seeking female companionship in the countryside, the guy's implication and lack of sympathy did not help lessen my fears for his safety. It was the rainy season. It rained often and without warning. There were no bridges in the rural areas. The lateness, it turns out, was due to a swollen riverbed. Al and his Nicaraguan colleague from the National Bank were stuck on the wrong side. Eventually the water subsided enough so that they could cross safely.

A second peril we faced was travel over secondary and tertiary roads—cow paths really. Once again I found myself in high-anxiety mode when Al was late to return home from a day in the campo. Al had set out with a Nicaraguan agronomist to visit a group of small farmers in a rural hamlet. As they began the descent down a steep hill on a rutted, narrow path, the brakes failed. Al looked to his left and saw no driver. With no warning, the agronomist had jumped from the careening vehicle. Al made a split-second decision to do the same, curling his arm over his head as he rolled out of the vehicle and landed feet from a huge boulder, breathless and stunned, but miraculously without serious injury. The jeep hurtled downward, eventually smashing into large rocks on the side of the path.

After that jeep accident, Al was sore and bruised, but had no broken bones. He stayed in bed for about ten days staring at the ceiling, saying nothing. If he was contemplating the meaning of life and death, having fleetingly stared both in the face when he leaped, he did not share those thoughts with me. I felt scared and alone.

After our first year in the Peace Corps and since we had always intended to adopt, we decided why not adopt a Nicaraguan child where there are so many children with little hope of improving their lives? We talked to Dr. Baredes, a dapper, dignified man responsible for the medical care of the volunteers. He was a board member of an orphanage in Managua where, until they were adopted or could walk, the infants' lives were confined to a crib, with little stimulation. Most of the babies were listless and took little notice of our visits, but one eight-month-old, Alba, was different. With beautiful brown skin and large, brown intelligent eyes, she held our attention and was eager to explore any gift we brought her. Unlike the others, she smiled and made eye contact. The doctor assured us, "Don't worry. The board will meet in a few months to make decisions about permanent placements. I will see that you are chosen to adopt Alba. She will be in your arms before her first birthday." Four months seemed a long way off, but we continued to visit Alba whenever we were in Managua—a 2-1/2 hour bus ride from La Trinidad. We were really falling in love with her and were anxious for her to be ours.

The orphanage board met. Afterwards, somewhat apologetically, Dr. Baredes delivered the painful news: Alba had been given to a single Nicaraguan woman. The board feared that, since we were a fertile couple, we would take Alba back to the States with the purpose of turning her into a maid for our future biological children.

My parents raised four children—two adopted and four biological. The idea that we would mistreat a Nicaraguan child, one of the very children to whom we were dedicating two years of our lives, was absurd. I'm not sure how the board knew or perhaps guessed our fertility status. We were using birth control, but our fertility had not yet been tested. No one had ever interviewed us or asked us why we wanted Alba as our own—and first child. We were devastated, but we were also ready for a baby. I went off the pill and became pregnant the following month.

At the end of our two years, the Peace Corps asked us to remain another six months in order to prepare sites around the country for the arrival of the next group of volunteers, and train those volunteers when they arrived. We both welcomed this opportunity to share what for us had been an eye-opening, formative, and immensely enriching two-year experience. As staff members we were paid a salary, but we were able to live on the *per diem*—$10/day each—which we received for travelling. We saved the salary.

Although we would have happily remained for the full additional six months, we needed to leave after only three. Our baby was growing fast and we wanted it to be born in the U.S. In addition, Al had been accepted into a graduate program at Ohio State University. It was time to move on with our lives.

Other conditions pushed us in the same direction. Our primitively constructed home had become overrun with rats. Apparently our home had become their favorite party spot. All night we could hear them running and chattering excitedly on the rafters above our heads. Toward the end of our stay, before a two-day trip to Managua, Al put rat poison all over the house. While in the capital, we said goodbye to the other volunteers. It was especially difficult for me to say goodbye to Kina who had been my closest friend for 2-1/2 years. She and John were moving to New York City to pursue further study in art. With everyone else departing and our staying on a bit longer, it was the end of an intense, enlightening, and formative period in our lives, a bonding experience for us that tested, strengthened, and readied our partnership for a lifetime of devotion.

By then we had purchased our own van in anticipation of the journey home. Thank goodness we were no longer travelling by bus because Al had to stop every twenty minutes or so on the way back to La Trinidad, for me to be sick. Now six months pregnant, I was emotionally and physically exhausted that night. When we entered the house, there was an overwhelming odor, a stink, as if someone had been cooking rotten cabbage nonstop. As I leaned down to get a pillowcase on a shelf, I nearly touched a dead rat.

I climbed into bed. For what seemed like hours, I dozed while Al cleaned up and discarded rat carcasses outside in the dark. For decades he refused to tell me how many he had found. Finally he did—seventeen. The party was over. The rats did not return.

After bidding goodbye to our many friends in the rural villages and in the town, and trying to fairly distribute all our goods among so many people eager to receive any item, we piled what remained into our VW van and drove from La Trinidad north through Honduras, El Salvador, Guatemala, Mexico, and on into Texas. Young Americans crossing all those borders could raise suspicion of drug smuggling, but early on we realized we had a powerful tool at our disposal—my big, pregnant belly. When I emerged from the minivan, the Latino border guards, guns at the ready, smiled and made the passage easy. We were grateful for the respect their culture afforded expectant mothers.

By the time we had driven up the East Coast of the U.S. to Worcester and then landed in what was to be our home city for the next seven years—Columbus, Ohio—I was eight months pregnant.

AL ON THE MOST MEMORABLE PART OF THE PEACE CORPS EXPERIENCE:

Witnessing and confronting at a very intense level the day-to-day life and conditions under which two-thirds of the planet live. Although we never worried about our next meal, we experienced poverty through neighbors, friends, and the faces of children we encountered daily. For the rest of my life, I'll carry with me that experience and the knowledge that billions of people live in such deprivation. Those 2-1/2 years also reinforced my desire to spend the rest of my life working in areas where I could contribute to social betterment.

AUGUST 1971
Students With Babies

Thanks to my mother's strong belief in natural childbirth, I always knew I would choose that path. It was she who sent us a book on the topic, complete with an exercise regimen. On the month-long trip, I practiced the breathing exercises and did my leg lifts in the back of the van. Mom also found for us an obstetrician in Columbus—not an easy task since the doctor had to be supportive of our birth method choice AND be willing to take us on so late in the pregnancy. Dr. Whitlatch turned out to be a jewel.

Al practiced with me and we felt ready for the birth. However, we had no place to live. On an August day, we began walking around the neighborhoods that surround the 50,000-student Ohio State University campus. There were quite a few apartments available, but when landlords saw my extended stomach, they turned us away: "My wife doesn't like to rent to people with kids because they want to use her clothes dryer."

With the baby due in three weeks and school starting in a month, we were starting to panic when we came upon a couple doing yard work. We told them our dilemma. They answered that they were preparing half of their duplex for new renters. They had, of course, noted that our family was soon to expand, so

I was holding my breath. "We like families," they offered. "They're stable and take better care of property."

For the next seven years, we lived in their white, wood-frame duplex, a three-bedroom, two-floor roomy apartment with an eat-in kitchen and back yard. We bought a swing for the front porch and spent hours there rocking our babies. For the first five years the rent was $75/month. In a gesture of support for Al's continuing education, Al's dad covered the entire amount. We made one request of the landlords—that they replace the old furnace that barely functioned and left us freezing during the Ohio winters. They did so immediately. When we moved to Boston, the rent had increased to a still-low $125/month. We felt blessed with the large duplex, its location, the low rent, and, of course, the generous support from Al's dad. But back to the baby I was expecting when we moved in....

MOMENT OF TRUTH—OR NOT. Standing at the hospital admissions desk holding my large belly, I have a moment of complete panic. Nothing to do with labor pains or first-time mother fears. I have just informed the clerk that I want no drugs, that my husband is my coach and that he will be with me for the labor and delivery.

"Oh," she says suspiciously. "Have you taken the Lamaze course?" Swallow. Didn't all those hours poring over a natural-birth instruction book and practicing breathing in the back of our VW van count as a course?

"Yes," I answer defiantly.

"What was your teacher's name?" she asks, apparently unconvinced.

Being away from Al for hours, facing labor and delivery alone, is out of the question. As a searing wave grabs my uterus, I think fast. Attempting to appear confident, I make a desperate attempt to recall the name of the book's author.

The clerk raises an eyebrow. Gail Wickford doesn't seem to ring any bells. I can see the clerk thinking that either there's a new class instructor she's unaware of or I'm pulling her leg. For good measure, I spell the last name. At least she doesn't ask me WHERE I took the course or demand a certificate of completion. She grudgingly writes Gail's name on the form and sends both Al and me to the labor room.

After that, the rest is easy! At least for me. I sleep through most of the labor. Al does all the work. He keeps track of every single contraction, learns the rhythms, knows exactly when one is going to strike and wakes me with a gentle five-second warning. "Another contraction is coming, Sweetie." At the sound of his voice, I open my eyes from what had been fifty-five seconds of deep, dreaming sleep and immediately begin the rapid Lamaze breathing that blocks pain messages from reaching the brain.

Hours later Al is standing behind me. We can both see the mirror where we will get our first glimpse of our baby. He cheers me on with words like "Push, Honey, push." Author Gail encourages coaches to help the birthing mother concentrate on opening up her vagina. So Coach Al urges, "Think open." Then inexplicably he adds, "Think *puta*." *Puta* is the Spanish word for cunt and for whore. I am a little startled, but am in no position to challenge his vocabulary choice. Afterwards, he has no memory of using that word.

"THANK YOU, Dr. Whitlatch," I swoon when he places my beautiful green-eyed, dark-lashed baby girl in my arms. I am totally in love with this infant, the doctor, the nurses, and everyone in the whole world in that moment. And more in love than ever with the baby's father. The smiling staff gathers round. It's a celebration. It's Kate's first birthday party.

"Nurse her right now if you want," Dr. Whitlatch suggests. "See, she knows exactly what to do." And boy, does she latch on.

In those days, babies were kept in a nursery separate from the mothers' rooms. Al waited until I was settled. I wasn't ready for him to leave, but I looked at him and saw that he was totally exhausted. This darling new young father had been standing and, yes, laboring for seven hours. I, on the other hand, was full of pep. I wanted to chat. Shoot, I wanted to dance! But I urged him to go home and rest.

All that energy was accompanied by a roaring hunger. It was 2:00 a.m. and the hospital kitchen was closed. So were nearby restaurants. Nothing I've ever drunk or eaten since was as welcome as the first taste of that hot tea and plain toast the nurse managed to conjure up. But snacking was quickly put on hold.

In the next minute, the nurse brought a demanding Kate to me. "I think she's hungry again," she said. It was a little difficult to set aside that delicious tea. My first motherly sacrifice. Forty years later, I can say that it's been well worth it. My oldest of three beautiful children has brought immeasurable joy to the two of us. I've switched to coffee by now anyway.

NEW CITY. NEW HOME. NEW BABY. NEW STUDIES. NEW WORK. Four nights a week Al was out until almost 10:00 p.m., either teaching a class or taking one. Even as a tiny infant, Kate refused to sleep until he arrived home. Lullabies, slow dancing, rocking—nothing I tried would close those gorgeous eyes until she had gotten a good-night kiss from her daddy.

I wanted to stay home with Kate and relished recording every new development. At her fortieth birthday party, "40 @ 40," Kate displayed forty of her art works along with the pink baby book in which her guests could see photos of Baby Kate and read my observations, musings, and delights.

For the first time in my life I had no work outside the home and no studies. I figured that nursing, changing, feeding, washing her clothes, etc. took six hours a day. And those were just the basics. There were also walks, La Leche League meetings, visits with other mothers and babies. My parents and younger sisters and brothers were an hour away—too far and too busy to provide a support group on a daily basis. After the first few months, I missed the stimulation of working, of making a difference beyond my little family. It was the last year of my life when I concentrated entirely on domesticity.

Meanwhile, Al was surrounded by colleagues and professors and other students.

Al on becoming a parent:

I felt very, very ready and it seemed completely natural that the baby should come when it did. I was also grateful that the birth took place in a safe environment, given that we were so transient in the weeks before. Judith was in the care of an experienced and skilled physician. Arrangements came together flawlessly. I was impatient to be a father even though, at twenty-five, I was still young. I was feeling competent and had high expectations that having a baby would bring great joy. Then during and after delivery, the baby was not only gorgeous but also curious, engaging, serious, focused—made in my image, I felt, except for the gorgeous. The adventure exceeded my hopes and expectations. I had feared I might eventually experience anxieties about parenting, but none materialized. I did underestimate the energy it took to care for one little human creature, but I felt completely up to the task. Kate became her own best judge of what she needed. She kept herself busy, was interested in so many things. She was creative and exploratory, an artistic child who spent hours playing with legos and blocks, designing and building whole cities. She was also intensely interactive. I remember talking to her, having substantive conversations when she was just beginning to walk.

Role changes. The summer that Kate turned one, we spent six weeks in a cooperative household in Kansas City, Missouri. Al was hired for a project sponsored by the National Science Foundation to document, analyze, and address locational conflicts over public facilities—in this case a proposal to build a major highway through the City. A north/south route would be an eyesore, as well as set up a barrier in the middle of an historic, largely African-American community. Just the anticipation of the project affected neighborhoods abutting the proposed highway. Outmigration and property depreciation were accelerating. Homes lay abandoned and decaying. A few years after this study, the project was abandoned. Thankfully, the highway was never built.

The three of us shared a first-floor bedroom of a mansion bought cheap and occupied by two men and three women—all single. We were the guests of the homeowner, a local social activist.

All of us were in our twenties. We sat in on the lengthy house meetings, but mostly listened as they heatedly discussed the formation of house rules and regulations. Once, after we had skipped out from a rambling meeting early, they informed us that they had agreed that there would be no sex between household members—with the exception of the one married couple—us.

We all added $5.00 each a week to the communal pot for meals, and took turns shopping and preparing dinner for the eight of us. These meals were often vegetarian though, and so skimpy that most evenings we'd spend another $5.00 each at Hardee's afterwards.

Yet we learned so much from that experience. Like the Peace Corps, it confirmed our values and showed us new ways of structuring our lives. The five residents—both genders—identified as feminists. Defining what that meant for a cooperative household was a main focus of all those discussions. Inequality was not tolerated. Although the men agreed in principle, the women often took them to task for outmoded thinking. For both of us, raised in the fifties where our dads went to work and our moms stayed home, becoming steeped in feminist philosophy was challenging, both intellectually and practically. Once, in the back yard I nearly stepped on a dead, decaying squirrel. I circumvented it thinking that I would need to ask one of the men to clean it up. Then I realized that if I were to embrace equality, I should clean it up myself. Yuck! I didn't do it. I was a coward.

They all had fun, though. The women refused to bend to societal expectations they felt demeaned or infantilized them—like shaving their legs, for example. One evening they organized a blind-folded smooth-leg contest. Melanie, a funny, hefty gal who rode a motorcycle, was really tickled to be declared the winner.

AL ON THE KANSAS CITY EXPERIENCE:

Formative, eye-opening, experimental beyond what we expected and perhaps desired. A growing, learning experience. A group of people who believed passionately in the need for change, in their ability to influence that change, and who were willing to live the life, walk the walk. Not just talk. Our first introduction to deeply committed American-style activism. Feminists, anarchists who wanted to see profound social change and were working for it.

Everything they did every day was aimed toward reaching their goal. They seemed beyond politics. Not particularly interested in who was running for office. Instead they spent hours asking questions about gender and the economic system, its agendas, flaws, injustices. We had great synergy with that group. It radicalized us somewhat. Pushed us politically more to the left. I became more advocacy-oriented, more impatient with slowness of change, more sophisticated in my political thinking. Meanwhile, my work that summer was at its roots a social justice project. In a small way, I was making a contribution.

The basic concept of feminism—equality between the sexes including equal work, study, and advancement opportunities—appealed to Al's sense of justice. It was part of the same belief system that originally brought us together, led us to the Peace Corps, and continually shaped his career. We started at home. We made lists of chores and divided them up, then switched chores so that we both became (reasonably) proficient at everything. We covered the basics, but neither of us had any fix-it skills, nor the inclination to learn them. We called in the craftsmen/craftspeople—plumbers, electricians, and carpenters—when we needed them.

Sharing child care was a little more complicated. With Al working and/or studying, and me running my foreign language education businesses from home for years, the hours of child care certainly did not approach fifty/fifty. Yet the time he spent with them was full of creative play, humor, spontaneous games, and delight. Kate and I sometimes visited Al on the Ohio State campus. When she spotted him across the wide expanse of grass in front of the student center, she would take off running straight for him. Just as she got to him, he would spread his legs wide. Like a one-car mini train passing under a bridge, she just kept up the same pace, ending up behind him. Then he would pretend to be stunned at her "disappearance" and would try to "find" her. When he scooped her up, they'd fall down on the grass giggling.

I WANT HER NOW. When Kate was 2-1/2 years old, we informed her that she was going to get a little sister soon.

"When?" she asked.

"In two days," we answered.

She burst into sobs. I thought she must be unhappy at the prospect. But no.

"I don't want a little sister in two days," Kate said through big tears.

"I want her RIGHT NOW!"

My mother, who raised six children—two adopted and four biological—said she felt freer to brag about the children who did not come directly from her. With that thought, I'll not hold back the awe I still feel thirty-eight years after meeting my second child. I often fantasize about our second baby waiting to be born.

First she must pass by God who is rationing the talents and gifts that make each individual unique. It's the end of the day and God wants to finish up the task quickly. "Have we given athletic talent to anybody today?" He asks an angel aide.

"Not today, My Lord."

"OK. Give her that one," God instructs.

With her new talent, she picks up a tennis racket and whacks a ball over the net. Spying a soccer ball, she runs right toward it and gives it an accurate kick that sends it flying into the gathered angels. God is impressed. He's also curious about something.

"Athletic talent does not necessarily indicate gracefulness does it?" He asks his advisors.

"Sometimes, My Lord. Humans occasionally describe top athletes in such terms."

"Mmm, let's see how this sporty little girl takes to dancing. Dance talent, please," He orders.

Dance? When she hears the word, she joyfully demonstrates her ballet steps, then her rock-n-roll sexiness. With red designs painted on her hands and feet and bracelets jingling up her arms, she shows off her classical Indian moves. She jumps, twists, turns, bows and finishes with a perfect cartwheel.

God is really entranced now. "Just one more talent," He says. "Musical."

"Musical, My Lord?" the angels object. "But she already . . ."

"Musical," God declares emphatically.

Once so endowed, our baby breaks into song. God closes His eyes and listens while the about-to-be-born goes through a repertoire of jazzy tunes and soulful ballads. She picks up a violin and plays a Haydn sonata. The angels gently remind God of the late hour. They urge God to send her on. "There are two more souls waiting to be born," they tell Him.

"With all that talent," He says, "she might get confused. Make her smart so she can figure out where to apply her considerable energy. Intelligence!" God commands. "Above average. No. WAY above average."

As God watches her traipse away, twirling and leaping, her sweet voice echoing, just in time He yells, "Oh, hell, make her good looking too."

If God was reluctant to let her go, we were impatient to welcome her. We named her Lena partly after a great aunt of Al's, partly after the Lena River in

Russia, home of Al's ancestors—but also because her natural tan and glorious lavender eyes reminded us of Lena Horne. That was June 1974. She was four months old.

I was finishing a second bachelor's degree. Whether I had to settle an administrative matter, attend a class, or grocery shop, I carried Lena around in a baby backpack. Initially, anticipating that she would tire, I set a goal of accomplishing one task at a time. But she seemed to love observing the world from that high vantage point. She was so intensely curious. I just kept going. She was my buddy. We might have an entire afternoon of walking and shopping, in and out of offices and stores. She never complained. Of course, she got a lot of attention too. Everyone wanted to interact with our exceptionally beautiful baby.

AL ON BABY #2:

Again I felt very ready. This child had her own mystery. You know where the biological kid comes from and when it will come. With an adoptive baby, you don't know the answer to either of those questions. A certain excitement. Difference in conception. With Kate, the deliberate attempts to conceive, making love with the intent to make a baby, to create a life through a loving partnership. With Lena, there was uncertainty. Yet, when the call came, we were euphoric. Couldn't wait to meet the mystery child. Moment of first meeting was breathlessly intense. We were so overwhelmed with this creature we were perhaps not as sensitive as we could have been to her anxieties. A whole storehouse of emotions unfolded for us. At 3-1/2 months, she was an extraordinarily alert, lively beauty. Holding her for the first time was magical. She was friendly and seemed receptive to us, but was still looking over her shoulder at the foster mother who adored her. She was probably concerned about who we were, although she may have had some sense. Leaving her behind after the first visit was very tough. Being with her seemed so right. So inevitable. We never for a second asked, "Is she right for us?" or "Are we right for her?"

Al took his PhD exams that summer. During the adoption process, we had informed the officials that Al had been awarded a Fulbright scholarship and that we would be moving the family to Lima, Peru for a year. Amazingly, given that the adoption would not be final until after a six-month review, they agreed to let us take Lena on this grand venture to another Latin American country.

But preparing for this venture would not be easy. During the summer of 1974 we experienced the most difficult period of our lives up until that point. Only decades later did we face months of upset that surpassed that summer's fears.

SUMMER 1974
Will We Get There Or Not?

After successfully completing the exams, Al fell ill with a mononucleo-sis-like disease. I was caring for a two-year-old, an infant, and a husband who mostly slept for five weeks. I also took the final exams that led to my securing a teaching certificate.

Then I discovered I was pregnant. I was probably two weeks pregnant on the day we welcomed Lena, but I didn't know it. During the first years of our marriage—even when the bold Nicaraguan roaches ate them—the pill worked great for us. But once I became a mother, I was afraid of the pill—afraid of the clots I had read about, fearful of the long-term effects. So we switched to other methods. Less effective methods, apparently. I'm sure my body knew I was preparing for an infant. It just started one when I was already "expecting" another. Slight bleeding did not alarm the doctor much. "Just rest," he said. "Rest? I'm packing up a family to move to Lima." "Oh no," he said. "No flying until you've completely stopped bleeding. You could hemorrhage to death on a plane. But don't worry, some women bleed through an entire pregnancy and give birth to a perfectly normal infant." Which left me where exactly?

Al, by now recovered, went to Peru alone, began his program and, hopeful, found a two-bedroom apartment for us and filled it with furniture. Communication was via ham radio. Al from Lima: "How are you feeling, Honey? Are you still bleeding?" And then, "Over," so that the operator knew to turn the switch. Me in Columbus: "Yes. Still bleeding. Over," I sobbed.

My sisters had all gone back to college. My mother was recovering from a hysterectomy. I felt isolated and frightened. My generous in-laws arranged for an aide to come during the day. Neighbors came a few times to play with the kids. Following doctor's instructions, I stayed in bed, wanting desperately to be with Al, to experience a new country.

To complicate life further, we had sublet our Columbus apartment. The new tenants had given notice to their landlord. We could not break the chain. The sub-letters agreed to let me and the girls use one of the bedrooms until the situation was resolved. They moved into the rest of the apartment.

After a month, Al flew back home. As if my body were waiting for his arrival, that very night I had mini labor pains for hours. The next day I went to the hospital and miscarried. We were relieved. After brief visits with both sets of parents, we moved to South America with our little girls. We arrived in the middle of the night. The next-door neighbor's maid had made the beds. We fell into them.

Early the next morning, we heard three-year-old Kate call out excitedly to her seven-month-old sister in the crib next to her, "Lena, I think this is Peru."

AL ON PERIOD BEFORE MOVING TO SOUTH AMERICA:

Second worst time of our lives. Absolute stew of mixed emotions. Excitement over Lena and the thought of Peru. Despondency over my summer illness and an unwanted pregnancy, neither of which could have been more ill-timed. Pressure of exams. Feeling weak. Having so many planning and child responsibilities. I couldn't contribute what I normally would have.

About a month after we settled in, at 9:21 a.m. on October 3, 1974, I was in our street-level apartment with two four-year-olds—our Kate and Danny, the son of the in-country administrator of the Fulbright Program, Marcia. Lena was visiting next door with Marcia's housekeeper who already adored her. Without warning the floor and walls began to buckle and shake. The rattling sounds were deafening. It felt as if a train was approaching from underground and was going to come right up through the floor.

I grew up with tornados. My junior year upon my fall return to Oberlin I could see a mile-wide swath where a tornado had flattened everything. It looked as if a giant roller had come through. An Oberlin College professor was killed. I knew what to do in a tornado. You take shelter in the basement.

But what if your building has no basement? We lived on the lowest level. I had no idea how to protect the children. I turned to Danny since he was the native Peruvian. "Es un terremoto. Qué se hace?" It's an earthquake. What do we do?" I asked the terrified four-year-old child, who was looking around in alarm and bewilderment. I didn't know if we should climb under beds, run out the door, or what. It seemed to go on for five minutes, but the official report was two minutes. When the shaking stopped, there was a loud pounding at the door. Our neighbors were worried about us. We were supposed to exit the building and stand in the middle of the street. They must have imagined us all smashed up.

Our apartment building was designed by a Peruvian architect who was also Marcia's husband. During its construction he had reinforced it to resist earthquakes. Even though it felt as if a giant had picked up the building and given it a vicious shake, there were no cracks. Cups that held the children's refreshment were still standing upright, although a few drops of milk had escaped onto the table.

We were fine. But I was worried about Al who was somewhere in downtown Lima. Again, no phones. When he returned, he had this tale to tell: At the moment the earthquake hit, he was in a taxi waiting at a red light in heavy traffic. Everyone got out of their cars and stood on the brick street, which was undulating and shaking. As soon as the quake stopped, everyone leaped back into their cars and began driving in all directions like madmen. They all wanted to get home to check on their loved ones. Passengers riding on buses were out of luck. Without suggesting the riders exit, many drivers simply made a beeline for their own homes, leaving the riders to get to their families in any way they could. Al convinced his taxi driver to bring him home.

Others were not so fortunate. The shock, which measured 8.1 on the Richter Scale, caused damage to churches, historical monuments, public buildings, and residences. Adobe homes were especially hard hit. Seventy-eight people lost their lives. Over 2,500 were injured. The damage was estimated at around 2,700,000,000 *soles*. With one sol worth about $.35 in 1974, that was about $945 million.[1]

Trembling-earth experiences aside, Al settled in quickly and began gathering research for his doctoral dissertation.

AL ON HIS ACTIVITIES IN LIMA:

A recent re-organization of metropolitan government had potentially wide-ranging equity impacts across the dozens of districts in the city. Who were the winners? Who were the losers? What was the overall effect of wealth distribution and well-being of city neighborhoods? The initiative was unusual not only for its boldness, but because it occurred under the leftist military regime that governed Peru in the early 1970s, a political orientation rare in a region replete with right-wing military strongmen.

The experience of doing the research was as interesting as the findings. I visited municipal offices in twenty districts that took me to the poorest on the periphery ("pueblos jovenes") to the wealthiest along the coast. I gathered public finance data in each district and interviewed the authorities regarding the impact and prospects for the reform initiatives. I became acquainted with every corner of this giant metropolis, interacting with rich and poor, delving into the lives of a sample of the 3.6 million residents. Urban reform was one among many expressions of the government's commitment to wealth redistribution. In the course of the research, I established a working relationship with the Consejo Provincial de Lima, the central agent managing the fiscal reform program. One relationship in particular was exceptionally enriching.

---

[1] "Historical Earthquakes in Peru," *LimaEasy*. http://www.limaeasy.com/ earthquakes-in-peru/historical-earthquakes.

Jose Maria Blandon—"Pepe"—a young man not much older than I, basically adopted me as an innocent and naïve young foreign student who needed guidance not only on substantive economic/data aspects of study but also on the politics of the study. Pepe was invaluable in guiding me through a labyrinth of municipal politics that enabled me to reach the right people, obtain the necessary data, and avoid the political minefields about which I was totally oblivious.

In addition to the practical aspects of that relationship, ours turned out to be one of the richest professional and personal relationships in my life. Pepe was both politically savvy and intellectually astute. Most memorably, his expressionless wit was a rarity in my Latin American experience. Droll, ironic, biting. During our frequent coffee outings, we went through all the characters and personalities with whom I interacted, each dissected for their flaws and foibles, odd habits, and personalities, including revelatory aspects of their personal lives. Hysterical and amusing conversations. Pepe also played an invaluable reality check to my unquestioning view of the benevolence of the military regime. He helped me cut through the propaganda, to sort out the real from the illusory enlightenment that was unfolding in those tumultuous years in Peru.

Al's Fulbright scholarship provided $365/month. Even in 1974 that amount did not cover shelter and food for a family of four. Like all middle-class families in the neighborhood, we needed a live-in *muchacha* (maid). In many cases, the *muchacha* freed up leisure time for the lady of the house. In my case, I needed domestic help so that I could work. We chose carefully and found an intelligent, skilled young woman who took our children to a neighborhood playground (*el club*) where they met other *muchachas*. The children the other *muchachas* cared for became our girls' daily playmates.

I secured a part-time job teaching business English to recent high school graduates who planned to become bi-lingual secretaries. The thirty young women were lively and full of humor, but also serious about learning. I thrived on preparing and delivering the lessons. Sometimes I used the lyrics from American pop songs to teach vocabulary. One of them was the Roberta Flack classic "Killing Me Softly." To my delight, one of the girls spontaneously sang the entire song in front of the class. Being the wife of a student did not allow me to obtain a work permit, however. That meant that any paid position I accepted was illegal. Both my employer and I risked fines.

One day I saw several official-looking men wandering the halls. I guessed they were inspectors of some kind, perhaps government officials. I panicked, fearing that they might be looking for illegal employees. I bolted from the classroom, abandoning the students. Then I realized I had left my purse in the room. A secretary retrieved it for me. I returned the next day to continue teaching without further incident.

AL ON THE GOVERNMENT SITUATION AT THAT TIME:

By 1974, General Juan Velasco, head of the leftist military regime, was being challenged by a second political figure, General Morales Bermudez. There were rumblings of dissent and divisiveness within the military ranks, and talk of a possible coup. As conditions deteriorated, a weeks-long, city-wide curfew was imposed by Velasco's government.

No one was allowed on the streets after 6:00 p.m. One afternoon we traveled from our home in San Isidro to neighboring Miraflores. When we exited the movie theater at 5:00 p.m., armored tanks rumbled through the streets. We hopped a bus with our little girls, arrived home at 6:00 and shut ourselves in. All night long we heard gunfire.

A year passed so quickly. As the end of Al's Fulbright year approached, we felt so at home in Lima that we seriously considered staying for additional years. Al's research was enriching and productive. We had moved to a larger apartment in the same complex.

Best of all, Kate was enrolled in one of the best schools we've ever experienced—*Leon Pinelo*, a private school serving the small Jewish community in Lima. Once we learned about it, Al visited. He came back on a high. It offered a stark, thrilling contrast with other preschools (*nidos*) where three- and four-year-olds sat at desks in rows. Kate was ready for interaction with other children on a regular basis, but we feared her bright, curious, artistic mind would suffer at the local preschools. *Leon Pinelo*, on the other hand, had roomy, airy classrooms with learning/play stations open to a large, outdoor play area. Classes were all in Spanish, of course, but Hebrew was the second language.

Proof of Jewish identity was required for admission. Al's dad promptly obtained a letter from the rabbi in Worcester. Kate's dynamic young teacher, Israeli-born Jenny, marveled at Kate's intelligence and rapid learning—"She can do puzzles OUTSIDE the frame!" she exclaimed with amazement. I too learned all the catchy Spanish songs and used them in my own Spanish classes for decades. One of my favorite memories from that year is greeting Kate wearing her standard gray school uniform, flying toward me every day when I arrived at the school to walk her home. At age three, she adapted instantly to the school. She radiated joy and confidence.

Through our work, neighborhoods, and the school, our social circles expanded. For dinner parties, we set up in the living room and made crêpes all evening as guests helped themselves to sweet and savory fillings cooked to perfection on our portable, gas-cylinder stove.

We had a series of live-in *muchachas,* but they were young and ambitious. Most stayed only a few months. Our final babysitter was in her fifties. She quickly became devoted to our girls and joined us for dinner every night. That meant that the meal was entirely in Spanish. What a thrill it was for her language-loving mother to hear Kate use complex tenses and idioms. If I had been fascinated with her rapid learning of English, I reveled in her quick grasp of a second language. Once during a garbage strike we were walking home from school. She noticed the pile-up of trash and exclaimed, "*Qué basurero!*"—What a mess! With school four hours per day, a Peruvian babysitter, and play with neighborhood children, her immersion in the language was almost total. I actually feared she might lose her English.

Lena's first spoken words were in Spanish. Not yet a year old, she would pat the seat beside her and invite me to sit, "*Mami, acá.* " ("Mommy, here.") She was a big animal-lover too and relished drawing our attention to creatures both in books and in real life, "*Papi, Mira. Vaca. Perro. Gato.*" ("Daddy, Look. Cow. Dog. Cat.")

What's more, I was growing my first foreign language business. More and more neighbors in our upper-class neighborhood hired me to tutor their elementary-age children in English. Having secured a degree in education and a teacher's certificate just before moving to Peru, I was ready to go. My methods were playful. The children were eager. Sometimes parents sat in and learned too.

With my income, we doubled Al's scholarship money. We also managed to save $500, although taking money out of the country was illegal. We hadn't decided how to solve that problem when I learned that, once again, I was pregnant. Unlike the pregnancy before we moved to Lima when I felt we had perhaps been lax because we were so in the mood for a second baby, we felt betrayed and angry by this unwanted development. We thought we had been making every effort to avoid it. I seemed to be breaking laws right and left. Although we were alone in the examining room, my gynecologist whispered the information he thought I probably wanted. In a land where even the sale of contraceptives was illegal, a week before we left we spent the entire $500 on an abortion. We did not make such a drastic decision lightly. We were not yet prepared financially or psychologically to welcome a third child into our family. We also knew Lena would have some complex identities to work out. We wanted to be able to give her whatever attention and support she needed. We did not want to burden her or ourselves with another child, a biological child, so close to her in age.

Although we had by then lived in Peru for almost a year, what happened on the day I returned to the doctor for a checkup showed how out of touch we still could be with the local culture. After the doctor's A-OK, I headed home only to find that the buses were either packed or not running at all. In two hours of wandering, I never saw a single taxi. I was still experiencing some pain and there were no available seats anywhere. All benches, restaurants, and bars were packed to overflowing.

Excitement and shouting filled the streets. Why? The entire country it seemed was focused on a soccer match. In those days, especially in the U.S. Midwest, THE sport was football. I hated football, especially since there was always an ambulance parked at my high school football games. I did not understand how people could be so enthusiastic about a sport where one or more of my friends were almost guaranteed to be hurt. In fact, some of them, fifteen-, sixteen-, seventeen-year-olds, incurred lifelong knee and back injuries.

I first learned about soccer at Oberlin but, because the emphasis was on academics, the competition was low key. Since that afternoon in Peru, I've also experienced the fanaticism of European fans, but this was my first introduction to soccer's global competition. Screaming packs of men and women, some drunk, filled every downtown street. We had no telephone. Finally, late in the afternoon, I did locate a taxi. I arrived to find my family playing calmly on the floor.

My sister, Molly, visited as we were packing up to leave. Since we were not sure when we would return to the region, we wanted to visit Nicaragua for a few days. Our toddler would accompany us, but Molly flew to Ohio with Kate in tow. The flight took off in the middle of the night. The terror of watching my precious child fly into the night sky is something I'll never forget. When we arrived in the states nearly a week later, Kate, having been spoiled by her grandparents, was quite content. She had also completely converted to English.

AL ON LIMA EXPERIENCE:

Overall, I'd say we acclimated quickly, notwithstanding the financial pressures, cultural adjustments, and political turmoil. Fluency in Spanish was not only a practical necessity but also a blessing and joy. Our days were rich and varied—shopping, transportation, interacting with our muchachas, building professional relationships, and nurturing a variety of friendships. Memories of my friendship with Pepe—his black humor and sardonic com-

mentaries--remain with me to this day. A bit crowded in the first months in our initial apartment, but the quality of the neighborhood was excellent. We walked often. Abutting the ocean. Safe. Minutes to an outstanding school. Local shopping. Friendly neighbors. Life was good. Reluctantly but resigned, we packed our bags and returned to Columbus. I often wonder what path our life would have taken had we remained for a few more years in Lima.

SPRING 1978
Boston Via Martha's Vineyard

A l discovered Martha's Vineyard at age sixteen and worked there the summer before and after his senior year in high school.

AL ON THOSE EARLY MV DAYS AND WORKING FOR HIS DAD:

I discovered Martha's Vineyard through my sister, Betty, who is twenty-two months older. Betty was still in high school when she followed our cousin, Joan, and a friend to the Vineyard, beginning a lifelong love affair with the island. Two years later, at age sixteen, I followed and worked the summer in various restaurants. A mixed bag, to be generous. I migrated between three jobs and was fired from Ralph's Restaurant for eating untouched food left behind by a patron. I wasn't starving. I just thought, 'What horrible waste!' But there was no discussion, no negotiation. I had mindlessly violated a cardinal rule of restaurant employment. Then there was donut making at Wesley House Bakery. The 5:00 a.m. start time was not compatible with my family culture that placed sleep second only to food among life's priorities. My main task was using an anvil-like device. Instead of blowing air on a fire, I blew jelly into the donut. Donuts came out of the oven fully baked, two dozen to the batch. I would impregnate each donut with lemon, strawberry, or raspberry filling. I arrived late several times. They said they'd look for someone else. Job #3 was dishwashing at the diner in Oak Bluffs near the ferry dock. The Captain's Table. The warmth of the owner and his family offset the meniality of the work. This is the one case where I decided to depart after several weeks, instead of enduring yet another insult of termination. It was a summer of hard knocks but, with such experience came introspection and self-reflection that brought one mid-adolescent a step closer to badly needed maturity.

I was not new to the concept of work. I had worked for my dad since I was thirteen in increasingly responsible positions, starting with being a stock boy, rolling goods into the store and stacking them on shelves. Wolf White and Sons on Water Street in Worcester. The name of the building—Mendel block—is still visible. Graduated to delivery. Fun for me because I got to go to all the "spas" in different towns. It was good knowing my work was helpful to my dad. He had a series of delivery men who were not always reliable. Before that I had mowed lawns in the neighborhood.

Forward to MV. I left Wesley House. I was getting terrible wages. Work was 5-8 in the morning. Meager pay. No redeeming qualities. Did not enjoy staff, hours, nature of work. I gave notice. Captain's Table I continued. I was there about six weeks. I was living in Menemsha in a hovel with Betty. Had to commute to Oak Bluffs with a motor scooter that kept breaking down. Sometimes I got off work at Captain's Table late at night, would start out and the scooter broke down. I hitchhiked back. Took scooter to Chancy Morey, a colorful Vineyard curmudgeon. Never saw the scooter again. A Labretta. I had ridden it all the way from Worcester to the Vineyard.

After our Vineyard honeymoon, except for our years abroad, we vacationed there every year—taking first one, then two, and eventually three children and various dogs with us. At the end of a week there, as we pulled away from the island on the ferry—knowing I would not see it for a full year—I watched the island get smaller until it became invisible. These Vineyard summers represented cherished continuity for Al and me, and the girls whose carousel rides and beach exploration remain ingrained in their childhood memories.

By 1978, after seven years in the Midwest (minus the one year in Peru), my East-Coast boy had had it. Having been born in Ohio, grown up there, graduated from college there, and spending six more years there as a wife and mother I, too, was ready for a change. Armed with a new PhD, fortified by two years working as a Research Scientist at Battelle Memorial Institute (later changed to Battelle Laboratories), Al began exploring positions in Boston. We were both anxious to live in another big city and this would allow frequent visits with his widowed mother, Sarah, in Worcester. Like everyone who met her, we and our children adored her warmth, humor, and generosity. We also loved her cooking.

I can't remember when I first fully grasped how witty Al is. He has been referred to as "stone-faced." Although his face has become somewhat more expressive over the years, he still rarely smiles broadly. I remember telling my mother during our courtship that I didn't know what his laugh sounded like. She thought that was awful. But I think he was too busy watching everyone else laugh when he made a clever, incisive, often ironic remark. I wish I could see into his brain because he comes up so instantly with connections that describe with deep humor exactly the current situation, be it a family matter, a work-related issue, or a global challenge. He avoids puns, dislikes schmaltz, and distains canned humor or telling "jokes" of any kind. Instead his humor is quippy and wholly original. I've been pretty healthy through the years and I'm sure it's partly due to the amount of laughter he brings into my life on a daily, even hourly, basis. I'm often chuckling heartily before I get out of bed in the morning.

Another quality I adore in Al is his problem-solving ability. When I'm faced with something that doesn't work, whether it's a computer that's shut down or a work relationship that is frustrating me, I tend to get flustered, swear, cry, scream, thus shutting down any possibility of being able to look objectively at the situation and apply some creativity to finding a solution. Al, on the other hand, quietly but incisively gets to the heart of the problem and quickly comes up with five possible solutions.

AL ON FIRST POST-GRAD SCHOOL POSITION:

From no collar to white collar. From poking doughnuts to prestigious research center. If I had received a reasonable academic offer, our lives would have been different. After teaching in graduate school, I did not teach again at the college level until 1984. Battelle Memorial Institute was only two blocks from our home, a rare convenience in a commuter-dominated country. My Battelle work and colleagues offered a rich variety of projects in the field of industrial economics, energy analysis, and community development. But the daily highlight occurred outside the walls of my office building. Every day as I approached our house, I would see Kate jumping up and down and waving her arms, waiting for me to cross the street so she could hold my hand and accompany me home. She was my precious, plump companion sharing a sweet smile and the daily news as we headed home to see Mom and sister Lena.

Kate, Lena, and I were building castles by the sea at one of our not-to-be-missed regular Martha's Vineyard summer hangouts—Menemsha. Al had left to use the pay phone. We looked up and saw him leaping through the sand toward us—his long bare legs kicking in all directions. He had been offered a position as a member of the professional team of the New England Energy Congress at Tufts University. It was a temporary job—only six months—but it was enough to get us going. He accepted without hesitation.

As we prepared for a move which would open up excellent professional possibilities for Allen, I pondered my own professional future. One of many things I learned while in the Peace Corps was how much I loved teaching. Yet student teaching in a school system taught me that a formal school setting was too limiting. If I were to teach, it would in a program where I was free to apply my creativity to developing my own curriculum. Women were beginning to dedicate themselves to full-time careers that sometimes took them away from their families. I wanted to be home for my young children. Within a year, I would initiate a home-based business which met all my criteria–offering small language classes in my home to children ages 5-12. It was a career which created the right balance of growth and challenge for decades.

We packed a small moving van and moved. Al's Tufts job ended up lasting a year and a half. By then we were thorough Bostonians and my first entrepreneurial effort, Foreign Language for Young Children (FLYC) was thriving.

But first, we needed to decide where exactly in that large metropolis we should settle. Wherever our treasured, bright little girls, now six and four, could experience an excellent education, we decided. Our hearts were drawn to the city proper, but the Boston public schools were in complete disarray. We had relatives in the nearby suburb of Newton and Newton had a national reputation for excellence in education.

There was also another factor. In Kansas City six years earlier, we had experienced the benefits of communal living. Shared resources meant lower living costs and a smaller environmental footprint, an issue about which we deeply cared. An extended-family-like atmosphere meant built-in mutual support and positive models for our children. On a whim, we posted a notice at the Boston Food Coop.

We soon received a response from a childless professional couple with a generous offer to stay with them in their current home while we looked for a suitable place to rent together—in Newton. We found the perfect place. A three-floor dwelling at the end of a cul-de-sac in Newton Center. Lesley and Bob took the third-floor rooms plus bath on the top floor. We took three rooms plus bath on the second. We all shared the first-floor living room, dining room, and kitchen. In retrospect, I must say that we probably got the best of the shared arrangement. Most of the furniture belonged to Lesley and Bob. There were four of us and two of them. Since they were away during the day, we used the house far more intensively than they did. As if our family wasn't already causing more than our share of wear and tear, I began a business in the dining room, teaching French and Spanish to young children. We also benefitted from their attention to our children and from the fact that Lesley was a professional chef, a talented seamstress, and a gifted carpenter, as well as a woman of exceptional generosity and humility.

As we approached the one-year anniversary of this arrangement, Allen took a job with the Center for Community and Economic Development (CCED) as a Research Scientist involved in urban economic studies, energy analysis, and job creation through renewable energy. Kate and Lena were responding well to school. We decided to move from renter status to home ownership in the same town where we were already living—Newton, Massachusetts.

Again we found a house that excited all of us. It was even in the same school district, but it would require the resources of three, not two couples to purchase it. Ultimately, Lesley and Bob decided to purchase a home with another childless couple. We bought the house with other friends, Steve and Becky, who were expecting their first baby. It was large enough that we were able to make up for the loss of one couple by renting out space.

When we moved to Boston one year earlier, my first purchase was a $600 piano I picked up at an estate sale. With Lena soaring on the violin since she began Suzuki lessons shortly before she turned four, and with musicians on both sides of our family, we felt it was a most necessary purchase. But it left us with less than $1,000 in a savings account—the only money we had.

Nevertheless, in August 1979, we closed on an 1858, Italianate, seventeen-room home on a large corner lot, with a circular driveway and a lake view. Our fifty percent share was $65,000 and we needed to come up with a down-payment of $22,000. We spent our entire savings account of (by then) $2,000 and traded in a life insurance policy for another $900. The rest of our share of the down payment was in the form of loans from my parents, Al's mom, and Al's Uncle Max. Except for $1,000 Al's mother eventually forgave, five years later we had paid back every dollar of the family loans.

We occupied the first floor, Becky and Steve the second. We rented the third which had a separate entrance. There was a huge front yard where Becky raised vegetables, including ten-foot corn and (much later we found out to our horror) several hidden marijuana plants. The house also provided a perfect arrangement for my foreign language classes. As you entered the front door there was a half bath straight ahead, a large library on the right, and on the left an over-sized open living room that was probably a double parlor in its Victorian days. Parents could easily drop off and pick up, wait in the living room, or sit in on the classes that I gave in the library. For parties we roasted marshmallows in the fireplace on the glassed-in porch and prepared s'mores.

During those years Al worked at Northern Energy Corporation/Northeast Solar Energy Corporation, followed by a consulting organization which he founded. He also spent five years in academia in various faculty and research positions at the University of Connecticut, Clark University, and Tufts University. In 1990, he joined Tellus Institute, a global sustainability research organization, where he remains as Vice-President and Senior Fellow. His bicycle commute to Tellus during the last 25 years remains one of the great joys of his life.

Thinking I would enjoy an article on the importance of studying foreign languages at a young age, the mother of one of my students gave me an issue of *Psychology Today*. I was always happy to see that theme treated in the media. Every day I observed and delighted in how easily and uninhibitedly children learned French and Spanish. I felt strongly that delaying foreign language classes until middle school was foolish and a missed opportunity in American education.

But it was another article in that magazine that captured my interest—a review of Ira Progoff's *At a Journal Workshop*. My only diary as a child, given to me by my writer mom for Christmas when I was in the seventh grade, had a gold lock and matching tiny key. The sound of the lock clicking into place and the careful hiding of the dainty key assured me that my secrets were well hidden from three younger sisters.

That diary is long lost, but some of the memories remain unexamined for decades and suddenly resurface bringing new insights. Take the choice of Al as my life-mate, for example. At age thirteen I didn't yet have a "type." Yet I now realize that a first serious relationship shaped my future choice.

Jimmy's influence was there when I fell in love with Al at first sight. In addition to their height, slenderness, and coloring, they have in common a natural sweetness, a calm, a quiet confidence, and a strong but gentle paternalism that makes others, including me, feel safe and cared for. I wonder if those appealing characteristics come from something else they have in common. They are both the middle and only son with an older and a younger sister.

Since that brief youthful foray into diary writing, I had felt too busy living my life to take time to document or analyze it. But the subtitle of Progoff's book, *Writing to Access the Power of the Unconscious and Evoke Creative Ability*, intrigued me. This was no ordinary fill-the-blank-page journal. With a dozen separate sections dedicated to daily entries, dialogs, dreams, relationship to work, relationship to society, etc., its organized approach appealed to me. When I learned it was out of print, I searched for it everywhere. In those pre-Internet, pre-Amazon, days, locating a specific book was challenging. Reluctantly, I turned my attention back to reading novels.

A few months later, while accompanying Al to an Association of American Geographers conference in Los Angeles, I wandered into a bookstore. Focusing on novels as usual, browsing with nothing particular in mind, I found myself pulled toward an area I normally ignored—the psychology section. I was about to continue on when a book leaped forward from where it had been lined up carefully with the others. It was as if someone were behind the shelf and pushed it toward me. I saw it move. The book seemed to be saying, "Here I am. Grab me while you can." Ira Progoff's *At a Journal Workshop* was now in my hands.

I bought a three-ring binder, set up the section dividers, and began writing. The interaction and influence of the separate entries fascinated me, but it's Progoff's guidance in accessing one's subconscious that has given me insight and provided a framework for making every major decision since. Following his methods gave me the confidence to regard my subconscious as not some hidden, mysterious, possibly even frightening and spooky place, but as an asset I could call on to enrich my life and inform my choices. Thirty years after discovering Progoff, I began writing historical novels. It's from that part of my mind that my characters spring often unbidden—with their unique personalities and desires ready to leap into my story—just as Progoff's book leaped forward on that shelf decades ago.

TWO MAJOR DECISIONS. As I approached forty, I felt I had to make some decisions about my own career. My language classes could be offered only after school. Although working from home was extremely convenient, I had only ten hours a week in which to earn money. I had seventy-five students, there was a waiting list and I did not want classes larger than eight. I supplemented that part-time effort by becoming an adjunct professor at University of Massachusetts/Boston and a counselor for foreign au pairs and their host families. When I made an appointment with a career counselor, I left in tears—not because of her, but because I realized that FLYC was my calling, that I was not finished teaching French and Spanish to Young Children.

There was more to do. I just needed to find a way to enlarge the effort and a way to use the materials I had developed over decades. I needed to scale up the work I loved. But at that time, in 1982, I felt blocked from concentrating on expanding my business. I couldn't move forward in my creative/work life because I wanted a third child. I wanted a boy child. Al was quite happy with his two precious daughters, but agreed to pursue the possibility of a number three. I continued to be concerned about the effect on Lena of being squeezed between two biological children, and of being the only adopted and only bi-racial child in our family. I was also clear that it was a boy child I wanted. I would love to have had two biological and two adopted children, but if I could have only one more child, it would be an adopted child.

Al and I did not want to begin again with an infant. We approached a private adoption agency with this wish: a bi-racial boy between the ages of three and five with no health problems or disorders. A big wish! Nine months later nothing was happening at the agency and I went searching in the Department of Social Services folders. After turning page after page, looking at scores of photos, and reading descriptions, I found myself looking at the handsomest, cutest kid I'd ever seen. Three years old and bi-racial. It turns out, he was also quite healthy and active. He had been in the same foster home since birth—a real plus—and he had recently been released for adoption.

When we pulled up in front of the foster home for our first visit, we heard a little-boy voice from behind the screen door. "Daddy." Doug understood that he needed a dad, but in his mind, Al should move to Quincy to live with him and the foster mother. Quite logical, really. Since he already had a mommy, I was initially a bit extraneous. On one of our visits when the female social worker was present, Doug wanted the attention of all four adults and called out "Mommy, Mommy, Mommy, Daddy!"

Adding Doug to our household was a markedly different experience from adding the two previous children—both infants. The social worker eased everyone through a process that took about five weeks of ever-increasing contact. Doug was old enough to ask questions and understand but, of course, Peg was the only mommy he had ever known. Although very loving, Peg was a single woman in her sixties. He seemed to understand intuitively that with us he would have a more expansive life with more opportunities. Yet switching families was difficult.

After the initial meeting, Lena and Kate introduced themselves to Doug by making a scrapbook full of photos and notes just for him. Then Al and I had an afternoon with Doug in person all by ourselves—just the three of us. A photo we must have asked a passerby to snap for us shows Doug and his soon-to-be mother sitting in the sand with Al stretched out behind us, all of us looking into the camera. Our beautiful, but anxious three-year-old holds tight onto Al's fingers. During a visit to McDonald's the same day Doug was engaged and somewhat more relaxed. Next Lena and Kate visited Doug for the first time—at his foster home. By then Doug had gone through the scrapbook many times. He knew exactly who they were. He knew their names. The girls were seven and ten and they all three had fun on the playground equipment.

It seemed pretty natural.

When Peg and Doug visited our house in Newton, the first thing Doug said when he walked into the living room was, "Look, Mommy (meaning Peg), a piano." There was no piano in the foster home. Our little three-year-old seemed to know already where his major interests and talents lay. After he was ours, he soon was spending hours a day at that piano, inventing tunes and sometimes singing at the top of his lungs. Once after meeting Rosa Parks, I heard him singing his latest tune, "Rosa in the Park." He was barely four. Eschewing formal lessons ("She's not teaching me what I want to learn"), he taught himself chords and came up with his own charming melodies. By age twelve, he already had a rich, full, strong baritone sound that astonished those who encountered it.

We saw Aunt Peg one more time, when she visited several months later to bring Christmas gifts. Doug was a little tense about the visit and he fell while playing in the driveway. I was standing right next to Aunt Peg. When Doug saw blood running down his leg, he ran toward Peg and me, crying, "Mommy. Mommy." I honestly did not know which of us he would reach for, but Doug and I had bonded. Every morning we spent time alone together while the girls were at school. While I taught in the afternoon he played at a small neighborhood family day care that he thoroughly enjoyed. The whole family was together every evening for dinner and on weekends. He was a big three-year old, but I could still carry him around on my hip. I was the mommy he came to that day for a hug, a cleanup, and a band-aid. I felt such pain for Peg. Peg died four years later. Allen and I attended her wake, but Doug did not want to.

Al on living at 21 Lake Avenue:

Improbable phase of our lives. Living in an 1858, seventeen-room house in an affluent Boston suburb seemed beyond our reach and misaligned with our lifestyle. Our paramount concern was quality of education. We could have found such education in Brookline, but it was unaffordable at the time. We could have found good education in Needham and Wellesley, but that would have been beyond our toleration for suburban living. Even living in Newton was unaffordable unless we co-purchased. It was safe and family-friendly and relatively close to Boston. But for me it was a seventeen-year residence of continuous impatience to relocate to a more urban environment.

Al on adopting Doug:

We had animated discussions about enlarging the family. I was concerned about finances. I felt it might constrain us further. We were always drawn to exploration and travel, to new places, new faces. I worried a new child would cramp our style. Ultimately, I knew that I would adjust. I also felt that not adopting now would represent for Judith a life-long loss. So on we went. Raising Doug was not easy, but we never thought it would be given that he was a mixed-race kid in a predominantly suburban environment, adopted at age three and a half. That he was bright, healthy, energetic, curious, and very handsome certainly helped. We dealt with the challenges. He's a great kid. Given the challenges we knew Lena and Doug would face growing up, we wanted to offer them the most stability possible. It was years before we went abroad again.

MAY 1996
New Love

I always thought that I would have several years between the time our third child left home and the birth of our first grandchild. Child-free time. Not to be. Shortly after turning twenty-two, Lena gave birth to Nicole on May 3, 1996. Three weeks later, Doug graduated from high school and soon left for college. Our beloved family dog, Sheba, had recently died. The last of several cats ran away. In August that year, Al and I moved out of the big Lake Avenue house and into a condominium in Brookline. Thus began a life more suitable to our new status as urban empty-nesters.

During our twenty years of raising children, Al insisted that Friday night was sacred. Couple night. Date night. Movie night. We hired babysitters. Al's mother stayed over. We usually couldn't afford a sitter, dinner, and a movie, so we would have dinner with the kids and skedaddle. Now closer to the allure of Boston city life, with no need to serve regular dinners for a hungry adolescent, no need to supervise homework, or enforce curfews, we realized, gosh, we could go to movies midweek, we could spontaneously show up at the box office and attend a Boston Ballet performance.

But there was a new love in our lives. We couldn't get enough of our green-eyed grandbaby. Nicole was my first thought when I woke and my last thought before I went to sleep. Grandparenting is a gift—one we were given while we were still young and active enough to enjoy it thoroughly. In our community of late births, we were occasionally and flatteringly mistaken for the parents. This was joy without primary responsibility. When a friend asked Lena, "Is there anything about becoming a parent that surprises you?" Lena answered, "Yes, how much I enjoy it." She was a natural, intuitive, responsive mother. We were free to play, sing, dance, and observe the wonder of a growing, rapidly learning child in a way we couldn't with our children.

When she was about six months old, I was carrying Nicole in front of our condo. She reached up to hold a leaf from a low-hanging branch. I watched as she examined the leaf, turned it over, studied its shape, traced its veins. Was I really so young once that I could be so entranced by a leaf?

Another time my brother Johnny (6'2"), Allen (6'3"), and I (5'8") all got on our knees and crawled into a plastic playhouse that Nicole enjoyed. With adult long legs and big feet sticking through the door and windows, Nicole happily prepared us "tea," arranged her dolls, and "read" us books as if climbing over giants in one's home were perfectly natural.

Nicole was poised. She was a connector. On the occasions when I picked her up at day care, the little tot would always proudly introduce me around, "Gamma, dis is Tessie. Tessie, dis my gamma."

The summer she turned two, after living in a number of different homes in Boston's western suburbs, she and her parents moved to Cape Cod. It was perhaps my favorite summer ever. We visited nearly every weekend. Until then the Cape was for us a place we passed through to catch the ferry to Martha's Vineyard. That summer we discovered its allure. When we arrived on Friday nights, after hugs, Nicole and I would put on some music, hold hands, and swing in circles. Then we spent the weekend exploring together. The individual charm of each village. The hidden lakes and ponds. So many beaches.

Less than a year later, we experienced one of our saddest evenings ever. I took a photo in front of a mirror, so that Al and our little darling are visible both from the front and the back. There she is with her black eyelashes, blond bangs and shiny ponytail, focusing her bleary eyes on the book Al is reading to her, *Boomer's Big Day*. On the cover is a forlorn-looking dog surrounded by boxes, some taped up, some half-filled with household goods. Al is holding her close. Reflected in the mirror is a bright light from the flash. Under that flash, I'm a barely visible, faded presence. Nicole's parents were trying to keep her awake so that she would sleep in the car. They were going to drive all night. They were moving to Florida.

AL ON BECOMING A GRANDFATHER AT AGE FORTY-NINE:

The arrival of the little queen was a seminal moment. Healthy. Beautiful. Engaging. Charismatic. Cuddly. I achieved something I had always wanted: carrying on a long tradition spanning the generations, I became a grandfather called "Zayde."

AFTER THEY LEFT TOWN:
She changed our life upon arrival. She changed our life upon departure. She was so prominent in our thoughts and activities. And we in hers. Now suddenly when she was 1,200 miles away, it was a shock to the family chemistry. We knew that our time with her would then be limited to two or so times a year. Precocious Nicole proved to be resilient and adaptable under the loving wing of her extraordinary mother. When Lena made the decision to move from Gainesville to Jacksonville, Nicole, age four, said, "OK, Mommy, let's get packin'." Thanks to the wise parenting of her mother and devoted father, our beautiful, talented, caring, extroverted eighteen-year-old granddaughter is building a life of great promise.

FALL 1997–SEPTEMBER 1998
Bold Idea, Then Shock

AL–FALL 1997:
The idea was hatched mid-1997 after a frustrating meeting in Chicago with companies regarding the idea of environmental reporting. Their attitude: "We don't understand the value or the audience for such reporting." Unspoken was the view that they were unconvinced that an entity such as CERES—the leading U.S. coalition of environmentalists and investors that I had advised since its creation in 1990— had the legitimacy and credibility to create a reporting framework that would be widely recognized as authoritative by companies, investors, NGOs and other stakeholders.

The same day over a beer, three people—Bob Massie, then Executive Director of CERES; Judy Kusziewski, a CERES staff member; and I—were debriefing after an underwhelming workshop. In a moment of epiphany emerged the idea of designing a program that would reach beyond U.S. boundaries and build a structure that recognized worldwide the standards of excellence for corporate environmental reporting. The concept of a global reporting initiative was born that day. It soon became the upper-case GRI. We believed history was on our side, the winds of change were at our back—it was the moment to mobilize around a big idea whose time had come.

Rationale: By the late nineties, there had occurred a series of corporate incidents that raised public awareness of the environmental risks of corporate activities. The two most prominent were the Bhopal Chemical tragedy in India and the Exxon Mobile oil spill off the coast of Alaska. These were

*seminal events, catalysts to public awareness that corporate activity creat-
ed environmental footprints which must be measured, managed, and disclosed. Environmental accountability must take its place alongside financial
accountability.*

*In the months following our meeting, we began a five-year journey to bring
this concept to reality. These were years of excitement, experimentation, and
exhaustion. This involved intensive networking to enlist corporations, investors, NGOs, labor, and government to collaborate on this great, global venture. It would require enhancement of the reporting architecture I had initiated
years ago at CERES—outreach to a global audience that would transcend borders and constituencies and, soon after its conception, expand the purview of
reporting from purely environmental to encompass economic, social, and governance issues. With my partner, Bob Massie, I would journey into intellectual
and political territory little known to either of us.*

*We traveled, organized, and spoke at a furious pace for five years. With
the help of a new invention—the Internet—we reached audiences from Argentina to Malaysia, South Africa to Japan, and Canada to Germany.*

*In a very early meeting at the CERES office on Atlantic Avenue in Boston,
the first steering committee was formed. The personalities in the room blend-
ed companies, investors, and NGOs who historically shared little common
ground when it came to environmental and social matters. It was a contentious meeting that portended a process that demanded consensus-building
skills beyond anything we had demonstrated. We were building not only a
process, but a brand—a "multi-stakeholder initiative" to address a gaping de-
ficiency in global governance—corporate accountability for the non-financial
impacts of business organizations. In that early meeting at CERES, Bob and
I witnessed the first step of a journey whose outcome we could not possibly
imagine.*

SEPTEMBER 1998–DIAGNOSIS. A year after that momentous Chicago
meeting, following a routine annual physical, Al's internist called and asked
that he come into the office. Usually if the doctor had any concerns, he discussed them by phone. This was unusual and we were nervous. Al was in De-
troit when he received the message. The flight home was filled with anxiety.
If there were a concern that was so serious that it could be discussed only in
person, what could it be? As possible answers to that question popped into our
minds, we pushed them away.

When we arrived in the doctor's office, I saw a word on Al's chart that made
my heart stop. "Leukemia?" I asked the doctor. I'm sure I looked stricken. "It's

not so bad," the doctor said. "Don't worry." In fact, as leukemias go it could have been a lot worse. As the visit ended, the Internist said, "I've found the best white-cell guy for you." A reassuring way, a soft way of saying "You're going to need him."

A high white-cell count on a routine blood test had prompted the doctor to do further blood testing. The diagnosis was Chronic Lymphocytic Leukemia (CLL). The intense emotions we shared in the next few weeks mirrored almost perfectly, I realized, Elizabeth Kubler Ross's "Five Stages of Grief": Denial, Anger, Bargaining, Depression, and finally, Acceptance. Well, Bargaining and Depression, not so much. Neither of us is the type to withdraw into a corner, tough things out alone, and feel sorry for ourselves. We immediately wrote our large extended family. We wanted sympathy. We wanted support. We got it . . . in abundance.

AL'S REACTION TO THAT VISIT:

GRI was in its infancy with high aspirations, little money, and surging momentum. The juxtaposition of all that excitement against the sudden diagnosis created a wrenching emotional experience. I knew that the project would take years to evolve and emerge in the way we aspired. But the "L" word suddenly exploded on the landscape of hope and determination. It felt as if the devil was knocking at the door of my professional life. A pall was cast over the survival of the project and over one of its co-founders—me.

My brother, Johnny, said, "It's obvious to me that Al wants to leave a legacy." Yet Johnny urged Al to quit his job and dedicate himself to working with his disease, to get out from under the pressure of founding a new organization, to just take it easy. Johnny later commented, "Boy, was I wrong. His work inspires him. It keeps him going."

The year was 1998. Al was fifty-two years old. We had been married thirty years—not nearly long enough, I felt. I wanted thirty more.

Part II

Living with Leukemia
1998–2009

FALL 1998–FALL 2010
Learning–Managing

For Al, knowledge is power. He immerses himself in learning everything he can about the disease. Most common form of adult leukemia. Fifteen thousand people diagnosed annually in the U.S. Mostly adults between ages forty and sixty. A cancer of the bone marrow. Early symptoms—only the high white-blood-cell count which Al's annual physical has uncovered. Later symptoms—swollen lymph nodes, spleen, and liver. Advanced stage symptoms—anemia and multiple infections. Cure—none. Average time between diagnosis and death—ten years. Early management—regular monitoring. Later treatment—chemotherapy, biotherapy, radiation. Ultimate treatment—a bone marrow transplant. With no guarantees.

Although a bone marrow transplant offers the most hope, it is rarely used in the initial stages of the disease because of its risks. Healthy cells are removed from a large bone of the donor, typically the pelvis, through a wide needle that reaches the center of the bone. The technique is referred to as a "bone marrow harvest." Then the healthy cells are placed into the hip bone of the patient. Isolation is crucial. The patient may come in physical contact with no one and must remain in a carefully controlled, germ-free environment in the hospital for several months. The prospects for a patient who after years of disease is severely immune compromised are not encouraging. The prospect of such a disruptive, dangerous, and demanding procedure looms over our lives for the next twelve years.

However, chronic is not acute. We are fortunate. Our children are all in their twenties establishing their independence. We can both continue to dedicate ourselves full time to work we love. We travel. What's more, Al is in the care of an outstanding oncologist at Dana Farber Cancer Institute—the "white-cell guy" the Internist referred to. In fact there are two such guys. Dr. G for five years and then Dr. F for the next seven during which the disease is relatively dormant.

When we moved to a cozy residential area of Brookline, Massachusetts two years before diagnosis, it never occurred to us that a nearby world-class medical area would become so central to our lives. For years we arrived at Dana Farber Cancer Institute or "Dana" as we called it, after a ten-minute car ride, a fifteen-minute bike ride, or a twenty-five-minute walk. For the first ten years those visits are sporadic. Eventually, as the sleeping devil awakens and begins to gnaw at Al's health and at our lifestyle and psyche, we will be there every day.

For now, over a period of many months, I watch Al grapple with what the diagnosis means for his future. Will he have the strength to see the Global Reporting Initiative realize its full potential? Will he live to see other grandchildren born and his beloved first, Nicole, grow into womanhood? Just how much time and effort will the disease require of him? When I try to encourage him to talk about feelings, he tends to use intellectual words. Although he's extremely articulate, emotional language in those years does not come easily to him. After sharing his diagnosis with family members as well as with the senior team at Tellus, he delays telling the staff of Tellus's Business and Sustainability Group that he leads.

Al on his Tellus work:

The Business and Sustainability Group began with three staff in the early nineties and grew rapidly. Because of Tellus's unwritten requirement that 'every new hire raise the average IQ in the organization,' the talent was extraordinary. Just to get an interview, an applicant needed a graduate degree and a 3.5 grade average. My group did international, national, and local work on environment and sustainability studies, drifting increasingly to the role of business in advancing the sustainability agenda. Over time, in order to lighten my supervision burden, I succeeded in grooming three managers. Those managers, in turn, developed their programs and hired younger staff in the image of their own exceptional talent. By 1997 the Business and Sustainability Group numbered seventeen and was the largest of four groups at Tellus.

Finally, after several months of pondering the best way to inform the group about his diagnosis, Al calls them all into his office. By then, some may have heard that he is ill, but others are shocked. A few cry.

Al on informing Tellus board members and program staff:

I told my fellow Tellus board members shortly after diagnosis: Chronic Lymphocytic Leukemia is chronic. It's indolent. The typical evolution of the disease would be uneventful for years, although, for reasons that are not understood, in some patients it turns acute. However, because of my overall strong health, I did not expect that to happen. I put off telling my program staff at Tellus for several months. I wanted to be as educated as possible and convey expectations that were probable and based on science. I did not want to have to answer questions with, "I don't know." I did not want to be seen as diminished, but I wanted to be honest, so that should I become incapacitated earlier than I expected, they would be prepared.

We crowded into my office. It was a bit delicate because I was already delegating a lot of duties to the more senior of my staff—not because of my illness, but because I was dedicating so much attention to GRI, the focus of my energy and passion. I didn't want my senior managers to feel anxious that the captain was fragile and, possibly, on his way toward debilitation.

What was that meeting like? It was intense. Some people already had a sense that something was wrong. They may have sensed my distraction. Those people seemed prepared to hear bad news. Others were stunned. The "C" word is always shocking. "It's a blood disease, not a tumor disease," I explained, "but it's still cancer. For now, it's business as usual," I told them.

Given the anxiety about what the future would hold in my work life, I felt emotionally on trial with a shadow hanging over my future. Physically I was performing unchanged. It was a short meeting, probably twenty-five minutes. I think they left feeling reassured, at least for a while.

Karen Shapiro, former Tellus Institute Senior Scientist and one of the Business and Sustainability Group's managers looks back on that meeting fourteen years later:

It's amazing because clearly this was something happening to someone else, yet it had a strong impact on me. It felt jarring and momentous. It's one of those moments you always look back on with a sharp focus. You remember where you were standing. The group anxiety. The feeling of being crammed into his office. Why are we not meeting in the conference room where we usually meet? The more intimate setting intensified the curiosity and self-concern. Oh my, how is this going to affect us as individuals? As a group? What strikes me from that day is that it seemed that it had been a tough decision for him to tell us, whether to tell us, plus when and what exactly to reveal to us.

I believe he was keeping the news to himself as long as he felt the diagnosis was not going to affect his work life. But then he reached a stage where he had to be cautious about his travel destinations. At the time he was on a new drug that had been approved in Europe, but had just been introduced in the U.S. He was just so thankful to have access to leading medical knowledge and medicine.

Allen was held in high regard by his staff. Hearing about this potential threat to his life was like hearing that my uncle had been diagnosed. I felt I was getting some information but not a lot. Part of me wanted to know more, but I felt I had to respect his privacy. Kind of tough to know that your work colleague has a horrible disease and what it might mean for him, but also that you're dependent on him to reveal information to you at his own pace.

The general reaction among us was one of total shock because we had not observed any change in him. As we walked out the door there was a lot of breaking up into small groups for conversation. What does it mean? His attitude seemed very positive, but we still wondered. But as time went on, I think we almost forgot about it. The way he took on the demanding tasks of creating Global Reporting Initiative convinced us he wasn't doing too badly. I never saw any decline in his health. Periodically I was reminded he was having blood draws, perhaps even transfusions. There was that telltale gauze bandage on his arm.

Yes, those blood draws. Al becomes adept at the language that describe the ups and downs of his condition. Hematocrit. Platelets. Lymphocytes. T cells. Stem cells. The printouts are long. The information they spit out is daunting. What helps Al grasp all this information and gradually be able to analyze it is in part due to the relating style of his doctor.

AL ON ADMIRATION FOR HIS ONCOLOGIST:

Dr. F is one thoughtful, understated physician, an oncologist with a long history of working with CLL. He has an unusual manner in terms of how he interacts with patients. I feel included in his thought process. He thinks out loud about the prognosis and options available for managing the disease. By doing this and looking at the lab results, he invites you into his mind and makes the decision-making process a mutual one with the patient. So different from being handed a set of orders by a higher-up, the process is empowering for the patient. I feel no doctor-patient divide, but rather like a member of a decision-making team. The approach invites thoughtful critique. That suits my personality.

Dr. F might muse aloud: 'Now if we start Rituxin next month, then we have to consider XYZ, we may control the disease earlier. On the other hand, we might opt to wait and begin in six months . . . because the sooner we begin a therapy, we have to be aware of building antibodies over time. We are at the point where the disease may be accelerating. We don't want to build resistance to later treatments.' By verbalizing that thought process, he is inviting questions from the patient. Not a shy sort, I fire away. His approach also leads me to my own research. I take those questions home with me and dedicate significant time to framing and forming opinions of what would be best. Then I return and say, "I saw this while scouring the literature at the Harvard School of Public Health and want to discuss it with you." I educate myself about risk factors, drug trials, who is most vulnerable and why, life cycle of the disease, new therapies.

During the decade after diagnosis, CLL accompanies Al on his global travels. Meeting far-flung colleagues and admirers of his oncology team provides its own set of adventures. The results of Al's blood draws are faxed to Boston from a French facility that dates from the seventh century—*l'Hôpital Hôtel-Dieu* on *Îsle de la Cité* next to Notre Dame Cathédral in Paris, for example; and from *Onze Lieve Vrouwe Gasthuis* in Amsterdam. Al also sometimes notifies international colleagues before visiting, explains his disease, and asks them to have a doctor's contact information at the ready—just in case. A close and caring colleague in Sao Paulo, Brazil, for instance, writes back immediately, "It's done. Not to worry." There are days when Al rises very early for a blood test and then heads off for a meeting or to speak at a conference, be it in New York City, San Francisco, or Washington. The occasional blood transfusion keeps him going, but he often looks tired.

I attempt to involve Al in visualization. The idea is that both of us together imagine his white cells as ripe and healthy, completely free of disease. I lead him on a guided meditation. Through his skin, his flesh, his muscles. We are tunneling right through his veins.

I am really involved in this journey, when he suddenly says, "Stop."

"What's the matter?" I ask.

"It's too invasive," he answers.

'And all those medical procedures aren't?' I think. I am disappointed and a little hurt. Going forward, I continue to visualize healthy cells, but I keep my visualizations to myself.

Early on the morning of September 11, 2001, I am chatting on the phone with our friend, Roberto. As the conversation ends, Roberto says, "By the way, a plane just flew into The World Trade Center. You might want to check it out. You better prepare yourself, though."

I run to the television, which is never on before 7:00 p.m., if then. After observing the smoke, destruction, collapse, and confusion for ten minutes, I watch with growing horror and fear along with the rest of the United States as a second plane hits. Meanwhile, Al is on a phone call in his home study. I can hear from the tenor of his voice that neither he nor whoever he is speaking with has heard the news. Finally I hear him end the call.

I call him into our TV room.

"Do you know what's happening?" I ask.

I explain briefly. But when I say my next sentence, the enormity of the situation hits me and I sob through my words: "They've closed down every airport in the country."

Al and I embrace, sharing mutual stunned disbelief and fear.

Two days later all U.S. airports are still closed—no planes are allowed in or out of the entire United States. Al has an important GRI meeting at Imperial College in London, part of his effort to bring the initiative to the attention of European companies, investors, NGOs, and governments. But how to travel with a shuttered U.S. air space?

The solution? With two colleagues, he rents a car, drives to Montreal and flies across the Atlantic. I am pretty frightened just thinking of him in the sky and on earth too, for that matter, negotiating borders at such a tense time. He is worried that if he does not go, the still fledgling Global Reporting Initiative will be in jeopardy.

Addressing the group of 200, who are amazed that he appears on schedule, he connects the recent horror to GRI's goals:

"Global Reporting Initiative has world-wide implications and potential impact to define a new era of corporate accountability in a global world. Its success requires the cooperation of all countries and cultures. We must continue this journey, now more than ever. We must dedicate ourselves to such cooperation, to participate in it fully. We must not let the destruction of a few madmen distract us from building a just and sustainable world."

SPRING 2002
Courtship, Choice, and Recognition
Global Reporting Initiative Finds a Home
And So Do We

From an initial list of ten possibilities for locating a permanent home for GRI after its launch at the United Nations in April 2002, the field narrows to two cities in The Netherlands. The Hague and Amsterdam compete to host the new international organization. During the courtship, mayors and other high officials from both cities entertain us in elaborately decorated centuries-old state buildings. The spaces, reserved for intimate VIP dinners, are designed to dazzle.

For three hours, they roll out the gold-plated china, the tall, thick silver candlestick holders, the large, linen embroidered napkins, and course after course of hearty native foods. A meal might begin with *erwtensoep*, a thick pea soup cooked with sausage or ham, then proceed to a first course of *hutspot*, a thick potato/beef stew with carrots and onions. There are mussels, oysters, their famous pickled herring, and a variety of breads and cheeses followed by creamy flans, *appeltaart* and chocolates, all accompanied by native beers, *jenever* (gin), and wine served in large-bowled, glazed goblets. Speeches and gifts follow. Both aim to entice, to convince GRI that their city can provide the best in family life, comfort, culture, business opportunity, entrepreneurship, belief in GRI's mission, and, most importantly, the needed financial support for GRI's startup.

INTRODUCTION TO US:
We are a professional, married couple from Boston, Massachusetts. One is employed as the Acting Chief Executive for a new international organization that is locating in Amsterdam. The other is an educator/trainer/writer and a consultant to nonprofit organizations.
OUR APARTMENT NEEDS/WANTS: Amsterdam City Center. Two-to-three-bedroom apartment. Two baths. Fully furnished. Appropriate for entertaining visiting international guests.
TIME PERIOD: 1 September until summer 2003.
PRICE RANGE: Euros 2000-2800.
CONTACT: glochild@hotmail.com   Tel. in U.S.: 617-976-2211

We will be in Amsterdam from 30 May to 7 June and wish to finalize an arrangement at that time for 1 September 2002 occupancy.

Yes, Amsterdam won and for the next year, Allen and I realize a long-held dream: living in Europe together. We explore the charming city itself, of course, and other parts of The Netherlands. But as temporary Europeans, we can also make quick romantic get-aways by train to Paris and Berlin, or fly to Italy. Most of all, we love waking up in this vibrant city, food shopping, entertaining, making new friends, celebrating Dutch holidays, attending concerts at the Royal *Concertgebouw,* and at dusk gazing out our living room window as the lights begin to illuminate the quaint arched bridges reaching into every direction.

ALLEN ON HOW AMSTERDAM WAS CHOSEN:
In choosing the optimal home for GRI, we applied three major criteria. 1) Cordiality—a demonstration that the country not only would welcome the organization but would support it in various ways. Governments needed to step up as we entered a new chapter. GRI needed a stable situation where we could

count on national support for at least a few years until we established a secure financial footing. 2) A location viewed externally as neutral, not tied to a particular way of doing business, or at least open to different views of companies, their corporate cultures, and their societal responsibilities. For me that meant steering it away from an Anglo-American location; namely, the U.K. or U.S. 3) Access and affordability. We weren't a rich organization. In order to attract talented staff, as well as attendees for workshops and meetings, an appealing, central, affordable location would be a great asset.

In early 2002, Dr. Klaus Topfer, head of the United Nations Environment Programme, our U.N. partner in helping to found and build GRI, sent twenty letters on his official United Nations stationery to government officials in Japan, Canada, The Netherlands, Denmark, and a dozen others, inviting and encouraging them to consider permanently hosting GRI. We received half a dozen serious inquiries. When we visited Amsterdam, it was clear it would meet the three criteria. The competition between two Netherlands cities gave me additional confidence that we were zeroing in on the right country.

In April 2002, GRI was officially launched with a ceremony at the United Nations in New York. About 300 guests, representing business, governments, NGOs, and labor groups, attended. The timing of the ceremony allowed us to complete a thorough screening of potential sites leading to my recommendation to the board and their approval. I stood up at the United Nations and announced that we had selected a permanent location—Amsterdam.

With a view toward moving in September 2002, Al begins searching in June for office space. I search for an apartment.

AL ON OFFICE LOCATION:

I thought 'If we're going to be in Amsterdam, let's be in Amsterdam. Let's locate in a canal house.' When we signed the lease for 209 Keizersgracht, highly skilled, specialized craftsmen were restoring in exquisite detail the main room of the seventeenth-century house. The site was suitable for a staff of ten. I could not have imagined that in ten years the organization would outgrow this elegant but limited space as it increased by more than a factor of seven to over seventy personnel.

While searching, we spend one week in a rented apartment located at the intersection of two major canals and the Amstel River in the city center, with water views from large windows on two sides. Our friend, Kien, who grew up in the city, calls it "perhaps the loveliest spot in all Amsterdam."

That week I spend one of the most delightful days of my life. While Al is busy at his new office, our rental agent drives Kien and me around the city and shows us eight available furnished apartments. Kien enjoys sharing her native city. I relish learning about it.

We have a large variety of choices, including several architect-designed apartments. One is on a corner in the Nine Streets—*de Negen Straatjes*—a pedestrian area with narrow cobblestone streets, three blocks wide, and three blocks long; full of cafes, restaurants, barber shops, boutiques, and small shops that sell everything from antiques to lace to chocolates. This apartment is on the second floor with rambling rooms one after the other, but ceilings too low for my 6' 3" husband.

Another is at the top floor of a stately, beige-stone, centuries-old building once owned by the University of Amsterdam, but recently converted to condominiums. As soon as we ring the doorbell and step into a bright, high-ceilinged foyer, a small white dog comes bounding down the stairs, greets us as if we are his dearest friends in the world, and leads us up three flights of stairs to the top-floor apartment. This apartment sits above what was once the university's astronomy lecture hall. In those pre-Power Point days, the professor rolled open the ceiling, thus accessing the universe and revealing the celestial bodies the students were studying.

Now that same ceiling has become the floor of an enormous open space surrounded by narrow balconies with decorative iron railings high up overlooking the city. It is spectacular. Ideal for one person or the right couple. But too open for us, I feel. We require some privacy from each other and from guests.

The next evening, I return to Boston to begin preparations for our move. Al stays behind for a few more days. I cry all the way to the airport.

My travelling companion asks, "Is it Al?"

"No," I say, "It's Amsterdam."

I feel like little crying Kate when she was so impatient for the arrival of her new sister. I don't want to wait another two months to live in that city. I want to begin living there RIGHT NOW.

Al and I agree that after my scouting expedition, I will narrow my choices to two apartments which he will explore the next day. One of the two has a large open kitchen with an island, and one bedroom and bath on either side of the kitchen. Other than the bedrooms and bathrooms there are no walls. The kitchen opens onto a dining room which leads to a lounge which in turn leads to a living room. The apartment just keeps going. It also has a sumptuous garden—beautifully kept by the landlady and available to renters—although it is four floors below this apartment.

Al, however, unhesitatingly chooses the second apartment, deeming my first choice far too spacious and opulent for the head of a new, financially-constrained, non-profit international organization. I am disappointed at first because the chosen unit is quite a bit smaller—the top two floors of a once-grand canal house with one two-floor apartment just below us and an apartment in the basement. The only outdoor space is a tiny balcony overlooking two canals that intersect outside our door. With an open floor plan, the first floor has a living room and kitchen connected by a dining room table. The kitchen, although new and bright, is apparently designed for a single young professional who eats all her/his meals out. The refrigerator is about a third the size of a standard American model. We soon learn to shop European style; i.e., daily.

When we move into the apartment two months later, I fall completely in love with it. Without our having planned it that way, it is a short distance from Al's GRI office on the Keizersgracht—Al's headquarters while he serves as GRI's first and temporary CEO, with the task of launching the entire program. I watch him from the balcony in the mornings as he unlocks his bike from the canal bridge outside our window, throws a leg over the center bar, and rides away. With his briefcase under one arm, he steers with the other, Amsterdam style.

Al once described Amsterdam as having "a busy-bee quality." The bustle begins early. Workers hammer into place a loose brick, repair a roof, replace a street lamp, take down a decayed tree and plant a new tree, dig the recycling out of the underground deposit stations, and haul it off. I observe someone spend days carefully spreading deep green paint on one of thousands of elaborately decorated iron bridges. With small brush in hand, admiring his progress, he whistles and sings and takes his time. Solitary, but bathed in fresh air and sunshine, poised over the water below, he seems so content as the bridge slowly acquires a shiny new look.

A pick-up truck pulls up to a residence. Several workers hop out. Only one enters the building. Soon he pokes his head out from the fourth floor and attaches a pulley to a thick wooden horizontal pole that is permanently attached at the top of the building. In the tradition of centuries-old canal warehousing, the men on the ground attach a piano to a huge hook at the end of the pulley. Slowly the dangling instrument moves up and up and disappears through the window. Later that day, the piano comes to life. Lyrical Chopin streams over to my own window next door.

A huge flat trawler moves through the canals, nearly bumping their sides. Men lower nets, steel baskets, and clamps. Up come cars, a refrigerator, and scores of rusted bicycles. People gather on the bridges to watch.

Twice a day one can observe the otherwise still canal water swishing rapidly forward in waves as if on its own power. The movement is actually the result of a pumping system that sends water from the River IJ to cleanse the entire canal system in a way worthy of the world's preeminent water engineers.

And, oh, those bikes! The Dutch become accustomed to the motion in utero and ride in a basket in front of their parents as babies and toddlers. Bikes are often custom designed to accommodate and adapt to changing family needs for transporting adults, children, and cargo. By the time they're in school, children ride their own bikes through the streets. Courting takes place during bicycle rides. The seriousness of a relationship can be judged by how a couple shares this favored mode of transportation. They may begin on two bikes, reaching across to hold hands. Then she moves to the back of his bike. By the time she's seen cozily perched in front with his arms around her, they're probably moving in together.

We pass female bike riders in high heels and men in suits and ties, one hand on the handlebars, the other holding a briefcase. Among the crowds there are always some riders who appear to be in their seventies and eighties. Relaxed and seemingly with little effort, a rider steers one bicycle with one hand, while carrying a second, riderless and suspended bike tucked under the opposite arm. The number of ingenious ways to cart, pull, move, and deliver all manner of objects on a bicycle amazes us.

Woe to anyone like me who prefers to walk. Once you've nearly stepped in front of a bike and been met with a scornful rebuke from a rider, you don't forget that bikes always have the right-of-way.

Al's work takes him to countries around the globe with the goal of promoting GRI to businesses, nongovernmental organizations (NGOs), investors, governments, and other parties who have a stake in advancing corporate accountability through a new form of reporting. I am visiting the GRI office when Al calls from South Africa where he is attending the World Summit on Sustainable Development—"RIO + 10." I take rapid notes so I can share the highlights with the staff.

AL ON THAT CONFERENCE:

We had two special events announcing and releasing the second generation ("G2") of the GRI sustainability reporting guidelines. One was a large ceremony to celebrate the G2 launch. The second was a workshop on global development. There were scores of other events and sessions. I had been invited as a guest to one of them on short notice. When I entered the room, slightly hurried and barely on time, I took my seat and looked around me. To my dis-

belief, I found myself in the company of heads of state and the U.N. Secretary General, Kofi Annan. Across the table sat Jacques Chirac, Tony Blair, and the presidents of Algeria, Nigeria, Senegal, and other countries. Kofi Annan called the meeting to order and said, 'We are pleased to have as our honored guests—to my right the Franco delegation and to my left the Anglo delegation.' Each group made their remarks in their respective languages.

Later that day, Al is delighted when he receives an unanticipated request from one of the titular heads of the Dutch delegation, saying she is attending the World Summit and would like a briefing on GRI. The next morning Allen finds himself in a corner of the conference hotel lobby in the company of Princess Máxima of The Netherlands, with two of her advisors on either side.

Seven months prior to this meeting, Máxima became the bride of Willem-Alexander, Prince of Orange, heir to the throne of the Netherlands. When they first met, her royal suitor introduced himself simply as "Alexander." When eventually he revealed that he was a prince, she thought he was joking. An attractive Argentine blonde married to a future king, Princess Máxima is a highly educated and accomplished professional. After receiving a degree in Economics from the *Universidad Católica Argentina,* she worked with large international finance companies in Argentina, New York, and Europe. Personable, inquisitive, and multi-lingual, she asks probing questions of Al and GRI board member, Sir Mark Moody Stuart, former CEO of Royal Dutch Shell, a joint Anglo/Dutch company.

Al reports that the princess, with her Wall Street background, was well-prepared and informed about GRI's mission and operations. She also seemed proud that The Netherlands was hosting the fledgling GRI and offered to help in any way she could.

Two days later Al flies from South Africa to The Netherlands. After he boards the plane and settles in, he looks up one row across the aisle and sees Máxima with her prince.

AL ON THAT TRIP:

Sitting next to me was Máxima's chief of staff. Lovely fellow. When Máxima got up to stretch during the ten-hour journey, she walked right over to me and stood there in the aisle dressed casually, recognized me and continued our previous conversation for about twenty minutes.

All the lights went out. Everyone grabbed a blanket, stopped reading and chatting. I had some difficulty getting to sleep after the exhilarating experiences of the past week. Although I'm not easily star-struck, it was especially difficult to doze, knowing royalty was across the aisle.

When Al arrives in Amsterdam, he shares with his staff the news that GRI has passed a critical phase of recognition. Proof is the precious reference to GRI in the official conference document released by the United Nations. GRI is one of two organizations mentioned by name as an exemplary business/NGO-government alliance. That's TWO among HUNDREDS represented at the Summit. The overarching theme of the conference was "Partnerships for Sustainable Development." The timing of such a theme couldn't have been better, communicating that GRI represents a leading example of a new generation of partnerships essential to advancing the global sustainability agenda. Better than any organization in existence at the time, GRI embodies the concept of a multi-stakeholder partnership.

News of GRI's prominence at the Johannesburg summit inspires and energizes both Al and his staff for the journey ahead. In the four months that have elapsed since GRI's launch at the U.N., GRI is quickly emerging as a leading initiative on the global stage. The vision that Bob Massie and Al conceived in 1997 is starting to materialize with a speed and impact that these two dreamers could not have imagined on that prophetic day in Chicago.

MY CAREER. When an American—or at least this American—visits Europe for the first time, she realizes she was born in a baby nation. Compared to thousands of years of European history, the U.S. is barely an adolescent. I am drawn to those historical periods prior to the creation of the United States of America. Middle Ages. Renaissance. Golden Age. With admiration for its clear, interactive exhibits, I devour the Amsterdam Historical Museum that traces the city's growth from a small fishing village in the twelfth century through the present.

I learn that the very building that houses this museum was for 450 years, beginning in 1520, the Amsterdam Civic Orphanage. Pondering a large exhibit that preserves its heritage, I can hear the patter of thousands of little feet moving through those spaces, up and down those stone stairs. I can hear children's voices coming from outside, from the large, stone courtyard. Children who lost entire families to plagues. Children whose mothers died in childbirth. I begin to imagine one child—a little girl. She is six-years-old. Why is she there? Where did she come from? How does she adjust to the confined and rigid, but also nurturing, life in this institution governed by the most prominent men of the time? How long does she remain there? I name the child Nelleke. My fictional character takes on a definite look, personality, and history, along with many needs, longings, and yearnings. I begin writing her story. And for the first time in decades, I actually have the time to dedicate to research and writing.

The thirteen years I taught French and Spanish from my home served as an extended hands-on workshop for me. I could test new methods and approaches and constantly adapt them as I gauged student reactions and learning. I developed enormous amounts of material. By 1992, I knew exactly what worked with grades K-6. Activity. Movement. Fun. I invented games. Wrote songs. Compiled files of visuals. I reached the point where I needed to share it all with a larger population.

When Carlyle Carter, the mother of one of my brightest little language learners, approached me about starting a language program for schools, I liked the idea immediately because it meant that we would send teachers to the students instead of requiring students to come to me.

What's more, Carlyle was a foreign-language editor and had set up a model program in two school districts already. We complemented each other well because I had the material in rough form. She had worked in publishing. Global Child, Inc. was born. Nine years later we were offering classes in thirty-five Massachusetts communities, had published twenty-four curricula, teachers' manuals, and cassette practice tapes. During the school year before we sold the company, I trained ninety-five teachers and we had three thousand students. It was spring 2001.

I was ready for an entirely new career. But what?

There's a certain emotion I rarely feel but, when I do, I pay close attention: jealousy. What does someone have that I don't? And do I really want it? I actually envied those people lining up to take the train downtown to work every day. I was sure I wanted to work OUTSIDE the home for a change. I also wanted to work in the nonprofit sector in a way where I could use my language, writing, and entrepreneurial skills.

Al's cousin, Carrie, was a fund-raising expert and enthusiast. When she and her daughters followed her husband, Hans, to Paris, Carrie convinced the Director of the International School of Paris (ISP) to lower her daughters' tuition in exchange for applying her fund-raising skills to identify and approach potential donors. Because there was little history of tuition-dependent international schools raising money or hiring development staff, her proposal was met with a mix of curiosity and skepticism. By the time Carrie and I sat together for tea in an outdoor café at Place des Vosges in 2001, Carrie was on her way to not only raising large amounts of money for ISP, she had formed a partnership with another experienced fund-raiser to do trainings and consulting for independent schools around the world.

"Judith, you can do this," she said. On the spot, she gave me my first lesson in fund-raising. I can point to the very chairs we were sitting in at the time. "If two people are speaking with a potential donor, which one should 'make the Ask'? The person who knows the most about the organization or the person who knows the donor best?" Carrie asked me. OK, so I had a fifty/fifty chance of answering correctly and I flunked my first lesson. Correct answer is the latter—the person who knows the donor best. But I was hooked.

I began educating myself watching videos, listening to tapes, attending conferences. Before we left for Amsterdam in the fall of 2002, I had convinced the Boston School for Adult Education to hire me to teach a fund-raising workshop on individual gift solicitation at their November conference. I did all the preparation before we left for Amsterdam. Two months later I returned to Boston for three days to deliver that workshop. I was an educator. I figured I could communicate and inspire on a topic, or maybe especially on a topic that I was still learning myself. Given that I was a fund-raising novice, I was pleased with the attendee reviews. In order to build on that experience and extend the learning of the workshop attendees, I collected emails for a website I was setting up—"Tuesday Tips."

Now, because I have no work permit in The Netherlands, I am free to fill my time with continuing the Dutch language studies I began back in Brookline, MA, learning the culture and history of the country, particularly the Golden Age setting where the fictional Nelleke is becoming a beguiling, active, and demanding little presence in my imagination. I join the International Women's Club and take part in an array of their programs including both Dutch and French conversation groups and, to my delight, a French chorus.

OCTOBER 2002
Dictators, Prime Ministers, Princes, and Queens

In Nicaragua Al and I lived under a dictatorship. In Peru we lived under a left-wing military government. Here, of course, we're living in a democracy in the form of a stable constitutional monarchy. Or are we?

I learned soon after I arrived never to compare anything Dutch to anything German. Not a vocabulary word, not a food, not topography, nothing. The Dutch groan if you do.

When at the age of twenty-five, the future Dutch Queen, Beatrix, fell in love with a dashing thirty-six-year-old German diplomat, Claus von Amsberg, her subjects recoiled in horror. Two years later at their wedding, police in riot gear subdued thousands of protesters. That was in 1966. The couple had a son in 1967, another in 1968, a third in 1969.

Beatrix became Queen in 1980. Prince Claus became fluent in Dutch. His charm, his wit, and his devotion to his three little blond boys wore down the Dutch. They embraced him. They loved him. He died just recently at age 76 from Parkinson's disease and the nation is mourning. He adored children and lived long enough to hold his first grandchild. There has been lots of footage of him dancing with the Queen and with African children, and holding a baby monkey that clings to him.

Seeing the three princes now in their thirties, all the same height, standing at attention in formal evening attire as Prince Claus's casket is brought to the palace is so sad. The sons wipe away tears and so do I. The Netherlands has lost a strong father figure and the world can never have enough of those.

But royalty doesn't rule here, of course. Elected officials do that. Yesterday, I was doing my little afternoon Dutch language self-study. I read children's books. While I struggle along looking up every third word, I keep the TV on to hear the adult talk to which I aspire. I don't understand much of it, but I hope I'm getting the feel of the Dutch vowels and intonation.

One afternoon, I thought it odd that all the Dutch stations were carrying the same program–some debate in Parliament. I also noticed that, unlike the usually placid Dutch conversation, this debate was rather heated, even nasty. Half an hour later, I saw these words on CNN: "Dutch government collapses." Collapses? Now that's a strong word. I looked out the window expecting to see people throwing rocks at each other across my canal.

But my Dutch friends explained this is good. This government was horrible and a better one will be elected within months. It's true that the Harry-Potter-looking Prime Minister did not inspire confidence. Meanwhile there is a caretaking government. No one seems concerned.

War Buildup. Unlike in Britain and the U.S. and some other parts of the world, there have been no demonstrations here yet. I seek the opinions of my family and friends in the U.S. It's hard not to feel isolated here from what's happening in the States.

Non-EU-Citizen Registration. Al and I are off to fight the bureaucracy and register with the Alien Police. Yes, that's what they're called. "No matter how many documents you take with you, you always have to keep returning," we're told.

Personal Grief. All of the above issues loom small in the Kline family right now. One week ago my youngest brother Tom's middle child, Christopher, age three, was diagnosed with a vicious brain-stem tumor. It's like being suddenly plunged into a nightmare. We've thought of little else for a week. I've spoken to Tom and his wife, Bonita. They are trying to be strong, but we will most likely lose Chris within six months.

NOVEMBER 2002

CHANGES AT GLOBAL REPORTING INITIATIVE. The GRI board has selected a new Chief Executive Officer. Ernst Ligteringen beat out 140 applicants and appears to be a terrific choice. He's Dutch but has not lived in The Netherlands for twenty years, since he was in his late twenties. He'll move to Amsterdam from Geneva in mid-November, but will not officially replace Al until mid-December.

Al always knew that his job as founder of GRI was to launch the organization and then turn it over to someone else. Nevertheless, for about two days after the announcement, he had a little difficulty thinking of letting go of an organization that he co-founded and directed during its critical start-up years. A little hard to turn over the great staff that he had carefully hired and the beautiful 1780 building whose renovation he oversaw. But he recovered from those feelings quickly and now feels a sense of relief from day-to-day management responsibilities in an organization that is shifting from ground-floor to mezzanine stage. He's pleased with the choice.

Al's new title is Vice President for Special Projects. His presence will assure a smooth transition as he continues to travel and speak: in Denmark and Geneva this week; in Milan next week; back to South Africa the following week. I'll accompany him to Madrid.

DUTCH CHARACTER, ESPECIALLY THE POLDER MODEL.[1] Out walking Sunday, we see a young guy in his twenties who deliberately or carelessly has lost control of the two dogs he is walking. An elderly woman who walks with a cane feels threatened by the dogs running by her and she berates the guy. I wouldn't do that in the States where I might be knocked to the ground and left for dead. Although pick-pocketing is rampant here, there's little violent crime. People confront people if they feel they've been treated unjustly or even if they

---

[1] The **polder model** is a term with uncertain origin that was first used to describe the acclaimed Dutch version of consensus-based economic and social policy making, specifically in the 1980s and 1990s. The term quickly took on a wider meaning, to denote similar cases of consensus decision-making in the Dutch fashion.

just think people are misbehaving.

When there is a verbal confrontation in public, passersby gather around to lend support to the person they're taking sides with and to give their own opinion. That's what happened with the young guy and the elderly woman. Soon there were six or seven people involved in the discussion while the dogs continued to run around.

Kate witnessed something similar. A woman bicyclist yelled at a car driver for cutting her off dangerously. He stopped, but was arrogant and unapologetic. The woman burst into tears and became nearly hysterical when she pointed out to the unrepentant driver that she had two children on the bike. Quickly, other bicyclists began to surround the woman in a show of support. Strangers calmed her and took up the argument for her.

Yes. . . *Maar* (the Dutch word for "however" or "on the other hand" pronounced with the double aa and r drawn out while moving the mouth from side to side), there's always a contrasting view. I mentioned to Kien how much I admired this handling of public confrontation. Everyone chips in to keep outlandish behavior under control. Everyone feels they can speak their mind.

She agreed. *Maar* . . . people also feel free to criticize or correct anything they don't like at the moment," she said. Such as? The way you're treating your children. She told me that people have berated her for speaking English to her children and for not sending them to Dutch schools. A woman she barely knew enrolled Kien's children in a Dutch school even though they were happily attending an English-speaking one.

I attribute both the public scenes and the speaking out as an extension of the Polder Model That goes for business and government. Endless meetings. But I do usually admire the outcomes.

GOALS. Moving forward on my goals of researching and writing what may become a novel; doing volunteer work; learning Dutch; and exploring the nonprofit world here; I have two interviews soon with organizations that serve children and just joined a Dutch conversation group.

UPCOMING. Friday Allen and I will be the guests of the City of Amsterdam Foreign Investment Office, GRI's sponsor, at a concert of the Royal Concertgebouw Orchestra. I was surprised to learn from the program that Sergei Rachmaninov died in 1943 in Beverly Hills. Somehow, I never pictured Rachmaninov lounging around the swimming pool with Clark Gable and Hedy Lamarr.

DECEMBER 2002–JANUARY 2003

We both feel blessed that living here (as opposed to passing through as tourists) allows us to go deeper, to experience another season, get to know the neighbors, continue the language studies. If I began by feeling that I was living inside a travel poster, after visiting the excellent Resistance Museum last weekend I now feel as if we're living inside a WWII movie. The streets are unchanged and still have lots of medieval remnants as well.

When I think of my otherwise lovely Brookline Street crisscrossed increasingly and recklessly with cable, telephone, and electric wires, I feel sick. There are no wires visible here. I'm looking out right now at a sunset reflected in the ice-patched canals, the gas lamps coming on, the bridges lighting up. Yes, old fashioned in some ways, yet the policies and values are so progressive. There's a national election on January 25, but it's far from heated. Since the previously-unheard-of assassination of a political leader last year by an animal rights fanatic, Holland has returned to its low-key politics. No candidates really, just parties campaigning. A few debates. No posters up. The parties that get the most votes will then form a coalition to select a Prime Minister.

JANUARY 2003–AL WRITES:

Dear all:

Warmest greetings and best wishes for the New Year. Like Judith, I am delighted with the opportunity to live in Amsterdam. The city combines history, enlightenment, and more than a bit of magic. We are blessed with a cozy, city-center apartment and a view of the canals, boats, ducks, and bridges that will remain with me forever.

It's a time of transition for me and the Global Reporting Initiative (GRI). I stepped down in early December as CEO and handed the reins to Ernst Ligteringen, the choice of the Board to lead GRI in its next phase as a new independent, international institution affiliated with the United Nations. Ernst is a wonderful Dutchman with great integrity, management skills, and experience in running international organizations.

GRI has entered its next phase. Conception and design are complete. An inauguration at the U.N. in April, a new Board of Directors, and a new home in Amsterdam (at the invitation of the Dutch government) all position GRI for its next chapter. Much has been accomplished, and we are very proud. But much remains to be done to secure GRI's future as an enduring force in advancing corporate accountability worldwide through new forms of economic, environmental and social reporting.

During a few months of transition, I will be advising Ernst, raising money, and serving as Interim Director of GRI's technical and stakeholder programs. This will keep us in Amsterdam through mid-May, and involve regular travel to Paris, Brussels, London, Berlin and other cities to spread the GRI gospel.

The post-May future likely will see some continuing work as a GRI "ambassador," primarily in North America. In addition to GRI work, I anticipate a mix of writing, teaching, and advising to business, government, and international organizations . . . unless, of course, I dream up some other wild and impossible idea as a sequel to GRI!

Good health and good fortune have been my blessings in 2002. I can only hope for more of the same in 2003.

As he travels around Europe promoting GRI, Al is meeting some European nobility. You can tell because they have five names that begin with something like "*Viscompte*" and end with the place where their family probably once played lord to serfs, like "*d'Avignon.*" Al wants an inherited title too and has renamed himself "*Viscompte Alain Lee White Shvetsky von Shtetyl.*"

PLOT IS FORMING. My fascination with the City Orphanage is growing. For months the only information I could find was an exhibit in the Amsterdam Historical Museum. Gradually, without really searching, I'm stumbling onto more information.

While browsing in a card shop, for example. No ordinary card shop, it has thousands of postcards filed by photographer and by subject: animals, bikes, buildings, children. I look under "Amsterdam" and find my first paintings of life in the orphanage—staff dressing children in uniforms that are half red, half black—Amsterdam colors. Children sitting at long tables as staff pour ale from pitchers and ladle soup into bowls. Another postcard of a rural child who resembles my character, just as I had imagined her before she was taken to the orphanage.

Later, Al and I set out to find a restaurant in the oldest part of town. We reject several and choose a place called *Haesje Claes*. I order a Dutch meal, look to my right, and see a glassed alcove with little orphanage objects. When I ask the waitress about it and tell her of my interest, she says to Al "I'm taking her with me." It turns out that *Haesje Claes* is the name of the woman who founded the orphanage in 1520. People give the restaurant their orphanage memorabilia and collections. The waitress leads me into a small room in the restaurant with more paintings and photographs and commemorative plates—far more than I have yet seen collected anywhere else. A complete surprise.

Since then I'm totally fired up. What was it like to live in the orphanage during the occupation? During the hunger of 1944/45 when 20,000 people died in the countryside? To have enjoyed outings to the zoo and befriended the exotic birds only to find one day the birds gone and German soldiers setting up offices there? To have befriended the Jewish bookseller on the corner and see him and his family carted off?

But before I answer those questions, I'm exploring the 1600s of which there is so much written, be it nonfiction like *The Embarrassment of Riches: An Interpretation of Dutch Culture in the Golden Age,* by Simon Schama; and *Tulip Mania: Money, Honor, and Knowledge in the Dutch Golden Age,* by Anne Goldgar; or historical novels like *Girl With the Pearl Earring,* by Tracy Chevalier; and *Rembrandt's Whore,* by Sylvie Matton. Soon I'll hit the city archives—armed with a dictionary.

The period reminds me alarmingly of the U.S.—economically and culturally powerful, but how long can the wealth and power last without moral leadership?

MARCH 2003

SWIMPOOL. I pay about $2.90 per visit to swim in a public pool behind the Rijks Museum, a ten-minute walk from my house. It's large, light, and immaculate. (They never seem to stop cleaning.) There's a time for every swimmer's fancy. They play live jazz there alongside the pool on Saturday nights. Two hours a week are set aside for those who prefer to swim "without attire."

Once I make the mistake of going at noon during the *pauze* (the "pause," which is "lunch hour" to us). It's more like a break here, long enough to enjoy the traditional cheese sandwich and large glass of milk. Young, fit men and women use this brief period to swim laps aggressively. With what I call "vertical" swimming—my kicking and jumping aquatic exercises in one spot—I'm in their way and they let me know it.

So I go on Wednesday mornings at a time set aside for "women and people over fifty"—a more easy-going crowd. My schedule changes this week, though, and I go on Monday morning for the first time to a general recreational swim (swimming attire required—good). No more just over fifty's, it was quite intergenerational.

I notice that eight tables are lined up in a neat row with diaper changers on top. There are also three net playpens. The parents with babies and toddlers begin to show up to enjoy a dip, splash, and sing in the shallow end.

When another swimming grandma approaches me, we chat in Dutch about our grandchildren for awhile, swoon over the babies, and return to our exercise. Swimming, conversation in Dutch, grandchildren as a topic, and beautiful, happy children to observe—now that's a wonderful way to spend a morning.

CHILDREN. I look at every one of the twenty child faces in the pool, so content and safe in their parents' arms and, of course, I think about the Iraqi families who are feeling terrorized, about the children our nephew Simon is working with in Rwanda, and about my three-year-old nephew who is suffering from brain cancer. I wish so fervently that all of the children in the world could someday soon feel as secure and be as well nourished and healthy as those chubby-tummied, round-faced beauties within my vision at this moment.

WAR. Many of my countrymen have asked what it's like to be an American here now. First, let me say that I have never felt safer. Safer from violence of all kinds—crime, terrorism, xenophobia, accidents. Al and I blend in completely, for one thing. I am never out without being asked directions. Eighty percent of the people ask me in Dutch. I'm thrilled that by now, I can respond accordingly.

We've attended four anti-war rallies since we've been here. The last one last Saturday attracted 80,000 people in a city with fewer than 800,000. The sentiment is decidedly anti-Bush, but not Anti-American. Unrelated to the march, but hanging out of a window, I see one "Yankee go home" sign, but it looks quite dusty and faded as if it's left over from some previous gripe.

The official Dutch government position is: "We support the U.S war effort, but we aren't sending troops until we reach a consensus." Typically Dutch. Agreeing is everything.

There is still a provisional government because, in spite of endless meetings, the parties that won the election in January haven't reached an agreement on who should be Prime Minister.

ARCHIVES. Think archives and what do you picture? Used to be that the word "archives" would make me sneeze from imagined dust and mustiness. I saw darkness and caves and endless shelves reaching back into time, guarded zealously by possessive librarians with their hair pulled back in tight buns, shaking a long finger. The message seemed to be—"stay away."

That was before I went to the Amsterdam City Archives in a beautiful seventeenth-century building along the Amstel River. Huge windows, helpful folks, great organization. I knew that the orphanage always kept immaculate records. I am looking for the names of orphans who lived in the Amsterdam City Orphanage in the second century of its existence.

Jos, my Dutch tutor, who is very knowledgeable about Dutch history but had never been to the *Archief*, accompanies me. First we get a pass, then we look in a big book, then we enter info into a computer, then we wait for our number to show up on an electronic board. A short time later, we enter an inner room where our materials are waiting.

We are both totally awed to be holding a Kinderboek from 1640—the very period on which I am focusing. We look at each other and are afraid to touch it. Of course, after we get up our courage and begin turning the crinkly pages, we are respectfully admonished to touch it as little as possible.

The ink looks as strong as it must have 365 years ago. Jos says they used beetle nut juice. We read numerous entries with names of parents, the dates the parents became Amsterdam citizens (the only way your child could enter the civic orphanage), the date and place of their marriage, the birth and baptism day of the child. I copy down lots of names. I hold history in my hands.

That pivotal experience will culminate in a second life-changing moment a decade later—the arrival by mail of *The Seventh Etching*, my first published novel and the first in a series of what will eventually become *Amsterdam Trilogy*.

I meet the curator of the Amsterdam Historical Museum who is also writing about the orphanage. Although he's not writing a novel and he's been pleasant, I sense a reluctance on his part to share information with me. Jos says he's feeling competitive. If that is the case, I'm flattered. Still, it's been good to talk to, and correspond with, someone with interests close to mine.

As we prepare to depart for a visit to Italy and a return to The Netherlands for a few days to experience what may be the most cherished Dutch holiday—Queen's Day—before heading back to Boston, I lose myself in a clever screenplay Doug has just written. When I wrote a screenplay last year, my favorite part of the experience was doing the re-write in response to his perceptive suggestions. "Mom, would she really have said that? Mom, let's look at the final scene. I think it can be stronger." I hope I can be half as much help to him as he was to me.

On our final full day, our friends, Kien and Paul, take us on a 35-kilometer bike ride into the country. They know I'm not confident on the bike. Every time we approach a curve, when my tendency is to brake, Paul's voice behind me urges, "Power, Judith. Power." I peddle faster. I do not stop. I do not fall. I round the curve. I continue on. It's a metaphor for what I'll be facing once we are resettled in the States. I need to establish myself as a fund-raiser/development specialist. I won't brake, I vow. I'll just power around the obstacles. I'll keep going.

JUNE 2003
Back to the U.S.A.

AL ON RETURNING TO BOSTON:

It was a time of change and some uncertainty in my professional life because, while I was in Amsterdam, a number of significant decisions had been
made at Tellus about its future direction. I returned to an institute that was
on the threshold of restructuring its mission, its programs, and its staff. While
I was away, I had occasionally contributed to these decisions, but much of the
new direction had evolved without my input. Within months of my return,
the process of reducing staff by two-thirds and changing the programs to align
with the new banner of the Institute, called The Great Transition, posed a lot
of changes and difficult moments on the personnel front.

While in Amsterdam, I left behind at Tellus the Business and Sustainability
Group which operated mostly independently, with only remote supervision on
my part. Suddenly I faced the uncomfortable and, in many ways, sad task of
notifying a dozen people in my group that the Board had decided to recon-
stitute the organization. It was a seminal decision prompted not by financial
challenges—indeed, our financials were in excellent shape—but by the desire
to refocus our work to create what might be called a "futures institute." Such
voluntary contraction was virtually unheard of in the non-profit world.

The re-organization meant that most of the staff would be moving on. Although this would mean an end to their tenure at Tellus, the Board structured
the departures in ways that we hoped benefited them wherever they landed to
continue their careers. We provided a bridge. They would leave with substantial projects and resources. Although their departure was mandatory, it was
cushioned by a generous lead-time plus projects to take away. The process
took about a year. By the end of 2004, Tellus was operating with a smaller,
refocused staff, prepared to begin its next phase, which would last for at least
eight years until the end of 2012. We committed to what we called The Great
Transition themes.

As for my own professional work within this Phase Two, I was growing
impatient with what I saw as incremental change in business conduct relative to the perils the world was facing: economic, social, and environmental
uncertainty and threats. It was a time to pause and reflect on the slowness
of change of the sort I had been promoting for many years. I went through
considerable soul-searching as to how I could contribute to an accelerated
trajectory for aligning business practices with 21st century ecological and so-

cial perils, and to moving from incremental to discontinuous change in the coming years.

Marjorie Kelly, a new acquaintance and co-founder and publisher of "Business Ethics" magazine, was at a point in her career where she was asking the same questions I was: How might we change business conduct by revisiting and redefining its purpose, by modifying what came to be called its "organizational design?" Repurposing and redesigning business became the two pillars of the new initiative Marjorie and I co-founded. We named it Corporation 20/20. Corporation 20/20 provided a focus for my intellectual and creative energy. It became the new anchor for my work within Tellus Institute and my focus for the next half decade and beyond.

On the medical front, there was not much to report. Periodic check-ins with my doctors were the only reminder of the lurking but still indolent condition diagnosed some five years earlier. The disease was inconsequential in terms of my daily life. I travelled to Latin America and to Europe. My energy and appetite were both good. I felt strong.

2004

For a short time in 2004, Al experiences an uncharacteristic "funk" as he puts it. The organization to which he has most recently devoted all his professional energies, GRI, is firmly established and growing. The excitement of watching the original concept take hold and Al's major role in that start-up with all the meetings around the world is mostly behind him. The ten-year survival rate of the disease he was diagnosed with six years earlier means he has passed the halfway mark. He begins to brood, to worry that he might not live long enough to see Corporation 20/20 and other new endeavors come to full fruition, may never have the chance to know and love future grandchildren.

Now in 2004, we are just beginning to experience some of the many supports Dana Farber Cancer Institute offers its patients and patient families. For the first time in his life, Al initiates an appointment with a psychiatrist—one who specializes in cancer patients. He meets with that doctor for two emotional sessions, openly reflecting on the possibility of a dark scenario wherein CLL snatches life prematurely from a victim who became a grandfather in his forties and who wants desperately to not only experience, but help shape, the future of both his family and the planet. The meetings help to restore his usual optimism and understated, steady verve. He feels better equipped to face the uncertainties that lie ahead.

2006–2009

NOVEL INTERRUPTUS. In 2006 I secure a position as Director of Development at a public health organization that serves over 20,000 Latin American families and individuals annually—the Latin American Health Institute. It is everything I want in a new career—the opportunity to apply a range of skills: program start-up, organizational, presentational, training, event planning, writing a video script for the organization's twentieth anniversary celebration. Another plus which I had not prioritized also materializes. To my delight I have the opportunity to use Spanish on a daily basis. For three years, I dedicate myself to building from scratch the non-grant aspect of the fund-raising program, focusing on individual gifts and events. At least two nights a week I attend networking gatherings where I meet outstanding Boston-area Latino professionals, many of whom I am able to attract and involve in the organization's mission.

When I leave LHI in 2009 with a sense of pride in what I have accomplished, I return to the novel I began in Amsterdam seven years earlier, *The Seventh Etching*. During the years of neglect, I imagined my characters sitting on a shelf like in a toy shop, dangling their legs, patiently passing the time, confident that I will return and set them in motion to continue their Amsterdam adventures. Nelleke needs a new family, one that will support her sometimes irritating inquisitiveness. Jos desperately wants to complete his collection of "playfully sensual" (as Al calls them) etchings. How will Pieter convince his father to allow him to marry the alluring Isabela when she's a devout Catholic? Will the reader ever learn who left that baby on the doorstep with half a playing card pinned to its blanket? I do find some time to move the story lines forward, but soon reluctantly place my characters back on the shelf once more as the demands of dealing with Al's illness suddenly explode.

At this point I am already a decade into the disease. I am fortunate in having a longer period of grace compared to most CLL patients. I am otherwise in excellent health. I have physical resources to fight the disease for as long as I have. But when the disease begins to intensify, it quickly takes on a character of no return. Now, by the end of 2009, the clock is ticking, leading to a crossroads, a choice looming on the horizon.

With the disease more active, I begin a series of management therapies to slow the CLL level. This is the normal approach to CLL. Control as long as possible until therapies no longer are effective, then—conditions allowing—ready the patient for a stem-cell transplant—a recently developed procedure that is somewhat easier than the dreaded bone-marrow transplant that was the only alternative at the time of my diagnosis. My slowly deteriorating health portends a pathway that will follow that course of action exactly.

Part III

Exhaustive Prep
September 2010–August 1, 2011

SEPTEMBER 2010
Letting Go of Normalcy

SATURDAY, SEPTEMBER 4, 2010. ISLAND RESPITE NO MORE. Since 2000, we've spent nearly every Labor Day weekend in our Martha's Vineyard cottage. Visits at any time of year, though, have become increasingly challenging. Five trips to the emergency room for example. One for each of us which required eye washing. Mine after dripping mold remover as I tried to scrub the front-porch rafters. One for Al after an incident with bird poop. The crow's aim was so extraordinary, it felt deliberate. Al was sitting in a narrow space between our cottage and the neighbor's painting the back stairs when a tablespoon-size whitish-pinkish blob came from above and landed behind his eyeglasses.

Another emergency visit for me when a thorn from our rose bushes pricked my thumb and it became infected—even though I was wearing gardening gloves, for heaven's sake! For Al twice after small mosquito bites immediately turned into green-and-purple blotches up and down his leg that looked like gangrene. They had become infected and he needed antibiotics which required coordination with Dana Farber docs. To avoid bugs, we must give up our treasured walks—those discoveries that take us through forest, up and down dunes, past abandoned farms, an old ice house. We could take a walk every week of the year and still not see all these enchanting out-of-the way spots.

Al continues to dismiss what I experience as increasingly urgent signs to sell and get out. Our favorite couple moves off island. Our favorite elderly neighbors are dying. Finding dependable help for cleaning and repairs inside and out continues to be an irritating challenge. One evening headed home, we drive off the ferry and fill up the car's tank for the trip back to Boston. The car begins to jiggle and resist acceleration. Al makes a desperate left into a parking lot, barely missing oncoming traffic. The car comes to an immediate and complete stubborn stop. We pay to be towed all the way to Boston. The next morning we get the diagnosis and the car repair bill: Al had mistakenly filled the tank with diesel fuel.

Back to the cottage for Labor Day weekend. The elderly neighbors whose company we had enjoyed are being replaced by their not-as-pleasant sons and daughters. One of these is staying next door with two dogs that simply do not stop yipping. We always keep classical music playing, but we can barely hear it above the barking. Not one to go complaining to authorities, Al approaches the dog owners about the problem. They not only refuse to do anything, they are defensive and nasty. Al then asks the cottage administrator about the issue. The administrator is emphatic. "No loud noises are allowed. That includes dog barking. We have in the past required owners of misbehaving dogs to ship or take their dogs off the island." That seems extreme and we don't want to press it. But like so many of our recent experiences here, it does not bode well for the future.

In the middle of the night, I reach over to hold Al's hand. It's like reaching into a fire. I feel his arm, his forehead. Same smoldering heat. The next morning once again he reluctantly goes to the only emergency room at the island's only hospital. One more time, the island doctors coordinate with his Dana Farber docs who urge Al to return to Boston. As he feels his island slipping away from him, Al insists on staying a few more days.

By the time we get to Dana, Al is worse. The diagnosis is pneumonia and they order him to enter the hospital. At first he doesn't grasp how immediately he needs serious attention. He thinks he has time to go home, perhaps work a little, pack, and return. But, no, I clarify. We're going right now. This very minute. The last hospitalization Al experienced was fifty-four years ago for an eye operation. He doesn't really feel that bad and he is kind of in shock about this turn of events. Soon and not for the last time, an orderly wheels him through the catwalk twists and turns that connect the clinic to Brigham and Women's Hospital.

DECEMBER 2010
Second Hospitalization in Three Months

WEDNESDAY, DECEMBER 8, 2010. Al and I get up early to go to Quest Labs in San Francisco's Chinatown for the required blood test. Results are emailed to Dr. F back in Boston. I'm alarmed at the familiar, telltale signs: heavy night sweats, swollen legs, ankles, feet, and the most worrisome, shallow breaths. Both of us perceive without saying so, that after more than a decade of living with CLL, we may be approaching a new chapter.

A day earlier, Al had moderated a workshop he organized on Corporation 20/20 held at the offices of Business for Social Responsibility (BSR). In addition to visiting with Kate and Maureen, this workshop is the main reason we've come to San Francisco. Kate, one among about twenty participants, reports her concern about her dad's stamina and pallid appearance.

AL ON THAT EVENT:

I think I looked like hell, but I was on an adrenaline rush. I was mentally intact and never felt any failing. It was a four-hour workshop. Most of the load was carried by colleagues who presented on various topics pertaining to the future of the corporation, the core theme of Corporation 20/20. Amidst the stimulation and intensity of the dialogue, I had no time to dwell on my health that, by any objective measure, was approaching a precipice.

After the workshop, he returns to the hotel to nap. That night at dinner with friends, nausea and dizziness set in. He rises from the table and barely makes it to the restroom to vomit violently. We leave friends in the company of our daughter. Halfway up on one of the city's countless hills, just off Union Square at the entrance to the hotel, he stops. Energy depleted, Al cannot take another step. Fortunately, we have arrived at the door of a gym housed on the lower level of the hotel. I swim there every day. I explain our dilemma to the clerk. We walk through the gym of exercisers, get in an elevator and go up to our floor.

THURSDAY, DECEMBER 9, 2010. I'm looking forward to a lunch at Union Square's *Café de la Presse* with two of my favorite women—daughter, Kate, and cousin, Betty. Just about to leave when Al gets a call from Evgeny, Dr. F's physician assistant in Boston, responding to yesterday's blood test results. "Call an EMT immediately. Your red cells are dangerously low."

I cancel the lunch.

I dial 911.

The responder asks, "Is the patient conscious?"

"Yes," I answer.

"Is the patient breathing?"

"Yes."

"Is the patient able to talk?"

"Yes."

We go downstairs and wait outside for the ambulance to arrive. Twenty minutes. Thirty minutes. I call again. I get the same questions. This time, I'm wiser. I figure out they're probably prioritizing the people who are NOT conscious, NOT breathing, NOT able to talk. I'm sorry for those people, but I have a beloved husband to protect. He's dangerously low on an essential element necessary for staying alive. He's low on oxygen, dammit. So when they get to "Is the patient breathing?" this time I answer, "Barely." Somewhat of an exaggeration, but panic has engulfed me.

An hour after the first call, the ambulance arrives. Neither of us has ever been transported in an ambulance. They direct me to the passenger seat up front. They put Al in a bed and slide him into the back. I can't be with him. I can hear only snippets of the conversation. The first is about insurance (only in America). Then they turn to the medical challenges. As in so many instances before involving new medics, Al must list his litany of medications. The conversations take another twenty minutes. We're still parked in front of the hotel. It's difficult being separated from Al. I can hear Al's voice, but not his words. At least he's still conscious.

AL ON WHAT WENT ON IN THE BACK OF THE VEHICLE ONCE IT STARTED MOVING:

San Francisco is not an easy place to be transported to a hospital under duress. The streets, cable car tracks, and hills provide less than a restful setting for dealing with an emergency situation. Judith could have answered a lot of the questions. The ambulance team seemed oblivious to the stress of our separation and the bouncing vehicle speeding to the California Pacific Medical Center, IV line dangling overhead. I think for the crew my case was undramatic and uninteresting relative to the blood and unconsciousness they routinely confront. I had no limbs dangling, no cardiac arrest, no gunshot wounds. Depleted of red blood cells, I was simply out of gas.

The worst part was the energy required to answer questions and the extended wait for the ambulance to arrive in the first place. Also, EMT's attempts to insert an IV as the vehicle navigated the city's hills, traffic, and cable car tracks. It was important to get fluids in me fast. I'm used to being poked; in fact, I'm often complimented on my "roadmap veins." But the twenty-minute, repeated search-and-poke en route to the San Francisco hospital was the worst I'd ever experienced

Al, Kate, and I spend four hours in the emergency room. Our competent daughter uncomplainingly makes who knows how many calls and is on hold for who knows how many minutes in order to cancel our return flight to Boston and get our flight money reimbursed.

Now we're in the hospital room. Al's roommate, a chronically homeless alcoholic had been found face down on the sidewalk. One of those "unconscious, not able to talk" people 911 referred to, no doubt. A steady stream of social workers, nurses, doctors, and various counselors approach the guy's bed. But the patient is quite befuddled, barely able to respond to their queries or understand much about his surroundings. Possibly delusional. I am nervous leaving Al in his company overnight. I'm trying to calm my fears about this guy when he gets out of bed, approaches us, and tries to make conversation. Although he's English-speaking, his words are barely decipherable. When we do not respond, he returns to his side of the small room. Will he wander over while Al is sleeping and pull out his IV? Mistake Al for a human or animal predator and pummel Al while he sleeps? A long night in the hotel room by myself.

After overnight infusions of fresh red blood (and no attacks from the roommate), Al's levels return to normal range. Kate and Maureen meet us at the hospital. I get my French lunch after all at a charming outdoor café a few blocks away—and this time with my husband included, temporarily restored to a functional human being.

Later, our Kate sends a handwritten note: "Just a quick note to thank you, Dad, for the invitation to join the Corporation 20/20 roundtable at BSR last week. I sincerely appreciated being at the table, meeting all those outstanding thought leaders in corporate redesign and the opportunity to examine my industry in a new, critical way. Thanks again for including me."

And thank you, dear daughter, for being there for us at such a critical time!

The next months are a blur of despair and anxiety, progress and setbacks, leaving both Al and me increasingly tense and unnerved. Uncertainty looms large. Could we, would we survive the unfolding ordeal? How will I cope with pressures of caring for Al while caring for myself? Should I prepare for a possible life alone? The stress is embodied in my journal entries during those tumultuous times.

FRIDAY, DECEMBER 17, 2010. Back in Boston. Back to Dana Farber Cancer Clinic. Appointment with physician's assistant, Evgeny, a Russian Jewish immigrant who has been in the states about a decade. Trained as an engineer, Evgeny retrained as a P.A. when he found his heart was with the caring professions. Of short stature, rotund from head to toe. Round face on round torso balancing on round legs. "Like a donut. Like the Michelin tire," Al says affectionately. Huge smile. Loves to laugh. Not being a retiring patient and always ready to engage, Al finds Evgeny eager to share his knowledge about the general status of the disease, about the many drug trials he has been involved in. These are complex trials which Evgeny—capable, witty and smart—explains clearly.

Evgeny is more than a P.A. to Al. He's a friend who is helping to make a difficult, uncertain journey more understandable and hopeful. Their friendship lasts for years until, to Al's distress, Evgeny returns to NYC.

BIOPSIES OF THE BONE MARROW. CLL causes discomfort, irritation, inconvenience, loss of sleep. It robs you of normalcy and time. But in itself, at least until this point, it has not been painful—with one exception. The periodic test required to measure how much CLL resides in the body. Through the years, Al has had several bone marrow biopsies. He never allows me to be present during the procedures. "The instruments alone are enough to conjure up terrible images," he says.

Since his first biopsy, Al no longer looks at those intimidating tools either. The marrow is "harvested" with an oversize needle to extract tissue. Traditionally, the procedure relies on the precision and strength of the human arm, pushing through skin, flesh, muscle and bone. Local anesthetic is helpful, but well short of an effective barrier to pain.

Recently though, Evgeny introduced Al to a technique using a high-speed drill as an alternative to the manual, elbow-grease technique used in previous procedures. Al dubbed it the "Black and Decker" approach. Hearing the drill is unnerving. But the procedure, accompanied by the usual dose of morphine, is decidedly less painful. More precise. Shorter duration. It also reduces the possibility of human error. Much appreciated, Evgeny. Thank you.

Report today: Al has had no flu shot and cannot get one while he has active infection. Chest cough and phlegm mixed with clear yellow because of irritation. No recent nose bleeding. No sores. Hematocrit high—good. Platelets low—bad. 8.2 hemoglobin unchanged—okay. No more shortness of breath. But also no infusion until infection is cleared up. CLL is crowding out platelets and will soon do further mischief.

Goal: To work on boosting platelets and red cell production. A supportive, management approach, but nothing curative. When we visit grandchildren in Florida soon, we will have his blood tested at a local Quest Lab there, one of several labs familiar to Al around the country.

RITUXAN TREATMENT CONTINUES. It is the first drug used to manage early-stage CLL. A biotherapy (vs. chemotherapy), it is the therapeutic use of biological materials or biological response modifiers, e.g., anti-cancer immunotherapy using therapeutic monoclonal antibodies, growth factors or vaccines, and genes. Serious side effects of Rituxan are rare. It targets and destroys B cells, the mutants that linger in bodies of CLL patients. Thank you, biotechnology industry.

WEDNESDAY, DECEMBER 20, 2010. APPOINTMENT WITH DR. F. Must postpone dental work. Dentists want platelets at fifty. Al's are very low at fifteen! These low platelets remind me of the time we were at the Vineyard, in the early 2000s. Our dear lively friend, Sylvia, was visiting from Rochester. Al called downstairs, "Jude, come up here a minute." He showed me the inside of his mouth, which suddenly had become covered with deep-purple blotches. We had never seen anything like that and haven't since. The next day he took the bus to Boston to have it checked out. I enjoy Sylvia's company so much and see her too rarely. I stayed on the island. Diagnosis: sores due to low platelets. This was the first time I learned that CLL threatened platelets and that they could drop so quickly. I've always felt guilty that I didn't travel with him that day. What if he had had an accident? Fallen? Cut himself? He might have bled to death.

TUESDAY, DECEMBER 28, 2010. More blood work. Still no dental work allowed. Al would bleed, not clot, and there's more risk of infection. Rituxan takes four-six hours to administer. Because it can cause hypersensitivity, and shortness of breath, they may have to interrupt therapy. If the procedure is going well, they accelerate the infusion. Chest rash is probably viral infection. Needs to cure itself. Take antibiotic to avoid secondary infection. Chest infection is suppressing platelets. Chest rash seems like a mild threat, but is soon to return. Fighting it will eventually occupy hours of our time every day.

JANUARY 2011
An Increasingly Active Beast

A seminal moment in two ways. With steadily worsening condition, the decision is made to prepare for Transplant. This means leaving the care of long-term oncologist, Dr. F. Al is being turned over to a Transplant team. New personalities. New approaches. New relationships. A glimmer of the emotional roller coaster is evident. The word "Transplant" conjures up the unknown, the uncertain. A signal that we have entered a new, decisive chapter in this decade-long battle with an increasingly active beast. A knowledgeable patient is an empowered patient. Al will take a deep dive into the scientific complexities of Transplant.

FEBRUARY 2011
Temporary Fog

WEDNESDAY, FEBRUARY 9, 2011. Appointment with Evgeny, who has not yet resigned from Dana Farber but soon will. Napping less than last couple of weeks. High energy. High appetite. Bruise gone. Mild, moderate night sweats. Ringing in ears begins later in the day. No hearing loss. Ringing may be drug-related. Stopping two among many meds. A mild middle-ear infection. Sugar a little high, but not yet alarming. Other levels good. One of those once-dreaded biopsies today, but Evgeny's slender drill reduces the anxiety. No biking to the clinic today. Because of the morphine, I must be there to drive him home. It's odd to see my usually alert husband temporarily foggy.

FRIDAY, FEBRUARY 18, 2011. Appointment With Dr. F who goes over possibilities and expectations. I take two pages of careful notes, but reading them 1-1/2 years later, barely understand more than this: ringing in his ears continues. He has no bacterial or viral infections. His spleen is a little large. He still cannot have dental work until platelets rebound. When they reach a certain acceptable level, he should run to the dentist before the platelets go back down again. That the level will drop is inevitable.

MARCH 2011
The Big Guy

A few years ago on my Brookline, Massachusetts street—a mix of three-level brick condo buildings and single-family homes—there was one odd little house set back as if it lived in the woods rather than an urban setting. One day I noticed the house was growing. For several years it expanded upward, forward, and sideways. A theme of three side-by-side windows emerged. New roofs at various heights slanted in multiple directions. A brick path now led to what appeared to be a mudroom. Vertically stretched decorative parallelograms sprouted. It became a two-family dwelling with a double driveway. Its color changed from grayish white to a two-toned pea green, befitting its quirkiness. It nearly reached the sidewalk. Only the tall bushes across the front hinted at its former timid isolation.

I had no way of knowing I would soon depend on one of the house's new inhabitants to save my husband's life.

WEDNESDAY, MARCH 16, 2011. Although he later redeems himself a hundred times over, our first visit with our assigned transplant surgeon leaves me shaking with rage. Age thirty-nine, half American, half French, Dr. A, is a medical oncologist with a specialty in lymphoma and stem cell/bone marrow Transplant. Graduated from University of California, San Francisco School of Medicine in 2000 with both an MD and a PhD, he has been at Dana since 2007. Online reviews are extremely positive: One patient writes, "When I was diagnosed with lymphoma, I went straight to Dana Farber and I think that decision saved my life. He is knowledgeable, honest, direct, sympathetic and dedicated. He answered (and still answers!) our calls and emails day and night. He will forever hold a place in our hearts." Another wrote, "I extremely highly recommend Dr. A to anyone who wants a caring, knowledgeable doctor on their 'kicking cancer in the bum' team."

While Al is in the bathroom, I have a few minutes alone with him. We discuss contemporary French literature in French. When Al arrives, Dr. A comments that Al comes "highly liked." Then he gets down to business. He goes over today's reports and asks Al about himself.

Energy and appetite both good. Weight gain. Now 187 which is lower than normal weight, but not alarming. Edema (leg swelling) reduced. No trouble breathing. No chest pains. Cough on and off. No nausea, no diarrhea, no pain. When was Al's last colonoscopy? Three-four years ago. Normal. PSA checked? Two years ago. Ashkenazi Jewish background. Not religious. Travel and biking and basketball can continue for now. Two aunts, Lillian and Pauline, had cancer. Father died of lung cancer. Neither of Al's two sisters is a match. For a Transplant, must either 1) find donor—an allogenic Transplant; or 2) extract, clean and reinfuse own cells—an autologous Transplant.

We listen carefully to our first introduction to "the procedure"—to what's involved in a stem-cell Transplant. I'm sure Al absorbs more of it than I do. In a few months I will be plunged into and live through every detail of what today sounds matter of fact, especially coming from Dr. A who I'm beginning to see lacks the humanity and warmth of our previous Dana doctors. The procedure will take place in Brigham and Women's Hospital across the street. A preliminary match search will begin shortly.

What will happen in the coming months? Four days of chemo followed by infusion of the donor's stem cells. In hospital a week prior to the procedure where various drugs will pave the way for the new cells to engraft into his marrow with least risk of rejection. Donor cells go into combat mode immediately, attacking Al's dysfunctional stem cells as dangerous foreign agents.

Risk: donor cells may "get confused," act as if Al's liver or kidneys "don't belong to them," and attack the organs as well as the intended dysfunctional stem cells. Therefore, various therapies concurrently work to suppress the immune system, to optimize engraftment of the newcomers while others act to temporarily protect Al from infection during the transitional period. This is a courtship. Al's body must welcome the newcomer cells at the same time the newcomers must embrace Al's body as their own. This balancing act can last several years until new stem cells are convinced that Al's organs are not the enemy and that, instead, their new home is right for them.

All the while, severe food restrictions, limitations on socializing, and a ban on public transportation serve to protect Al during the critical adjustment period during which the new stem cells, hopefully, adapt to their new home.

Despite all the preparations and precautions, a stem cell Transplant is a risky business. A fifteen-twenty percent risk of a failed Transplant, including the possibility of a fatal reaction within two years after Transplant. A thirty-forty percent probability of disease reactivation within five years. Best scenario? A forty-fifty percent chance of freedom from CLL for five years after Transplant, generally reviewed as the marker for long-term remission. That would bring Al to age seventy.

Having outlined the procedure, Dr. A explains options. He repeats that forty-fifty percent of stem cell Transplant patients go into remission. When I ask what would happen if we choose NOT to have the procedure, his nonchalant response reminds us that our medical supervision has changed.

"If it's not successful," the surgeon answers, "well, you've already gone beyond the average survival period for this disease which is ten years. Options are few. Without the Transplant, you might live another two years."

Then he looks at me, shrugs and adds,

"If that's enough for you . . . well . . . ."

I am stunned. Enough for me? For Al? Two years more? It feels as if the doctor is doing a hard sell of a product, then threatening us if we don't agree to buy it. It feels cruel. It feels manipulative. I'm shaking with anger and despair.

I am reminded of some of the degrading remarks doctors have made to people I love. When my mother was trying to adjust to the sudden announcement that she must have an emergency hysterectomy, she said, "But I have a meeting at the League of Women Voters. I'm directing a play. I'm committed to babysit my grandchildren." Using words that could have been delivered in a reassuring tone, the doctor instead said with a contemptuous sneer, "Well I'll bet they'll all get along just fine without you." Another time when a friend in her thirties was enduring an invasive painful procedure, she moaned and the doctor said, "What's the matter? Not quite the painful experience you had hoped for?" Was he accusing my lovely friend of being masochistic?

Fortunately, Dr. A's remark today is the low point of a relationship that will eventually rebound into one of mutual respect, admiration, and deep gratitude. Meanwhile, I'm furious.

When I get home, I call my daughter, Lena, and tell her about the casual two-year remark. "If that's enough for you . . . well . . . . " meaning without the procedure Al would die, probably an unpleasant death and be gone. I am sobbing. She is sobbing. Then Lena calms me down by telling me about the surgeon personality. She has worked in the medical field her entire career. "They tend to be detached," she says. "They prefer to relate to comatose patients rather than alert ones. They don't get emotionally involved because patients die."

I realize how spoiled I've been with our decades-long oncologist, Dr. F. A few weeks later, we say our goodbye's to Dr. F. Although he will be consulted occasionally, we belong to surgeon Dr. A now. I find an empty clinic room and have a good cry.

Immediately after that first appointment with Dr. A, we meet Toni, the nurse who arranges the donor matches. Charming, competent, lovely, playful, and funny. Mutual respect and affection between Dr. A and Toni is obvious. The tone of the meeting shifts dramatically.

In the following months, Toni will be our point person for coordinating the world-wide search for our perfect donor. For potential donors, the matching process involves a simple saliva swab followed by a blood test if a potential recipient is identified. The matching is based primarily on the human leukocyte antigen (HLA) system. Human leukocyte antigens are proteins found on the surface of most cells. They make up a person's tissue type, which is different from a person's blood type. The closer the HLA match between donor and recipient the higher the probability of a successful transplant. Gender? "We prefer male donors because of the higher volume of stem cells they produce." Toni explains. "A courier brings the stem cells to the hospital on the day they are donated. They are kept cool, but are not frozen."

Recovery: Al will be alert the whole time, but will probably experience nausea, loose stools, fatigue. Appetite can be a challenge. But he will be seriously immune-compromised. All food must be prepared and consumed at home. Take-out food possible perhaps after three months. "Can grandkids visit?" we ask Toni. "Only with great caution," she advises. "They're little germ factories."

About match potential. The International Stem Cell Registry contains some seven million potential donors, so there's an excellent probability for a good match. Toni reaffirms what Dr. A said an hour earlier using different, gentler language: "Without the procedure, almost constant treatment is necessary and the treatment becomes less effective over time."

Toni uses catchy metaphors—sports, actors, war. "Donor cells at their best are muscular and aggressive. They're on a search-and-destroy mission with the goal of decimating any residual diseased cell and clearing the marrow for their own engraftment. It's a Darwinian process. Survival of the fittest."

What are the determinants of successful treatment?

1. How clean the marrow is. Once infused, stem cells immediately begin looking for their "home." Once there, they set up residence and propagate both themselves as well as red and white cells. I love the Spanish words for stem cells—"Celulas madres"—mother cells. Lymph nodes are hangouts for bad cells. That's why they swell, or in clinical terms, engorge.
2. Age—Al turns sixty-five in July—a good age for this procedure.
3. Over-all health and physical condition: Excellent. No other major illnesses like diabetes or heart disease.
4. Nonsmoker.
5. Supportive family and community.

Leading up to the Transplant requires multiple treatments to optimize the body's receptivity to the arrival of the donor cells: **Purge** the lingering mutant cells with various chemotherapies to cleanse the marrow, creating fertile soil for newcomers; **Suppress** Al's immune system to minimize the risk of rejection; **Protect** against infection the risk of which, we're told, increases steadily during the preparatory period.

During the actual procedure, Al will be fully awake. Transplant technology has shifted dramatically in recent years. Rather than the former intrusive and painful bone-marrow-to-bone-marrow transfer between donor and recipient, most Transplants are through peripheral blood. This essentially amounts to a blood draw from the donor, processing the donation to extract the stem cells, and infusing these cells into the recipient. Deceptively straightforward, but still laden with rejection and infection risks. Neither donor nor recipient requires an anesthetic and they do not experience any pain beyond that associated with any ordinary blood draw or transfusion.

Recommended:

Speak with someone who has had a successful procedure. When I telephone the contact Dana provides, I feel reassured by her warmth and encouragement and by the fact that she had the procedure a dozen years ago and is in full remission and feeling great.

Take part in discussion groups which Dana organizes.

Al and Zen. Somehow these discussions remind us both of an experience Al had decades ago during a yoga class in Columbus, Ohio. As the class progressed, Al became increasingly detached from his physical self, guided by the tender voice of the instructor through a journey of separating the consciousness from the physical self. "Relax, and let your consciousness rise above your body and drift upward to the ceiling, enabling you to look down at yourself resting on the mat below."

And that was exactly Al's experience—a state of euphoric separation of body and mind bathed in deep repose (perhaps facilitated by Al's lifelong love of naps). As the students slowly returned to the normalcy of mind-body integration, Al remained unmoving. Finally, after most students had left the room, the instructor gently tapped Al to bring him back to Earth. "Did you enjoy that?" the instructor asked. "Yes, I did," he replied, with a mix of astonishment, mystery, and refreshment.

We refer to that incident as his "out-of body experience." Wouldn't it be something if he could leave his body behind for a year of repair work, then return to it when it's all healed? Alas, this fantasy would remain just that, trumped by medical realities that were becoming more ominous each day.

APRIL 2011
Respite. Support.

MONDAY, APRIL 1, 2011. Al emails me:

Platelets broke the 100 mark (105) up from 91. Yes! Reds higher as well. (29.5). This is more fun than watching the Celtics . . . when they're winning. I have the car. Will connect later re: plans for tonight.

THURSDAY APRIL 7, 2011. Berkeley, California cousins, Nat and Nina, email: "Allen, dear —We just heard via the efficient family grapevine that you are scheduled for a bone marrow Transplant soon. We're going to take a cue from your confidence that a matching donor will step up. We're focusing on the payoff: a healthy, vigorous Allen—an outcome that will more than justify the daunting treatment and subsequent house arrest. If love of life and a super-abundance of fortitude are the major determinants of a long remission, you're a model candidate for a smooth recovery.

How typically thoughtful of you is your plan for a website with continuing progress updates, we know there'll be hordes of well-wishers who'll be checking in regularly. As you may have guessed, Nat and I are ardent fans of yours. We'll be cheering you on from the other coast. So much love, Nina"

AL ANSWERS:

Thanks so much for your sweet note and encouraging words.

Yes, I'll soon notify family of website where updates and comments will be posted and, hopefully, misinformation will be corrected. The stem cell Transplant likely will be three-four months from now. After thirteen years of disease management, it's time. Happily, a perfectly matched donor is highly probable, my health is otherwise excellent, and my medical team is world class. The most difficult part, as you suggest, will be the tight restrictions on socializing for several months. But limited guests at home are welcome and I'll be free to wander outside (even ride my bike!) as long as I stay away from closed spaces with lots of people.

I hope all is well with you. We think of you often. Much love, Allen

Friday April 8, 2011. A Dr. W. calls from Dr. A's office. The biopsy two days ago did not harvest enough CLL cells. They need more to prepare the vaccine as part of the preparatory process for Transplant. The irony, Al points out, is that the drug, Campath, is destroying the very cells—the bad guys— which they need from the body to use in the vaccine. But in the past two weeks, Al has had two such biopsies through the hip into the bone. Even with a dose of morphine, they are painful and trying. He can't face three biopsies in three weeks. He asked them to wait another week. Dr. Wu says she'll perform the biopsy herself, but Al always prefers Evgeny and his "Black and Decker" technique.

In a telephone follow-up to this visit, Dr. Wu calls to reverse herself and says she can use what she already has for the vaccine after all. Another biopsy is probably not necessary. Al says something that makes her laugh. I can hear her laughter coming from the phone. They've never met.

I email Kate: "We're doing some major cleaning out and cleaning up— partly because I need to re-organize my office in order to give attention to two new writing projects, partly because I want as little old dust around as possible after Dad's procedure. His platelets have gone from a low of fifteen to a current ninety-one. That means he can schedule the dental work he's needed without risk of excessive bleeding, including the extraction of at least one tooth. For months, he's been chewing on one side.

He remains very upbeat, is occasionally drained by what he calls a one-quarter-to one-half-time job—dealing with all the medical issues. Numerous appointments in various departments. A growing number of new doctors and assistants. Insurance issues. Scheduling and rescheduling consultations and procedures. But he bounces back and continues to pursue the professional activities he loves. For him, remaining professionally active is every bit as therapeutic as the battery of drugs and preparatory procedures that fill his days. So work continues, sandwiched between medical commitments, sometimes the opposite. With one significant change. Business and personal travel are fading fast, the victim of both time pressures and the need to avoid setbacks. Still face months of complicated preparations."

Allen the professional. Taken from his current biosketch, this is who my husband is at this moment: *Dr. Allen L. White is Vice President and Senior Fellow, Tellus Institute, Boston, USA, and directs the Institute's Program on Corporate Redesign. In 1997, he co-founded the Global Reporting Initiative (GRI) and served as its Acting CEO until 2002. In 2004, he co-founded and is now Director of Corporation 20/20, an initiative focused on designing future corporations to create and sustain social mission. He has advised multilaterals, foundations, corporations, and NGOs on corporate responsibility strategy and policy. A former Fulbright Scholar in Peru, Dr. White has held faculty and research positions at the University of Connecticut, Clark University and Battelle Laboratories. He was Founding Chair of GAN-Net/iScale and has served on boards, advisory groups and committees of the International Corporate Governance Network; Civic Capital (an SRI fund); Instituto Ethos (Brazil); the New Economy Network; New Earth/Earthster; and the Initiative for Responsible Investment, John F. Kennedy School, Harvard University. Since 2005, Dr. White has served as Senior Advisor to Business for Social Responsibility. He is co-author of "Corporate Environmentalism in a Global Economy," and has published and spoken widely on corporate sustainability, accountability, and governance.*

Monday, April 11, 2011. Al emails Drs. A and F:

I am reading material regarding the trial for prevention of Ocular GVHD at Mass Eye and Ear contained in the DFCI Transplant Information Guide. May I ask for your views on this trial? Description indicates that fifty percent of Transplant patients may experience "severe dry eye and inflammation, leading to irritation, burning, light sensitivity, and decreased vision." (Temporarily, I hope?) Thank you, Allen

Dr. A replies quickly, saying he recommends it if Al's up for it.

Welcome Inspiration: With friends I attend Mendelssohn's *Elijah* at Symphony Hall performed by the Boston University Symphony Orchestra and Symphonic Chorus, conducted by the luminous Ann Howard Jones. The libretto, adapted from 1 Kings: 17-19 and 2 Kings: 2, is about the curse Elijah has placed upon Israel. A community begs God for rain, pleads to be delivered from a drought that is killing their crops and livestock and also bringing tempest, earthquake, and fire. Toward the end of Part I, a youth spots a little cloud and notes that the heavens are black with cloud and wind. "The storm rusheth louder and louder."

The Chorus sings its joy and relief repeating over and over: "Thanks be to God! He reviveth the thirsty land. The waters gather, they rush along! They are lifting their voices! The stormy billows are high, their fury is mighty. But the Lord is above them, and Almighty!"

The music produces images of streams filling, rivers flowing. I can imagine the people rushing as a group, reaching upward, lifting their faces, dancing, wanting to be drenched to the core by the welcome drops. I can feel the Israelites' relief in my own body. I feel my burden of fear lifting, drowned away in the downpour. I feel hope. I feel gratitude. It is thrilling.

I memorize those words. I carry them with me in the months ahead. This is what I expect to be feeling a year from now or sooner. Renewal. Out from under threat. Back to our "wonderful lives" as Al's sister Betty says—travelling, visiting our kids and grandkids, working, writing. "The waters will gather. They will rush along."

WEDNESDAY, APRIL 13, 2011. No more edema. Return of Al's gorgeous long slender legs and perfect ankles. Great visits with friends Peter and Claudia. Niece Eve, here for two days. So great to have a young person around. And for dinner tonight, Steve, always a source of wisdom, concern, and loving support. A dear friend since 1978, Steve confided to me that he cried when he first learned of Al's diagnosis. Tonight he also shows me some needed sympathy during a moment when we are alone (looking up photos of Doug on Facebook). "How are *you* doing?" he asks. I do so need to hear that question from time to time. "I'm having a hard time," I answer.

THURSDAY, APRIL 14, 2011. Clinic meeting with Toni. Trying to kill last vestiges of CLL cells that are now at thirty percent. Would prefer to get them down to five percent before Transplant. Another dreaded biopsy looms.

SATURDAY, APRIL 16, 2011. DONOR LOCATED! Allen emails Toni.

Toni, Thanks for the update re: donor search. Very good news. Nineteen-year-old male. Is it known how perfect the match is? We'll find out just how good later.

Since blood levels are so good, appointments are shorter—thank God. Just a blood check and a Campath injection yesterday. In a mocked accusative tone, the nurse says, "Allen, you didn't tell me!" *I'm sorry. What did I not tell you?* "That your platelets are over 100!" Al wonders if Dana's Human Resources Department screens applicants for warmth and charm. Such qualities are not really trainable but, with few exceptions, all staff members possess these qualities, a true blessing for patients and their families battling serious illness. Of course, it's also possible that Al brings out such qualities in people.

SUNDAY, APRIL 17, 2011. When Al writes occasionally in his own journal, he finds it brings up fears. Since he reads in Transplant prep material that whole-body radiation may be in the offing, he worries about hair loss and the ghostly complexion that usually accompanies such treatment. His hair is a lovely soft white, a bit thin, but not beyond anything I'd consider age appropriate. Anyway, that fear was set aside. He inquired and found he will not have the full-body radiation.

AL WRITES DR. F ABOUT TRANSPLANT TIMING.

All things considered (Campath cycle, possible lymph node therapy, personal considerations), it appears that the earliest would be mid-June and latest mid-August. Does that sound about right to you? At this juncture, my preference would be the first half of August. Of course, I understand timing of donation may be another factor. Thank you, Allen

Tonight, between the necessities of feeding Al's steroid-fueled appetite with croissants and a Blondie bar at Au Bon Pain, plus fish soup and lobster bisque with a tortilla/apple/goat cheese/grilled shrimp salad at Legal Seafood, we see "Poetry," a lyrical but disturbing Korean film at The Stuart Playhouse. We enjoy their films, but have never been joined by more than an audience of five. "Maybe we could continue to go out to the movies here during your convalescence," I speculated, "since it is crowds you are supposed to avoid when that time comes and there certainly are no crowds here."

It's an odd, haunting theater in the middle of downtown Boston. The floor under us rumbles at intervals for the first fifteen minutes. Feels like the beginnings of an earthquake—like we experienced in Lima more than three decades ago. Attendant acknowledges that it happens, but has no explanation. Theater seems like someone's hobby, not a serious business, although they did have 300 people earlier today for an animated film event. They are still cleaning up when we arrive. It's part of a hotel complex. Feels like it belongs to another era.

MONDAY, APRIL 18, 2011. Great news. Toni calls. Donor is perfect match. Seventy percent of all matches meet all twelve markers. This match is one of them.

AL ON NIGHT SWEATS:

Came in cycles beginning perhaps two years before Transplant. They varied in intensity as the disease itself intensified. Very common, but poorly understood symptom. I once asked Dr. F, "There surely must be a Dr. Night Sweats who has been dedicated to figuring this out." He smiled and said, "Not that I know of. I think more than anything it's a composite signal that a body is in deep distress and is furiously searching for equilibrium."

In the lightest version they cause only mild sweat around the neck and collar area. I can sleep through the night and wake up with some dampness in those areas. In the worst case, I am up every hour, drenched as if I had dressed after a shower without toweling. Every part of the body from the head to the feet is soaked. It isn't hot perspiration like that from exercise. Isn't a cold sweat, either. Temperature is neutral. But it is just so damn prolific, as if my body were a faucet that I can't turn off.

There's no immediate treatment. There are only coping mechanisms. My strategies include six changes of sleepwear during the night. Towels on top of the sheets. Frequent showers during the night. I can't put on fresh clothes without cleaning up. I must also drink enormous quantities to rehydrate. That, of course, leads to even more trips to the bathroom. I consume huge volumes of talc that absorb the sweat temporarily. Night sweats persist and are expected to last up to the time I am hospitalized for Transplant.

Later he adds: As the transplant preparation period came to a conclusion, the sweats finally, mercifully, petered out.

Half dozing in the middle of the night, after seeing Al in night-sweat get-up. I think about nicknames I've used for him through the years. Months ago Al said that he feels like Andrea Boccelli—only he's wearing hand towels around his neck instead of a sexy scarf. So Andrea is one nickname. Several years ago when he was visiting cousin Carrie in Paris, she introduced Al to a friend of hers. Al heard the woman whisper to Carrie, "He looks like Gregory Peck." Al has also been described as an Abraham Lincoln look-alike, but being compared to Gregory Peck was a first. I adored Gregory Peck and had to agree there was a resemblance. So it was "Greg" for awhile.

He's been mistaken for a number of bearded Jewish men, including Boston local, Paul Levy, who was Executive Director for Massachusetts Water Resources Authority and CEO of Beth Israel Hospital. Al was sometimes approached by a citizen disgruntled with high water and sewage fees. He listened politely, but informed the disappointed stranger that there was nothing he could do to help since he was not Mr. Levy.

Several years ago when were visiting the Getty Museum in Los Angeles, a man approached Al, handed him a document which he apparently always kept in his back pocket and began a sales job on his screenplay. When Al looked bewildered, the guy stepped back and said, "You are Steven Spielberg, aren't you?"

Quite a range of men, but all attractive in my opinion.

Tuesday, April 19, 2011. Al is taking part in a Speed Networking Event at MIT's Microsoft NERD Center. Net Impact Boston, the society of sustainability students and young professionals, will host the premier networking event. The invitation reads: "NIB Speed Networking is one of our most popular events. Attendees rapidly move from table to table in order to maximize the number of contacts they will meet. Conversations are engaging and dynamic. This event is surely to be a hit—join us as we strive to connect and to grow Boston's CSR community!"

VIP guests include:

Mark Albion, Founder, Net Impact

John Hawthorn, Founder and CEO, MassChallenge

John Katovich, Founder, Katovich Law Group

Lori Van Dam, President, PlanetTran

Allen White, Senior Fellow, Tellus Institute

THURSDAY, APRIL 21, 2011. Al emails Judith.

Kick-ass platelets—115. I'll start donating them soon. :)

FRIDAY, APRIL 22, 2011. Al emails Toronto sister, Betty.

Hi dear Sister: Back in Boston?? From where?? We've been here for many weeks, since a March visit with Lena. Somehow family and friends imagine us constantly on the road, which used to be somewhat the case, but no longer is. Your Passover sounds wonderful. Doing well here. I'm in the last four-six weeks of what is likely my final therapy before a summer Transplant. Three visits/week to my clinic is a grind. But feeling terrific—all blood indicators are strong, which is the objective in preparation for the procedure. In the hospital about a week afterwards, then home for a long recuperation, with guests in small numbers (with masks and gloves) warmly welcomed. My guess is the timing will work out so that you and Lisa will visit me at home before or after your August time on Martha's Vineyard.

On May 12 we fly to Ohio for Judith's fiftieth high school reunion and an overdue visit with her sister, Molly.

FRIDAY, APRIL 22, 2011 CONT'D. Earth Day. More than ever, I'm feeling how tiny is our earth. As if I could hold it in two hands.

- The Western World focuses on the royal wedding of William and Kate in London.
- Much of the United States focuses on today's activity of another couple—middle aged, but married only three years—U.S. representative, Gabrielle Giffords and her astronaut husband. In order to watch him lead the last liftoff of the spaceship, Endeavor, she's taking her first break from rigorous physical therapy after a gunshot wound to the head.
- Practioners of Qi Gong/Tai Chi gather today to practice this ancient art. The events begin at 10:00 a.m. in New Zealand and continue, fol-

lowing the time zones around the globe. Led by our expert teacher, Rick, I and a dozen others go through the soothing movements up on Corey Hill overlooking Boston. I'm not good at sitting still and meditating, but this suits me well. It's meditation in motion. It's peaceful. It's relaxing. I need it.

Monday, April 25, 2011. Colleague and friend, Andy, emails Al re a close colleague and friend of Al's running for the U.S. Senate: "If you were to run, Allen, I might want to reconsider my position because you are selfless as far as trying to make change is concerned, or at least as selfless as one can be. But, of course, you aren't running and probably never will, for just that reason. But let me know if you change your mind, and I might then change mine :-). I support all of your efforts and will continue to do so."

Our youngest child, Douglas, turns thirty-three today. His love for and talent for music were obvious very early. Once among his experiments with chords and melodies, I heard several bars of *"Für Elise."* "Doug," I said, "that's Beethoven." He just smiled and continued playing. Now thirty years later, he's living in Los Angeles, still playing, still writing songs, but also exploring every aspect of the entertainment industry—screenwriting, playwriting, theater acting, film acting, casting, and coaching.

We always knew we wanted to move closer to the city—to The Hub as Boston is affectionately called. We looked in Cambridge and Brookline and found the perfect place. I realized later that the reason I knew from the moment I took my first step inside that condominium, was that the seller was an architect like my father. When he renovated he knew just what to keep—like the gumwood paneling in the dining room—and what to change. He opened up the 1920 design by removing doors and stripping one wall to the studs and painting them. Now fifteen years later, it has proven to be the perfect abode for us. We can sleep five guests, entertain up to forty people at once, work in separate offices, and sleep on a second-floor sun porch with views of trees, sky, moon, stars, and sun.

We also love the location—Coolidge Corner—walking distance of a European-like bakery, two swimming pools, the library, scores of restaurants and shops. Although when we purchased the condo, we were somewhat aware it was also near the medical district, the idea that someday such proximity might prove to be so important did not occur to us.

Now we have one more reason to be thankful for choosing this place. We are a ten-minute car ride, a twenty-minute bike ride, a thirty-minute train ride, a forty-minute walk from Dana Farber Cancer Institute. I just dropped

Al off there. After his appointment, suitcase in one hand, computer case in the other, he'll fly to Washington D.C. where he has a dinner tonight and meetings tomorrow. Patients come from all over the country and the world for treatment at Dana Farber. We are blessed to have it in our back yard.

Last month, for a trip to visit our daughter, Lena; son-in-law, Larry; and three granddaughters. Al packed two pieces of reading material: a thriller written by our friend, Leonard Rosen, entitled *All Cry Chaos;* and a large, heavy binder entitled *Stem Cell Transplantation: An Information Guide for Patients and Families.* He was amused by both the juxtaposition of the two works and their relevance to his current situation.

Guidance–Both practical and Spiritual

A BOUT THAT BINDER. (Herewith capitalized because it becomes our Bible, our Ruler, and the Guide to our Survival): it's the procedure laid out to the last detail, step-by-step. It takes what Dr. A and Toni outlined for us briefly just a few months ago, but with ten times more detail.

By now Al has read through the entire Binder, including Section 4, "Coverage for Medications." The fact that Congress is debating and cutting and trying to change Medicare is unnerving, but Al shrugs and says, "*Oh, those issues will be debated for years.*" Today's news is full of stories of voters reacting with anger and scorn to Republican Congressmen's proposals to alter Medicare.

FRIDAY, APRIL 29, 2011. INSPIRATION. Our youngest granddaughter, Bridgette, is seven months old today. She's spending so much time on her knees that her mother bought her protective knee pads. She rocks gently, about to figure out how to coordinate moving forward so she can explore more of her small protected world. Sometimes she takes practice breaks and returns to an activity she's already fully mastered. She rolls over and over, surprised to find herself so far from where she started. A whole world beckons—first the other side of the room, then the other rooms in the house. When that happens, her family will have to watch her every minute as she plunges into discovery everywhere. A young life unfolding. We want to witness her growing up. A reminder of the life-threatening CLL Al and I face.

INSPIRATION. Allen and I watch a documentary on the volcano at Mt. St. Helens in Washington State. On May 17, 1980 it was a gorgeous, symmetric, snow-covered mountain surrounded for miles by all life forms: pines, flowering plants, elk, a lake full of plants and fish. Suddenly it erupted. Boiling lava slithered down its slopes, destroying homes, rails, bridges, and highways. Fifty-seven people died—some of them as far away as thirteen miles. Elk, pines, all bushes and flowers were burned or disintegrated. All plant and fish life in the lake were choked. There was no longer any oxygen in the lake to support life. The entire area looked like the moon—pieces of gray, jagged barren rock. No sign of life remained.

One year later, scientists saw some color in the distance. It turned out to be a knee-high plant with purple flowers, swaying happily all alone in the breeze surrounded by desolation. On another exploration soon after, they saw some dirt moving. A close examination uncovered a gopher energetically and determinedly digging tunnels. Whole families of gophers had survived deep underground. Young life unfolding. GO SURVIVAL!!!

Birds flying overhead dropped seeds and more plants sprouted. Plankton in the lake produced oxygen. Several years after the eruption, when the scientists stocked the lake with fish, they thrived. Five years after the volcano appeared to have killed all life, the area had recaptured much of its pre-eruption beauty. The scientists were amazed. They had predicted it would take far longer. The wonder of Earth's regenerative capacity!

MAY 2011

SUNDAY, MAY 1, 2011. Before co-hosting a house party to raise support for Bob Massie's candidacy for the U.S. senate, we walk in Riverway Park along the Muddy River and come upon a "Studios Without Walls" exhibit with the theme of "Sanctuary." Eleven Brookline artists. Outdoors, most exhibits hang from trees or are tucked between branches. All are captivating and inspiring. I am especially drawn to two: one by a man who is both an artist and a doctor—a Mexican recently caught in the middle of drug war violence. Entitled "Intensive Care," it outlines bodies in white chalk lying on a small hill with their heads on pillows made of moss. The work projects a feeling of caring, tranquility, and hopeful recovery.

The second work I'm drawn to is a delicate, lace-like woven work entitled "Chrysalis" (the hard-shelled pupa of a moth or butterfly enclosed in a cocoon). I immediately think of the protection of my husband's arms and the cocoon-like nature of our sleeping porch. I ask Al: "What for me is like a chrysalis?" He immediately answers, "Your husband and your sleeping porch." Can the guy read my mind or what?

TUESDAY, MAY 3, 2011. Our oldest granddaughter, Nicole, turns fifteen today. She is a natural blonde beauty with green eyes, and a sweet mild, gentle, caring manner. We adore her to the core.

SPRING 2011. Al's relationship to clergy has always been rough. There was his childhood Rabbi, Rabbi Klein. Al labels that relationship, "*Uneven.*" Against the wishes of Rabbi Klein and others who felt he was more misbehaving than spiritual or mature, Al was elected president of his Temple's confirmation class by his peers. There were rumors about efforts to disqualify him, but those were short-lived, especially after the adults orchestrated a second election. When those votes came back, Al was re-elected by an even higher margin. The powers that be accepted the inevitable.

Al: *For me it was a sign of my classmates' confidence in me, deeply gratifying for a peer-conscious ninth grader. I took the job seriously. Fortunately, by junior high I had matured, and was eventually able to reverse the years of poor conduct and my well-deserved reputation as a miscreant. Rabbi Klein and I made our peace and developed a comfortable working relationship.*

Then there was the Springfield, Ohio Rabbi who refused to marry us unless I converted, even though Al had no interest in my taking such action. Perhaps we function best, we thought, with no clergy involvement as during the five years we were active members of a lay-led Unitarian Fellowship in Columbus in the seventies.

The first exception to the clergy unease was the Arlington, Virginia Unitarian minister who did not object to making our relationship legal and permanent in 1968. But the major exception was Boston Arlington Street Church's Reverend Victor Carpenter whom we befriended and so enjoyed and admired. ASC, a bastion of faith activism, was our religious home in Boston from 1979 until 1996 when Doug graduated from high school. During that time we served on a number of committees but, most importantly, made enduring friendships and at least attempted to give our children, if not a well-defined creed to live by, at least a community of like-minded, progressive families.

Coming from a family of Protestant ministers, I'm more accepting of clergy than Al is perhaps. But I have always recoiled from medical chaplains, especially Catholic ones. It began when I gave birth to Kate in a Catholic hospital in Columbus, Ohio. I feared if it came down to a choice, they would save my infant rather than me. That made no sense to me since, although of course I would grieve terribly, I could have another baby. My fears grew into nightmares of priests leaning over me as I lay dying, crucifixes dangling in my face, forcing me to confess (what exactly?), attempting to give me the last rites, whatever that is.

Now in the spring of 2011 as we prepare for the frightening stem cell procedure and recovery, Richard enters our lives. All my previous—and albeit prejudiced—fears of chaplains are reversed. Al is good at summarizing personalities: "Accelerating" means someone who begins talking slowly but gets worked up and excited and keeps going and doesn't stop. Because he's so calm, I think Al attracts such personalities. We had dinner with someone recently whom Al described as "smoldering." "*It's like sitting across from a tinderbox,*" he said. To begin to describe Richard, take the descriptions "accelerating" and "smoldering" and come up with their polar opposites. "Calm," certainly. "Humorful too." "Fabulous listener." Yet with many rich stories of his own to tell.

AL ON RICHARD:

He poked his head around the corner of what I had dubbed the "Executive Suite" of the infusion room and introduced himself as the "chaplain on duty." By then I had met five other chaplains. Until he introduced himself as a rabbinical student on assignment at Brigham/Dana Farber, I hadn't realized that THIS chaplain was a member of my tribe. He said he was there for conversation and to give support. He asked about my condition and treatment. "What are the next steps?" he wanted to know. There was an instant sense of warmth and authenticity. He was intent on understanding what I was facing, what I would be dealing with. The chaplaincy did not seem like just a job. I began to sense that this was a dedicated professional and a very special human being. My medical issues quickly receded as the center of the conversation and the focus of attention shifted from me to Richard. I had a hunch there was much of this man's life and values that I shared.

As our relationship with Richard deepened over the next weeks and months, Al's first impressions were confirmed. We enjoyed and admired him and sought his advice. It was a relationship of mutual discovery as we learned more and more about his background and current life: Married to Will, a public school special-needs teacher. The couple lives in our former town, Newton. Like us they have three kids. Theirs are all adopted. Richard's former professions include architect and investor.

Richard suggests to Al that he make lists of friends and family—both first and second tier—whom he would like to see during convalescence. Then set up a schedule. He also asks Al, "Is there a project that you've been putting off that you could devote yourself to during that period?" Yes, as a matter of fact. Beef up his French. Complete a book on rewriting the social contract.

They discuss Al's current work projects, how he might notify clients and colleagues that he is taking personal leave, the emotional challenge of handing over unfinished projects and teaching and writing commitments where his presence is necessary.

THURSDAY, MAY 5, 2011. NURSE BANTER AND SUPPORT. Melissa has been Al's principal oncology nurse for five years. He adores her. A mix of Japanese and African American, she is smart, compassionate, and tough. After serving in a supervisory position for a short while, she asked to return to her former direct patient contact. She missed her patients. Married for the second time six years ago to a Navy guy, Melissa became stepmother to a fourteen-year-old. Tomorrow that child is graduating from Old Dominican College in Virginia. It's a ten-hour drive, but the whole family is going. "Gonna cry my eyes out," Melissa says. Al had emailed her before today's appointment. "I've got a ferry ticket for 1:30 to Martha's Vineyard, so if possible kick me out the door by 10:30 a.m." Half an hour later Melissa says to a fellow nurse in front of Al: "See what I have to put up with this guy? He wants to go to the Vineyard and that impacts my work." The other nurse says, "Throw the bum out." They all three chuckle.

We make it to the ferry on time. Need to prepare our cottage for sale, a decision we made based on health risks from island insects and the desire to spend more time with our three, far-flung children in California and Florida. Also because of the headaches finding dependable workers to sweep debris off the roof, remove all the damn mold that accumulates every winter, repair moldings, paint, clean up the garden. An excellent realtor is proving indispensable. With a condo in Massachusetts and an apartment in Florida, I am so ready to rid ourselves of the Vineyard cottage. I feel bad, though that this represents a loss for Al. The island has been part of his life since high school.

WEDNESDAY, MAY 12, 2011. Our final night in our cottage. As we cuddle in bed, Al's skin feels very hot. The last time that happened, he was hospitalized for three days with a lung infection. Sure enough his temp is 101 degrees—higher than his team permits. No way can I fall asleep. He takes his temperature every two hours until, finally, at 3:00 a.m. the temp falls within normal range. We both collapse for a few hours of deep sleep.

"If we get through this," Al says, "we'll spend a month in Spain." In the past month he has turned down opportunities to speak, lead discussion groups, moderate panels, or teach in Spain, San Francisco, and New Delhi. He will be teaching a webinar, however, for MBA students of the Presidio School of Management in San Francisco. This is on top of many other writing and research projects he continues to do.

Anticipating that this will be our last visit for many months, we take advantage of the island's rich cultural offerings. Watch Australian aborigine movie, "Samson and Delilah." See "His and Hers" at the Martha's Vineyard Film Society. Attend a concert and dance at the local high school. After that performance we discover we've both reacted the same way—weepy from the talent, but also from nostalgia, thinking of how much joy our own three kids gave us performing throughout their school years.

THURSDAY, MAY 13, 2011. Leaving in a few hours for Ohio—for my fiftieth high school reunion. So excited to see everyone. Plus, along with three of my best buddies, I'm being inducted into the Hall of Fame. We'll all make acceptance speeches. Plaques with our photos and bio's will earn a permanent spot in a display case in the school lobby.

Tomorrow night a banquet for anyone who has ever graduated from Greenon High School—held at the school itself. Will also attend brunches, lunches (including one to celebrate my birthday), dinners, visits with two sisters, four nieces, two nephews, Peace Corps friends. My bag is packed with gifts, three possible outfits for the festivities that my sister, Molly, can help me choose from, along with matching shoes, jackets, earrings, necklaces.

My dad designed the school in 1958. I have been reminiscing about my three happy years there—easy years compared to what many high-schoolers experience these days. I thought pot was something you used for making homemade soups or fixing the popcorn my family munched on every Sunday night. In my crowd there were no drugs, no alcohol use, no sex. Yet we shared so many good times. There's a photo of six of us in a friend's basement. We built a human pyramid, three boys on the floor on their knees, two girls (including me) on top of them, knees digging into the backs of the boys, and the lightest girl on the very top. It was an innocent time. I haven't been inside the school for decades.

I also have an appointment with Suzanne, owner of Yellow Springs' only B & B—the Morgan House—to discuss the possibility of using her facility to celebrate my seventieth birthday in 2013, hopefully reuniting my three delightful children and their spouses.

An hour before we are to leave for the airport, just after I close my suitcase and roll it to the front door, Al calls from Dana. He's still running a fever, still coughing. They want to put him into Brigham and Women's Hospital until his temperature stabilizes. At first I think I could go to my reunion alone, but when he calls back with a diagnosis of bilateral pneumonia, I begin telephoning and emailing to cancel my plans. I feel pretty sorry for myself and cry on the phone with my sister, Molly, who spent seven hours cooking the previous day in anticipation of our staying at her house and entertaining some family members. MY fridge, on the other hand, is completely empty. But I would not be able to enjoy myself, worrying about Al, not being there to make his hospital stay as comfortable as possible. CLL is taking its toll. Bummer!

Al had parked our only car at Dana, so I take a taxi there and wait with him for three hours while a bed opens up at Brigham and Women's Hospital. We read and eat and talk and joke with the nurses.

Once we're finally checked into a room, a nurse finds us napping side by side in the narrow hospital bed and asks, "How long have you two been married?" Another nurse, seeing us like that asks, "Which one of you is the patient?"

We grab Al's laptop, prop our feet up, and watch "The Way We Get By," a documentary about three elderly people who live alone and make every effort, any time day or night, to meet troops returning from Iraq. By the end of the film, they had greeted tens of thousands of troops with handshakes, hugs, and free cell phones to call their loved ones. "Mom, I'm home." "I'm on U.S. soil, Honey." "Can't wait to see you and the kids, Babe."

"Thank you for what you've done for our country," the elderly greeters say. The troops react with surprise and gratitude being welcomed home just seconds after entering their country for the first time in many months, some longer. Yet the real story is that the lives of Bangor, Maine residents Bill, Jerry, and Joan are less isolated, and made richer and more meaningful by their daily volunteer work.

The film is absorbing and moving. Seeing the soldiers arrive home, knowing what they've been through, and then the three elderly folks whose lives are given meaning by their dedication to greeting the soldiers—it all puts our troubles in perspective.

INSPIRATION. Whenever I'm in the car alone—a rare event because neither of us drives often or far—I listen to my *Champs Elysées* CDs—a monthly audio and print magazine with segments on French politics, the economy, food, culture, literature, theater, cinema. During that brief ten-minute ride between the clinic and home today, I pop a tape in the tape deck and find myself listening to an interview with author and dramatist, Eric-Emmanuel Schmidt. I'm shaky these days, anticipating and dreading Al's procedure. Schmidt's words are exactly what I need to hear. Years ago he found God after inadvertently spending a night alone in the Algerian desert. I hear Schmidt's voice saying: "Et puis maintenant, j'habite toujours dans un mystère, mais au lieu de l'habiter avec l'angoisse, je l'habite avec la confiance. Je m'abandonne à l'inconnu. Je lui fais crédit, a cette vie que je ne comprends pas, a cette mort que je vais rencontrer. Voilà. J'ai confiance."[1] Translation: "And now since then, I always live inside a mystery, but instead of living with anguish, I live with confidence. I abandon myself to the unknown. I place my faith in the future, in this life which I do not understand, in that death I will one day encounter. That's how it is now. I am confident."

Once, home alone for the evening I begin reading Schmidt's short novel, "*Oscar et la Dame Rose.*" It's another volunteer story. A "*Dame Rose*" (pink lady) is a hospital volunteer. Their pink uniforms distinguish them from medical personnel. I know the outlines of the story, but not that the other main character—a dying ten-year-old boy—has leukemia and only days to live. With the help of la *Dame Rose,* who has her own story to tell, in one week's time, Oscar lives a lifetime of experiences: he falls in love with another patient, "marries" her, says goodbye to his parents, to life. It's a deeply moving story that was wildly popular in France where it was made into a movie.

I also read the AARP bulletin and immediately feel cared for. These articles may provide comfort for such time when either of us is alone without the other.

Friday, May 14, 2011. Al's second day in the hospital with para-influenza in both lungs. It's a viral condition which means it cannot be treated with antibiotics, only with supportive care. Mostly just have to wait it out. Temperature still fluctuating. Still coughing a great deal. Just spoke with him. He's talking to Kate on the phone now. She encourages me to attend my reunion, but it just won't work. All my high school friends are in long-term marriages. One of my dearest friends, Steve, writes, "Any of us would have done the same."

Thursday, May 19, 2011. Tough going here. Al's cough has lessened, but his temperature spikes continue. He's back home and working, involved in several conference calls a day, but is fatigued. Bowed out of a call early yesterday. Sleeping a great deal. His quick, shallow breaths alarm me. He has experienced headaches and blurred vision, which he attributes to a new antibiotic. The one the hospital prescribed would have cost $300. This one is $7, but he's not going to take it anymore. We're seeing his internist, Dr. L, at Harvard-Vanguard this afternoon.

---

[1] Champs Elysées Série 24 numéro 11, p. 64.

Al emails sisters Betty and Lisa:

Hi, Sisters: Hope all is well. I've been delinquent in keeping you informed of my recent situation. I was hospitalized three days late last week to treat para-influenza pneumonia. This is a fairly common virus that attacks the respiratory system. With a compromised immune system, I'm a juicy target. I was discharged on Sunday and have been recuperating at home under the watchful eye of Judith. My orders are to keep myself away from crowds of people in closed spaces as a protective measure for both sides. Assuming I continue to make progress, I expect to return to the office Monday.

The most distressing and disruptive part of the whole episode is that we had bags packed for a flight to Columbus for Judith's fiftieth high school reunion. With profound disappointment, all plans were cancelled, including her participation in an award ceremony to induct her into "Greenon High School Hall of Fame." So that's it. These kinds of surprises are no longer surprises any more. It's exactly why a Transplant is on the agenda. Date is still not fixed, but likely early August. Will keep you posted. Much love, Al

6:00 P.M. Harvard-Vanguard Internist, Dr. L, calls Al in for post-hospitalization, follow-up appointment. Losing weight. 182 lbs. fully clothed with fat billfold in pocket. Blood pressure okay. Temp normal. But oxygen level low—93 whereas it's usually at 98/99.

My current concerns:
- Al's fast-paced, shallow breaths that go on all night. I try to feel his pulse without disturbing him, although I don't know what I would learn if I succeeded in finding it and counting. I try to count his and then compare it to mine. I'm afraid to sleep.
- The sores on his face. Pink sores around his mouth. On his cheeks.
- Continued use of antibiotics. Is he reaching a resistance level after which they'll no longer work?
- His fatigue.
- Is it safe for him to fly?
- Can he be left alone at all?

Diagnosis after one week in the hospital:
- Generally on the mend.
- Cough much better.
- But antibiotic resulted in blurred vision and headaches which are known side effects. Doctor said to take a break from that drug.

Warning:
- In the next few days, should stabilize or at least get better.
- If he feels worse, he should return to the hospital.

Conclusion:
- The dirty triplets—cough/temp/energy—all are improving.
- Para-influenza is slowly resolving. But it's viral and can last eight weeks!
- Until (I coil away from using the word "unless") the influenza clears up, there can be no transplant.
- Dramatic shifts unlikely. The short breaths at night are consistent with pneumonia. The lungs are less efficient. I get the explanation, but I'm still afraid to fall asleep.
- Sores could be viral rash.

Ten days later, pneumonia has cleared up. We grab these healthy days and plan for a trip to Ohio after all. Most of my friends have gone home to other states, but I will see my family. Yellow Springs, here we come.

MONDAY, MAY 23, 2011. With doctor.
- Night sweats are constant. Up at least three-four times a night, sometimes up to seven times. When I get up in the morning there are undershirts and pajamas hung up to dry all over the bedroom. Daytime, Al feels as if he's moving in slow motion. His hematocrit is going down. Why? Bone marrow is not producing sufficient red cells. Viral infection is running its course. On the other hand, platelets are 139. Highest in a long time. Bone marrow working better. But still needs a blood transfusion.
- Fever persists. Immune booster once a month.
- Will need chest x-ray. Infection has delayed transplant by a couple of weeks. Need one month of prep, then possibly more therapy.

Lymph nodes small. GOOD! But still need to be smaller. I feel like screaming, "Oh you gunk in the lymph nodes of my love—get the hell out."

TUESDAY, MAY 24, 2011. Al spends a whole day at downtown office yesterday for first time in ten days. Arrives home exhausted, but rallies with a before-dinner nap.

My sore throat and congestion are nearly totally gone. I've been fatigued too, worrying about Al, up early for 7:00 a.m. appointments. Purchasing prescriptions. Another one today. Another forty bucks.

Al often asks me, "How did you sleep?" Having watched me as he got up to change into dry clothes several times, he knows full well when I've slept seven-eight hours without moving. He finds satisfaction, he says, in knowing and watching even though his question is asked in a slightly amused tone.

Wednesday, May 25, 2011. Usual routine: Drive to Yawkey Center. Hand car over to one of six red-jacketed, polite—"How are you today, Ma'am?"—well-trained valets. In an attempt to avoid germs, use the knuckle of an index finger to push the elevator button for the eighth floor. Check in. Squeeze on antiseptic hand wash. Get vitals check. Temp 99.6. Too high, but holding steady. Then Al takes command of a corner of the infusion unit which he dubs "The Executive Suite."

About that "Executive Suite." In Dana's old building the waiting room was so crowded it felt as if patients were sitting on each other's laps. Little privacy to discuss very private matters. With all the confusion and movement of patients and personnel, Al sometimes worried he might be administered the wrong drug. Now all cancer treatment has moved across the street to the spanking new, roomy, state-of-the-art Yawkey Center. Al stakes out a place for himself in the infusion unit, a corner on the eighth floor with floor-to-ceiling windows. The view offers a sweeping vista stretching from across the Charles River as far as Cambridge on one side, and parts of Back Bay in Boston to the mouth of the Charles River where it merges with Boston Harbor on the other side. Because he arranges his appointments for very early in the day, it's a quiet spot. Good for working on the computer, talking on the phone, and napping during his endless intravenous treatments. There's competition for that spot, though. One woman told a nurse, "When I see that tall white-haired man on the elevator in front of me, I know he'll get there first."

Al lowers the blinds to just the level he prefers. Very bright sunlight needs to be modulated for work and napping. He arranges a stool for his feet, another for his papers/phone/computer. Gathers drinks and snacks so they're within reach. Moves the various parts of the big cushy chair until it's the right height and provides support level for his head. He arranges a comfortable chair and stool for me too. I read while I keep him company. Nurse Melissa starts the infusion. For the next ninety minutes to six hours, depending on the drug, Al checks emails, works on a document, participates in conference calls. This "Executive Suite" is his third office, invisible to colleagues with whom he regularly communicates–colleagues who may be nearby in Boston, somewhere else in the U.S. or thousands of miles away in another country.

Today he also surfs the Internet to find the best deal for a rental car. We're escaping to Vermont for the weekend. It's quiet except for the low-volume TV of the patient in the next cubicle, separated by a retractable curtain.

Because of soreness, Melissa places a warm pack on the spot where the needle enters the arm. Deep crimson droplets slide down the clear tube into Al's left arm (the side he chose for today). Fresh, healthy blood enters his veins. Goal: to keep him functioning a while longer until another transfusion is required or until he's temporarily healthy enough for the ultimate procedure. Transplant beckons and teases with promise, but it's on the horizon, still out of reach.

FRIDAY, MAY 27, 2011. Al mentions the word "funeral" for the first time. Though I have not dwelled on the subject or discussed it with Al, I have thought about his funeral these past months. I had decided I would ask Bob Massie to speak. Bob and Al co-founded Global Reporting Initiative. They spent days and weeks traveling the globe to build the program. Bob knows, respects, and cares about Al. He's also a dynamic and inspiring speaker and an ordained minister. But I had never broached the subject with Al. Before I say anything, Al says, "*I would ask Bob Massie to speak at my funeral.*" Sometimes I think we're just disgustingly in sync!

TUESDAY, MAY 31, 2011. AL EMAILS ME:

After a three-week hiatus to recover from pneumonia, I've restarted the drug treatments. Overall, strongest results in four-five months. Must be that Yellow Springs nourishment (no kidding). We have a birthday date tonight. Will see you about 7:30, I assume.

AL EMAILS DR.

Hoping to have extended visits with grandchildren in June. Could be a long while before we see them. What do you think?

DR. WRITES BACK: "Okey-doke."

JUNE 2011

THURSDAY, JUNE 2, 2011. I'm in D.C. for a few days for a board meeting with Campaign for the Fair Sentencing of Youth. Al reports on today's Dana visit:

Strong blood. Minor fever—100.5. Will do additional blood work and chest x-ray to check for any new virus. Window for transplant expanded from first two weeks in August to entire month of August.

AL READS ME THIS EMAIL FROM ONE OF HIS DOCTORS: "The rash is not from the chicken pox or shingles virus. It is Herpes Simplex Type 1, which is the virus that typically causes cold sores. We are talking with the infectious disease folks about which antiviral we will need to switch to while we wait for the culture results to be finalized, which can take one-two weeks. We will be in touch with you as soon as we have an appointment for you with one of our infectious disease colleagues and a plan for treatment."

My life-long Democrat husband then makes the shocking statement that he's becoming a Republican—because of all the specialists and waste. One doctor after another. Later he says something about taking a handful of barbiturates rather than continue to deal with all these medical issues and uncertainty. He is not serious about becoming a Republican or taking barbiturates, but these extreme comments show how wearing this ordeal is for him. It's alarming to hear these words. He's such a steady guy, heading out to be prodded and poked and infused and drilled. It's all taking a toll.

"Chronic disease is like a slow drain, robbing you of energy and time and spirit." Al says.

Al joins me in D.C. where he manages a panel for a new project—a corporate sustainability ratings initiative project. He insists on flying after he seemed knocked out yesterday by a combination of morphine, herpes, up-and-down fever, and general fatigue. It's his last business flight, he promises. The event goes well. Adrenaline trumps fragility. Looking frail and peaked, he rises to the occasion as a speaker and panel moderator.

In our hotel room together, relieved that the main event is behind him, we both need to make love and cannot fall asleep. We are reluctant about intimacy because we don't have a clear answer about the possibility of my becoming infected from the herpes rash virus on his chest. Should we wait until it begins to heal? During lovemaking, I keep unconsciously pulling up his T-shirt to get to some flesh. He keeps yanking it down to protect me. But as long-time lovers, we overcome the challenges and slip into a deep sleep.

When we arrive at the airport to fly back to Boston and check in for the flight, Al discovers that he does not have his cell phone. Panic. We search all bags, luggage, pockets. I use my Mom's old trick. "Think about the last time you used it." He thinks he may have left it on the table at Le Pain Quotidien where he had a breakfast meeting. I call the restaurant. The manager has the phone, but is leaving for the day. He'll give it to someone else for safekeeping.

Jet Blue is reassuring: "You're already checked in. When you get back to the airport, just go directly to security."

We grab a taxi back into the city and tell the driver our dilemma. I have a feeling this is not the first time he's heard this kind of passenger panic. The driver knows how to avoid heavy traffic. We zoom along on a side street, but can see traffic stopped completely on a parallel street. We double park in busy

Dupont Circle. I run into the restaurant and return triumphant, waving the phone. We make the flight. A good omen for the recovery that lies ahead?

Inspiration. On the return plane trip to Boston, my seatmate is a teenage American boy with Down 's syndrome. His feet do not reach the floor. He is one of the calmest, most self-sufficient kids I've ever seen. For 2-1/2 hours, he entertains himself in a highly intent manner with a large notebook, a pen, and an iPod, all of which he uses to coordinate with the book he has propped up on his tray: *The Ultimate Japanese Phrasebook.* So he is listening, reading, and writing at the same time—in Japanese. His equally calm and pleasant mother sits across the aisle from him, absorbed in her own book. Occasionally she glances over or they exchange a few words. Then he continues his studies. As a linguist, I am more than curious. I would like to ask him if he is going to travel to Japan, but he is wearing earphones and is totally immersed. I don't want to interrupt him. He never glances at me. He could never imagine that he's providing me inspiration when I'm in need of it or that I'm writing about him in *Autumns of Our Joy.*

Friday, June 3, 2011. An evening home alone. Strange after being in Ohio with fourteen people at every meal, talking, laughing, and sharing stories followed by a barrage of attention from friends and family. All my kids had contacted me by noon on May 31st. I am now sixty-eight years old. For the two West Coasters, that meant wishing Mom Happy Birthday before going to work. Love my kids.

Kate and Maureen sent me five French pop albums; Doug emailed me the lyrics to a dedication to Mom song he had written and is now setting to music; Lena was the first to call. She sang Happy Birthday in a most entertaining mock operatic soprano. I had already received a home-made card from Lena's family and opened it on my birthday. One whole side designed by granddaughter, Zoey; the other by Lena with granddaughter Nicole and husband Larry's signatures. Lena promised a "literary gift" plus a party with cake when we visit in June.

Al is at a Red Sox game. For the first time in a long time, I'm home alone. I like it, listening to my own music, singing along, reading the French lyrics. But now I have to wonder: if this were forever? If he doesn't make it through the procedure? Would French pop still give me this much pleasure?

Saturday, June 4, 2011. Al gets up early this morning and heads for the clinic as he must now that pneumonia is past—very little cough, slightly elevated temp at times—three times a week. It means he never gets to sleep in and since every night he is up as many as seven times for bathroom visits and/

or disturbances caused by those incessant night sweats, it's quite a mental and physical grind. He's always been extremely adept at taking naps, though—on planes, at his desk, surrounded by grandchildren, watching TV, in the movies—an invaluable talent in these anxious, trying times.

By the time he returns home for a second breakfast about 10:30 a.m., he has listened to NPR during the twenty-minute round trip to Dana and read some of today's *New York Times*. I've read some of *The Boston Globe*. We discuss tidbits of interest we have learned or thought about since we last talked the previous night:

- Harvard is expanding and rebuilding its board after a disastrous six-person board was "asleep at the wheel" and let former President, Larry Summers, make all the decisions—many of them disastrous.
- Several Republican Presidential Candidates have said they believe that global warming is real and that humans are contributing to it. Romney went so far as to say we must turn to alternative sources of energy.
- An NPR interview with the only U.S. female orchestra conductor— in Baltimore—and how she responded when asked if conducting a moving piece about the Holocaust was difficult emotionally.
- How the word "architecture"—meaning structure and design— is finding its way into many fields—including music.
- Whether Al should remain on the board of Civic Capital, an investment firm, which meets once a year.
- Retirement monies including the advantages of delaying social security until age seventy.

I wonder during our daily conversations on diverse topics: What would it be like to live alone or to live with someone who does not have Al's wide diversity of interests, alertness, thoughtfulness, and listening skills?

If I don't stop myself, I can quickly become maudlin. Who would hold me? Who would calm me down? Who would bring perspective to my fears? Who in the world could make me laugh as often and as raucously? Who but a joint-parent can share my pride and relief when our children experience small and large triumphs? Who but a joint-grandparent can find such joy in watching the next generation—our granddaughters—take that first step, pronounce those first words?

All I can do is enjoy each day with Al. Our niece, Anna, once said to me that I know how to make myself happy. I think that is generally true. I don't tolerate much longing or sadness in myself, and am rarely depressed. But could

I ever again be able to "make myself happy" if I lose my closest companion?

SUNDAY, JUNE 5, 2011. I EMAIL KATE. "Dad is doing pretty well. Cough gone. Such a relief. Fever comes and goes, mostly normal, but every day rises for awhile to 99 or 100. His stamina is still down. He rests a lot. Has a very hectic week this week. Must go to the clinic on Monday, Tuesday, and Wednesday; has a four-hour seminar on Wednesday. Trying to wind up a bunch of projects, is refusing others, and saying no to a lot of speaking invitations. He hates telling people he is going on 'personal leave.' But his mood is good. We've had a fun weekend with spectacular weather.

While hoping for the best outcome from this procedure—remission—we talk a little more about funerals and about what my life might be like without him. Every day is precious."

MONDAY, JUNE 6, 2011. DRUG TRIALS. Al generally agrees to participate in trial drugs not just for the possible benefit to him, but for other patients, future patients. After all, his survival the last dozen years and, hopefully, the next twenty, stands on the shoulders of patients who agreed to earlier drug trials. The drug companies, of course, hope for winners that eventually the federal Food and Drug Administration approves. But trial drugs are just that: unproven and risky. I'm nervous when he's in a drug trial. It's also time-consuming. Keeping records. Answering questions. On top of all the already demanding self care. It requires a degree of selflessness. But my darling has lots of that.

Dr. A informs Al that the vaccine protocol (a drug trial in which Al has been participating) has been frozen. Twenty-two to twenty-four CLL patients have been treated successfully, but one recently did not react well. Dr. A seems upset. It must have been a serious reaction. Al feels bad for the doctor and for himself.

Al continues to work every day. The Transplant date has already been delayed twice, each time leaving us increasingly impatient and anxious. He agrees, though, that by the end of the month he will refuse all requests to speak, travel, serve on panels, etc. We'll see how that holds up!

During recuperation he hopefully will still be able to be active and creative. For now we can walk and go to restaurants. But after Transplant? No travel. Not for a long time. Before/ during/after Transplant, things can happen. The clinic's message is, "ANTICIPATE MAJOR DISRUPTIONS."

THURSDAY, JUNE 9, 2011. ALLEN EMAILS DANA DERMATOLOGIST, DR. C.

Thank you for your voicemail yesterday. Unfortunately, the quality of the message was very uneven. I understand your initial assessment is that the skin condition on my neck and torso is not shingles-related, but rather connected to a herpes virus of a different kind. Is that correct? I'm reachable via cell today.

Friday, June 10, 2011. Dr. C emails Allen: "Yes, while you continue to develop new areas and have small blisters or pustules, these are contagious—similar to how cold sores are contagious. HSV is transmitted by physical contact only (unlike the chicken pox virus which can be airborne)."

Keeping the areas covered by clothing should be sufficient to prevent transmission to someone who has never been exposed to HSV. (Of note, by adulthood, the vast majority of people have already been exposed to HSV1). Hope this helps."

But this raises issues of infection for our granddaughters and our planned visit to see them—probably for the last time for many months until we can travel again. Mutual questions of infection. Al to them. They to Al.

Saturday, June 11, 2011. Al emails Lena.

I know you're concerned about Herpes Simplex Virus (HSV), the cause of spots on my torso. My dermatologist describes the condition as similar to cold sores. I'll need to be sure the kids do not physically contact the affected parts of my torso. At the same time, it's possible that with medication I'm now taking, the HSV will have passed entirely by the time we visit—I hope that's the case. xxoo Dad

Sunday, June 12, 2011. Al had a good night's sleep, but wakes up with a fever. Now they say this fever is caused by the herpes virus. Up for brunch with houseguest, our much-loved cousin, Carrie, who always brightens things up. Al heads back to bed for a nap and says, "I feel ravished." "I know, Honey," I say, "but that's why we're having the procedure." "I know the solution," Al replies. "I just want sympathy." And he adds again, "I'm sorry I'm such a burden."

Monday, June 13, 2011. Al unexpectedly sent to hospital because of herpes virus rash on torso. Darn. Second hospitalization because of this insidious stuff. CLL sees destruction on the horizon and is making itself felt more strongly than ever, looking for weaknesses, infusing Al's blood and lymph nodes with its mischief. We vow that we will get rid of this fucker and Al will have the Transplant someday soon. He feels okay, though, and insists on leaving the hospital for short periods, after signing an agreement that indemnifies the hospital against any mishaps while he is outside the building. Long spirit-restoring walks. Beautiful days. Fens. Gardens. Once walked all the way to our favorite café on Newbury Street. Once foolishly shared a bench with a homeless person while eating our lunch. Yikes! Infection risk! I schlep dinner every night and heat it up in the hospital pod's microwave, then clear a space among medical paraphernalia, newspapers, computer, and cleansers, to sit and eat more or less formally.

The virus is not healing and is spreading. In the worst scenario, it could become meningitis and affect the BRAIN! Al's been so discouraged. He is forced to cancel still another presentation on Wednesday this week. Our valued chaplain, Richard, responds immediately to my call and finds Al, who had not yet been assigned a room at Brigham and Women's Hospital and is stuck waiting at Dana Farber. Al calls me after Richard visits. They talked for forty-five minutes. Al tells me, "It was emotional and extremely helpful; Richard is a good ear, a shoulder, such a great listener."

HOSPITAL ROOM 9:00 P.M. Chatting with a transplant nurse, we learn that Floors four (our current floor) and six are dedicated to transplant patients. Struggling with various stages of transplant, they lie in silent, closed-door rooms all around us. "How are they doing?" I ask. The nurse sort of shrugs and answers nonchalantly, "Fine."

We then learn that the actual transplant will take place right there in the hospital room. I can be there wearing a mask. "It's really anti-climactic," the nurse says. "Like a blood transfusion." She's the second person to offer such a description. Perhaps it's just routine for the nurses, but for the patients and their families, it's a unique life-changing and life-saving experience.

We had heard earlier about someone who officially changed his birthday to the date of his Transplant, what is referred to as Day Zero—his new-life date. When nurse Katlin leaves, Al becomes weepy. "But many patients must be emotional," he says. He sits on the bed shaking his head and tearing up. The drama of it all. After all he's been through.

Tough day for me, though, dealing with still another hospitalization plus my own dental challenge. Doesn't hurt much, but I'm worried the infection could reach the brain through the sinus. (Oh, so both our brains are being threatened now?) Needs to be pulled along with wisdom tooth next to it. Desperate to get to Florida one more time before the procedure. May not see Lena, Larry, and grandgirls for many months. Plan is for me to leave Sunday, the 19th; Al to fly to D.C. for his "last" work-related flight, then to Florida on Friday, the 24th; returning with me to Boston on July 4th. We're both going to celebrate our birthdays while we're there. But that means I'll be away from Al for five days and I will not be able to accompany him on the trip.

Very nervous about not being with him, but I have to get these teeth pulled, the infection cleared out, and a bone graft put in place. The bone comes from a cadaver (creepy) and the doctor lowers her voice when she says the word.

TUESDAY, JUNE 14, 2011. EMAIL FROM COUSIN CARRIE AFTER HER WONDERFUL THREE-DAY VISIT WITH US BEFORE SHE RETURNS TO PARIS "Dearest cousins. Arrived safely in upstate New York (even got upgraded on the flight to New York from Boston in a first-class seat . . . too bad it wasn't a longer flight!), and am still basking in the warmth of your hospitality, wonderful conversations, and love. Thank you both so much for all the time you gave me during this great visit . . . I so wish we all lived closer to each other.

Al, I will be thinking of you in August and, in between, sending you only good vibes for a successful procedure. You are a remarkable human being, with strength and courage beyond anyone else I know. Let that take you through this next stage, and know that you are surrounded by family and friends who are wrapping you in a warm blanket of love. And of course there is Judith—what you have for each other continues to inspire me and serve as a model of what great marriages are made of.

This comes with all my love and support, Carrie"

WEDNESDAY, JUNE 15, 2011. Courtyard of Brigham and Women's Hospital with visiting oldest daughter, Kate. Reading hospital brochures. "Keep sanitizer near and offer it to your doctor, politely saying: 'I'm sure you've done this a hundred times already, but would you mind?'" So we have to police the doctors?

All day with our Kater. She and I enjoy a water aerobics class with the excellent instructor, Sean, then shop at Whole Foods and bring Al—still hospitalized—a lasagna, spring rolls, salad, and pie. Kate and Al set up the *Caring Bridge* website while I nap. Now we can notify family, friends, and colleagues to check that site for updates on Al's condition and progress. We take a long time choosing the right motif. Among the many choices are: patriotism, an ugly banner that spelled out hope, seasonal, religious, teens, child, and adult. Al asks if the adult themes feature anything erotic. We all agree on the "Go Green" theme which features lots of trees plus some symbol we can't read, but which seems to be about recycling. Nothing sexy. I choose the password, "Life Ahead." Al chooses "CLL Sucks."

We sit outside in the sun (an activity now referred to by many as "absorbing vitamin 'D'") to eat our Whole Foods lunch. When we return, we see that Richard has been by. Clue: a *New York Times* has been delivered. Happily, he returns and we have a wonderful chat that reveals still more things in common. He owns property in West Tisbury on Martha's Vineyard and may retire there someday. Like us he has taken his three kids there since they were born.

Richard also owns an apartment in Montreal and updates us on the Buckminster Fuller designed geodesic dome where I worked during Expo '67. There was a fire several years ago and all the windows were destroyed, but the structure still stands. He's not sure what it's used for now, if anything. "When this is all over," Richard offers, "I want you to use my Montreal apartment. Stay as long as you want to." This is a prospect that entices us. Eventually, many months later, we take advantage of Richard's generosity and spend a delightful five days in his apartment in the charming old part of the city.

When Al's feeling down after still another hospitalization, I feel his personality fading. But tonight, his spirits and body are much improved. Kate's presence—loving, generous, luminous—always has that effect. Third night in hospital tonight, but at least he has had several hours outside the damn room. Long hugs and tears from Kate as they say good-night, but we'll see him again tomorrow.

THURSDAY, JUNE 16, 2011. Al chastises me for not taking a nap. I'm sleeping only about five hours at night—instead of my usual seven to eight. We share a long embrace before I leave, but the tension of dealing with the disease, the herpes outbreak, the hospitalization, my infected teeth, on and on . . . it's getting to both of us, and not being able to relax in each other's arms for the fourth night in a row is so tough.

FRIDAY, JUNE 17, 2011. EMAIL THIS MORNING FROM AL:
Sorry if I sounded brusque yesterday. I know how restorative your power catnaps are and want you to be as rested as possible during these difficult times. Your teary eyes at the time you departed yesterday, which flashed through my mind last night, spoke to the cumulative stress this f-g condition has created for us. At the same time, it toughened my resolve to conquer the beast with the help of my precious partner.

Looking forward to movie date and hugs tonight. Plan is to stretch out on the hospital bed, download from Netflix, and share the laptop resting on our thighs.

Writing from Hospital Room—still there.

Speaking of our mystery lifesaver, Al says, "The donor could be from Paris, Puno, or Peoria." I can see his geographer's mind rapidly passing over the globe to gather those "P" towns.

Boston wins the Stanley Cup tonight. 4-0. Trounces the Vancouver Canucks. Al says, "*The Canadians got pucked over.*" Fireworks can be heard from my bed all night. Joyous celebration in Boston streets, but the usually calm, undemonstrative Canadians rioted, turned over vehicles and set fire to them.

At one point in the crowded hospital room, Kate is on the phone with my local periodontist since I cannot have the procedure in Florida after all. I'm on the computer working on a document for the Campaign for the Fair Sentencing of Youth, which I serve as board member. The alarm on the intravenous apparatus begins to ring insistently. Al picks up a phone message, saying his Transplant is now scheduled for July 6—four to eight weeks earlier than we expected. When, with all this noise and confusion, I shove a paper at him giving Kate permission to access our checking account if necessary—and ask him to sign it—we all three burst out laughing. Three people in one tiny room bursting with noise, activity, imminent decisions, surprises, more decisions.

Bone marrow biopsy shows that CLL interference is down to ten percent. Very good. He's also reacting well to the herpes virus treatment. No side effects. He's had few side effects with any drugs actually. Seldom any nausea or fatigue. He has a full head of beautiful white hair. He's now back to his take-charge, analytical, problem-solving personality. Waiting for visit from Kate's friend, Vikram, who is interning at Brigham and Women's Hospital. He just texted that he's in the building and is going to stop by for a visit.

Fifth day in hospital. Tears and Turmoil. All of us, especially Al, are attempting to adjust to the sudden announcement that the procedure is scheduled for July 6. That's three to eight weeks earlier than we thought. Al had planned to use all of July to wind down all work projects, say some goodbye's, get organized for the long semi-quarantine. But Lena and Kate urge him to seize that date since all the stars seem aligned. Choosing a date requires an algorithm: Four weeks after the last treatment of Campath. Maximum five percent presence of CLL in the marrow. No infections. No temperature. Donor availability. Surgeon availability.

SAME DAY. SAME HOSPITAL ROOM. Al on phone with Dr. A. Since Al must be off the drug Campath for four weeks before the procedure, the procedure will now be delayed. The disease must not go above ten percent of where it is now. But Campath is creating collateral damage making him too vulnerable for the Transplant. Possibly mid July or mid August now. All this must also be coordinated with the donor's schedule too. Maddening.

Over breakfast, Kate and I make a list of needs and divide up another list we've made of caregiving resources. Lena calls to urge us to cancel Florida trip and get my dental procedure done wherever I can here in Boston after all. Kate, Richard, and Al have planned to meet over lunch today. Al has 3:00-4:00 business call. Then more discussions, hopefully some decisions, and that movie.

Kate and Al have lunch with Richard who also encourages grabbing any available transplant date, regardless of how hurried the preparation may have to be. I stay home and remain out of the discussion. Although I agree, I think

Al will listen better to them and I might become too shrill. Bottom line: Al requests July 14 and Dr. A says okay. Only part of the formula not in place is that presence of CLL in marrow is closer to ten-fifteen percent. It's best if they can get it down to five percent, but Dr. A says they'd deal with that. As of today at 7:00 p.m., only other pieces missing (barring surprises like recent pneumonia and herpes outbreak, of course) are Dr. F approval and donor availability.

After the lunch, Kate texts she couldn't be sure but she thinks they convinced her dad to stop travelling (he has a D.C. meeting next week). Kate needs a break from the devoted caring of her parents. She's on her way to spend the rest of the afternoon and evening with her dear friend, Geeta, and Geeta's four-year-old, Rajan. I call Kate. She says her Dad teared up a few times talking with Richard and seems reconciled to a July date.

The most difficult thing about this sudden transplant date change is that we are forced to cancel the two-week trip to Florida to be with Lena, Larry, and the grandkids. Lena said she would come visit a couple of times, once maybe with Nicole, another time with Bridgette. At the thought of not seeing Zoey for months, though, I nearly collapse. I am horrified. It is probably about that time that Al is tearing up too at Dana. Lena and I decide that he probably fears he may never see his grandchildren again ever. We both sob on the phone. A short time later Lena calls back to say they're making plans to come to Boston. All five will come up for a four-day visit! Friday morning to Monday night. Relief all around. What a daughter!

Meanwhile, in the hospital room while we fight the herpes virus, every day is a picnic. Because Al hates the hospital food, I continue to prepare and schlep meals. Sometimes during past hospitalizations there has been a refrigerator in the room. Not this time. I keep food in a pink rubber bowl filled with ice. A handy microwave at the nurse's station is shared by patients, caretakers, and staff. It's like living in a co-op. Very communal. Tonight: turkey burgers with purple onion, tomato, pickle, and mayonnaise; kettle-cooked chips; green beans with olive oil, almonds, and lemon; blueberry pie from Whole Foods, and chocolate whiskey cake from Clear Flour. Guy's gotta have his sweets.

We arrange two chairs to face the window and enjoy a calm dinner. We now have a date for the procedure that Al can deal with emotionally (although two factors to make that date certain are still missing); our beloved Florida family is coming up to visit; I now have two Boston dental appointments—even earlier than we originally thought; plus Kate had put together a list of resources for us and made some calls. It's obvious we cannot continue without more support.

Al and I take a long wonderful walk in 70-degree weather and talk about our needs going into the procedure and during the six-month-plus convalescence. We're only ten minutes from home and it's tempting to scoop him up and take him there, but he says that would be too disorienting. We plan to talk to our lawyer to tweak our wills slightly—mostly because of the new Florida apartment we're building above Lena and Larry's house, and to have a few meetings with a psychologist to help us face the unknown—and the worst scenario. Thinking of me living without him, after our wonderful visit with my sisters in Yellow Springs, Al asked me if I could see myself spending extended time there. It feels important to me to have options near family.

I stay at the hospital until about 10:30 p.m. when Al's IV treatment ends. Then he walks me to the car and gets in while I drive out of the underground parking lot.

"Gee, I'd forgotten what it's like to be in a car," he says about this minutes-long return to normalcy.

I call him from home to let him know I've arrived and to make sure he has made it back to the hospital, since he said something about taking a long walk. He answers his phone in a whisper.

"Where are you?" I ask.

"I'm not supposed to talk in here. I'm in the hospital chapel," he says quietly.

"Is anyone else in there?"

"Not now. Some guy came in and said—a prayer, I guess—but he left."

I picture him in a medieval grotto surrounded by stone walls, a large crucifix dominating the small, cold space. But, no. It's comfortable, modern, restful, soothing.

"Another guy just came in," he says. "He removed a small rug from a pile, placed it on the floor toward the front of the chapel, knelt low on his knees and leaned over until his head touched the floor. They must have built this place so that it faces Mecca. Now he's chanting."

"What's the chapel look like?"

"There are Bibles and Korans. There are three rows of chairs. The front row is for the believers; the second row is for the agnostics like me—that's where I'm sitting; the atheists are shoved into the back row. There are two chairs on either side in the way-back for the humanists. They don't get a whole row."

I ask him how he feels when he's in the chapel. This time he gives a serious answer.

"I tear up . . . well weeping is more accurate. I feel sorry for myself that I have to stay here. I hate feeling limited, shackled. That's not my style. I was

just thinking that I'm almost at the age when my father died." But then Al adds, "I also mentally thanked all the people who contributed to my birthday yesterday."

Ah, giving thanks, I think. It's always so uplifting. I find that verbally expressing gratitude, especially for something very specific, makes sense of the struggle. It helps diffuse fear.

DANA SUPPORT. Blum Resource Center right on the first floor. Here are some examples: patient support groups, post-Transplant groups, social workers, financial advice, one-on-one phone call support, and family support groups plus much reading material for all ages. Free child-related stuff. Everything from pipe cleaners for art projects to books on sick grandparents.

I attend the first of four monthly caretaker support groups where every one of the ten attendees is coping with a relative who has cancer. At this first meeting, led by the immensely capable and sensitive volunteer, Ruth Cope, one young woman has come from Japan to support her sister through breast cancer treatment. Another woman, about forty, is dealing with her mother's complicated illness and the challenge of communicating with her mother's doctors long distance in Florida.

One appealing, articulate guy from Maine is caring for a brother. They have living parents and other siblings, but he seems to have been assigned the caretaker role in the family. We learn that if your loved one dies while you're participating in this group, you may attend one more time after the death. Then you move on to a bereavement group. At the next meeting this caretaker says goodbye to all of us. He expects his brother to live only a few more days.

A very feminine woman in her fifties, all decked out in bright colors, makeup, and jewelry, is caring for a recalcitrant, difficult husband who is not doing well on his SECOND stem cell transplant. An attractive couple in their sixties is coping with their son's liver cancer. The son is married and has two young children. They feel his wife is in denial and is not coping well.

Ruth Cope has a PhD and a Social Work degree and she is an ideal discussion leader. She listens intently and occasionally makes a comment based on years of caretaker counseling after she lost both her husband and her son to cancer. She also has had cancer herself. Ruth follows up each meeting with an email summary, with words of personal encouragement and support directed to each participant.

First, because the group changes some each month, we introduce ourselves and explain our situation. Based on what we've heard from others, we follow up with questions and share suggestions. Every meeting is different, but she often asks us what we are taking away from the day's conversation. Feeling over-whelmed and exhausted seems to be a common denominator. Focusing on the present helps. Communicating and sharing feelings with your loved one is crucial, but often difficult. Ruth reminds us always to take care of ourselves too. Do one thing we enjoy each day, no matter how briefly. Grab a five-minute quiet time, alone. Invite a friend to go shopping. "Do not neglect yourselves," she urges. "Stay healthy."

It's obvious that, like me, these caretakers find it tremendously helpful to be able to share their challenges and seek advice in a confidential, supportive en-vironment. Compared with most of these folks, however, I feel fortunate. One mile from the clinic is a lot better than coming all the way from Japan, for one thing. These out-of-towners must find housing and learn to navigate—some-times in a language foreign to them. There's often conflict and confusion too in these patient/caregiver relationships, whereas Al's and my communication is pretty smooth. At least so far.

AL EMAILS JUDITH FROM THE HOSPITAL:

Spoke with Linda about home assistance. She'll ask the social worker to stop by at our next clinic appointment. She casually referred to "Elder Ser-vices." Are we elders now? When did that happen?

PAUL RASKIN, PRESIDENT OF TELLUS INSTITUTE, forwards an email, to Allen along with a request that Allen respond. This email is from someone who identifies himself as "a professional in the field of sustainability" and comes from Mauritius in the Indian Ocean. It is one example of the requests Al still receives and responds to every day. He may be cloistered in a hospital room, but he continues to "interact" with people throughout the world.

EMAIL FROM ALLEN TO DANA STAFF:

Pending agreement by Dr. F and necessary arrangements with the donor, we agreed on a Transplant admission date of July 13 or 14. This assumes we halt further Campath treatments to allow for four weeks between cessation of Campath and Transplant. Allen White

The next morning, Al continues to talk about the chapel. He says it feels isolated in a good way. Being there is calming and conducive to contempla-tion. His mind wanders to his father, Yale's, boyhood on Millbury Street in Worcester, MA. His mother, the same age as his father, grew up near there and he wonders if they attended the same school or even knew each other when they were young. They married in their late twenties after an introduction by one of his mother's brothers. Al had an image of his father's father, Wolf—a dictatorial figure—packing up a suitcase for his father and taking him to Paris.

Al's grandfather felt that his prodigiously talented musical son could advance on the clarinet only by studying at the Paris Conservatory of Music. So he enrolled him there at the tender age of fourteen and knowing no French. This was in 1926 when darkness was descending in Europe—a frightening time for Jews. Yet Yale stayed four years, lived with a French family, became fluent in French, and perfected his mastery of the clarinet. He returned to the U.S. in 1930 as the Great Depression descended on the country and ominous signs of conflict in Europe were emerging. After a stint with a few orchestras and as a teacher, he began work in his father's wholesale dry goods store, eventually inheriting it. He played clarinet for the rest of his life, but never as a full-time professional. Trained in classical, he taught himself jazz and swing à la Goodman and Gershwin.

Al drifts into those thoughts because his dad died at sixty-four of lung cancer, just like Al's grandfather, Wolf, did at age seventy-two. Al's parents did not tell us of the disease for two years because they did not want to stress their children. We, on the other hand, told the entire large extended families on both sides thirteen years ago as soon as we received Al's frightening diagnosis. Unlike us, Sarah and Yale did not depend on their children for emotional and practical support in dealing with the illness, but they had many siblings living in the same town. We have no sisters or brothers nearby. Al says that we both have great families. They are incredible people, but they are also far away. Our visits with them are joyful, he says, but so short. In the chapel, it occurs to Al that he has now outlived his dad by two months. He is sixty-four years, eleven months of age, turning sixty-five on July 2.

Tonight's hospital-room picnic lunch prepared by yours truly: turkey chili and peach almond cornbread. We went for a three-hour walk around the Fenway, slept in the grass, stopped for frozen yogurt, each talked to a sister on the phone, and brought Chinese take-out back to the room for dinner. Kate just called from Martha's Vineyard where she and her friend, Anna, and Anna's three-year-old, Noam, are staying for three nights in our cottage. They've been to the beach. So glad she has this time in our cottage with a dear friend.

SATURDAY, JUNE 18, 2011. 7:00 p.m. Time for Al's second daily three-hour IV treatment. I'll be here until about 10:30 again tonight when he'll walk me to the parking lot and we'll kiss goodbye in the car—for the seventh night in a row. There's no privacy in the hospital room, of course, because you never know when someone will pop in—a doctor, nurse, cleaner, or phlebotomist. The most frequent and irritating are what Al refers to as "the invasion of the vitals takers." Four to seven times a day, one arrives, sticks a thermometer in his mouth and wraps his arm for a blood pressure reading. Some also take blood. The Foscarnet he's getting can deplete magnesium and potassium levels. Even when those levels are nearly normal, they give him magnesium via IV and potassium orally. The potassium tastes terrible. I'll be chatting away, not realizing he's trying to swallow the yellow creamy stuff until I notice that he's bent over and gagging. The taste is that repulsive. Generally, though, his magnesium and potassium levels have remained strong, even when they increased the Foscarnet by fifty percent two days ago.

We try to steal a kiss in the elevator, but we're on the sixteenth floor. Every time we get close, the elevator door opens and we jump apart guiltily like a pair of teens. Someone in scrubs might get on pushing a wheelchair or heading for another floor and occasionally say emphatically "CODE!" to communicate that he/she is on the way to an emergency call. Sometimes whole families get on carrying flowers, balloons, babies. The place buzzes 24/7. Illness knows no clock. Once when I was leaving late, a large group arrived with pizzas as if they were going to a party.

I have been waking up at 5:30 or 6:30 a.m. all week and have been exhausted with the tension and fear. Last night—perhaps because he's almost home—I slept seven hours—until 8:15 a.m. What a difference! I'm more patient and cheerful and productive—at least for a while.

I arrive about 1:30 today, with a suitcase full of what it takes to meet Al's daily needs and wants: clean clothes, the Sunday New York Times, the mail, and today's homemade meal: pasta primavera. He lost twelve pounds with the previous hospitalization—the pneumonia a month ago—but has gained back three pounds this week.

Tomorrow marks one week with this hospitalization. Al is trying not to hope too much that he gets out tomorrow. Three doctors have to approve.

Oops, time out from writing to call a nurse. The IV in Al's arm is dripping onto the floor. Everything requires monitoring. They're changing the location of the IV now. AND the nurse just told us she read the order: GOING HOME TOMORROW—NOON AT THE EARLIEST, BUT STILL HOME! We are so looking forward to a respite from what he calls "medical incarceration." Lots to do before Transplant. Florida family arrives IN FIVE DAYS!

This morning my neighbor, Dr. Debbie Frank, asked if I would be working the PICC for Al when he returns home with it. I said, "Oh no, a nurse will come to the house to do all that." When I arrive at the hospital, I learn that I have an 11:30 a.m. training tomorrow to learn . . . oh, God . . . how to operate that PICC. Help! I'm no nurse! What if I make a mistake and mess up the whole dangling, earring-like apparatus that has a wire running up Al's arm, inside his chest, and ends near his heart? That generous heart I love so much? That heart I cozy up to often to be sure it's still beating more or less regularly? Too much! Too much responsibility!

I love speaking French, Spanish, and Dutch, but medical language has never interested me. Too bad. Nurse Judy is becoming immersed whether she likes it or not: "PICC, pump, purge, port, saline, syringe, swab." And then there are the drugs, including the star of the moment, "Foscarnet." I memorize this one more easily than most because it has a French word in it. "*Carnet*" means "notebook." I've got one of those with me at all times. The drugs, their dosages, their timing, their side-effects—Al takes charge of all that. One less duty for "Nurse Judy."

MONDAY, JUNE 20, 2011. Al is home and he's wasting no time: after some cuddling, he dresses in jacket and tie and drives to Harvard Business School for a conference followed by a Unilever-sponsored dinner at the Institute of Contemporary Art. Lots of people he knew.

Just the intense business/social event he needs on freedom day. Some people's comments: "Al, I haven't seen you for awhile. Where have you been? You look so good! Where did you get that tan?" These are folks who have no idea of his condition and would probably be shocked to know he had just left the hospital after an eight-day stay.

Other comments: "Allen, wanted to tell you, I just quoted you this week in the class I teach." Or "Allen, I was thinking of you this week when I reread that paper you wrote on . . ."

The event and the comments provide needed sustenance for my struggling sweetheart.

SO HOME, YES. Treatment continues, however, administered by a highly untrained incompetent individual—me. Dining room table has been turned into a hospital center. It's covered with everything from bags of liquefied drugs to packages of alcohol swabs, saline solution, ubiquitous bottles and packages of hand disinfectant. Self-administered Foscarnet treatment takes about six hours of our time daily. Each treatment takes two hours and the prep and cleanup another hour. That's if everything goes according to instructions. Al has two ports (access points into his body via a line) hanging from his arm, close to his wrist. I use one port to inject a saline solution that pre-cleans the line. Through the second, I inject the medication. The ports have been surgically implanted in order to avoid his having to visit the clinic and undergo twice-daily poking for IV lines. Yet the ports, too, cause discomfort and irritation. "*Like an intrusive and repugnant companion following you around day and night at very close range,*" Al says.

Al tries tying them up so they don't flap during the few non-treatment hours. Other methods such as putting temporary mesh sleeves over them work best. With white mesh from wrist to elbow, Al feels he resembles a white-gloved Michael Jackson.

There is constant pressure to keep everything germ free. Both of us wear plastic gloves. We are drowning in green disinfectant soap. Also in medical waste. Throwing out large bundles of it every day. The portable injection pump keeps malfunctioning. When it beeps, we have to stop the injection and figure out what's wrong. Sometimes we call an 800-number for advice, adding still more time to the whole procedure, as well as increasing tension and emotional turmoil. "Always pull back on the syringe to get rid of the bubble," they might say. "Then push until you see liquid. Then re-attach." When none of this works, we call once again.

Looking back, Al says:

As stressful as that experience was, at least I was at home in familiar surroundings. Eventually, I was able to perform the operation myself, freeing up Judith's time. I had more control over the situation. It was a huge emotional and time drain, but not as dehumanizing as staying in the hospital.

TUESDAY, JUNE 21, 2011. AL EMAILS KATE.

I hope your flight was uneventful and your nap deep and dreamy. So glad the weather cooperated. I love the thought of the four of you enjoying the cottage, towns, and beaches. Please phone in the next day or two for a "debrief." I jumped into two meetings and one reception in the last 24 hours. I'm feasting on professional contacts before my semi-quarantine. Don't worry—I won't overdo it. Your visit was pure joy for us—your Kharma nourishes everybody you touch. Thank Morna again for her caring call; I loved chatting with her. xxxooo Dad

BLESSINGS. Our generous, caring neighbor, Sibyl, who is getting me a resident parking sticker, is also looking into getting a handicapped sticker, and brought us a Clear Flour strawberry/peach tart.

Kate called from airport on way back to S.F. Has spoken with still more resources and supports for us. I'll follow up. I'm feeling a little insecure with her no longer in MA. Even when she was at the Vineyard, she still felt close.

I'm off to buy cutting boards—just one of those dozens of items we need. Binder Bible says we must have different ones for raw and not-raw foods, wash them in dishwasher every day, on and on. I find the perfect item at our neighborhood home goods store two blocks away: a package of three thin plastic cutting boards that are dishwasher safe. Al says we are blessed with what he calls, "Coolidge Corner shopping amenities." Before we moved here, someone referred to us as "Coolidge Corner Wannabe's." No wonder!

WEDNESDAY, JUNE 22, 2011. LEAVE FROM BOARD WORK. Reluctantly, I email Jody Kent Lavy, National Director of the Campaign for Fair Sentencing of Youth, who is also a dear friend: "I'm taking your advice and withdrawing from 'active service' to CFSY beginning now, but hopefully starting up again late August. I still plan to work with Beth on the joint September fund-raising house party. Of course, I would love to attend November events in D.C., but I'll have to see how it goes. You've got some terrific people on board now working hard and I'm completely confident that the fall event and everything else you've got going will be successful.

I will really miss working closely with all of you over the next 2-1/2 months. Please do not delete me from relevant emails (board, fundraising committee, host committee). I may not reply, but I want to follow progress."

REHEARSING. All my life I've rehearsed life's events. Sometimes a speech looking in the mirror. Sometimes dressing up and prancing around in a carefully chosen outfit. Rehearsals of emotional events provide me with the opportunity to work through all the possible feelings that the actual event is likely to induce. Mostly, I cry through my imaginings. My H.S. graduation, for example. My younger sister Molly's wedding rehearsal in Minneapolis too. We had just adopted Doug and I hated leaving him behind for a few days. Also because I had responsibility for all the piano accompaniment, I knew if I cried during rehearsal, I was less likely to break down during the ceremony itself. But the minister became so irritated with my weeping during the rehearsal that he turned to me and sharply asked me to stop.

I do not know how to predict how I might be if Al does not make it through. Rehearsing such an event by prancing in front of the mirror wouldn't cut it. Especially immediately afterwards. Would I collapse? Be totally dysfunctional? My children would arrive within days, but until then? Without wanting to dwell on that possibility, trying to concentrate instead on complete recovery, feeling guilty that I should even give that terrifying scenario any thought, I've nevertheless become anxious. I've known I needed to ask someone to be there for me. It had to be someone close by. Someone reliable and sensible. Someone who will give me permission to wake them at any hour. Someone I trust, but not necessarily— and in fact perhaps preferably—not someone Al and I are very close to emotionally. Then I thought of the perfect couple. I called my neighbors, Neil and Debbie.

Debbie is a pediatrician who has received numerous awards for her work as Director of Boston Medical Center's Grow Clinic. Neil is a retired rabbi who lost his father three weeks ago. We sat shiva with them and donated to Debbie's Center in Neil's father's name. They are a mature, solid couple only two doors down. As professionals, they've also dealt often with death issues. So that I could get through my meeting with them without breaking down, I first cried by myself at home while I rehearsed and imagined what I was going to say to them.

At the meeting they were warm, understanding, and reassuring. Neil offered his cell phone number and gave me his travel schedule. He will be gone from July 14 (procedure day) until July 19, but Al will be so delicate for many months and I will feel nervous during the entire recovery. Knowing where I can reach Neil is reassuring.

This was a rare instance when I discussed with Al neither my fears nor my plan before implementing it. I told Neil that, and Neil said I should tell him and that having a plan— hopefully one we never have to put in place—will give us both peace of mind. That was all I needed. The reassurance. That advice. I did tell Al right away. I tucked my plan into the back of my mind. I didn't worry anymore about what I might do immediately upon learning I had lost him. I concentrated on the present. I concentrated on healing. I concentrated on a long, shared life after Transplant. Thank you, Debbie and Neil.

THURSDAY, JUNE 23, 2011. Al's in D.C. for 24 hours—his last flight until he's recovered.

Referring to that trip, he says:

Traveling at this time was a difficult choice. The risks weighed heavily on me. I was feeling strong, but if I contracted any kind of infection it might have set back my Transplant preparations. I mulled the go/no-go options again and again. The event was critically important—the launch of the Global Initiative for Sustainability Ratings, a project I had nurtured from concept to early stage. Lena vehemently objected to travel. I had earlier discussed it with Kate and my chaplain now dear friend, Richard. Ultimately, the decision was "go." My calculus—dubious in retrospect—was that the despair and morale that would accompany cancellation outweighed the real but small risk of a medical setback. Thank God, all went smoothly.

FRIDAY, JUNE 24, 2011. For an inside look at his chest, abdomen, and pelvis, Al has a CAT scan in the DFCI Radiology Department.

I spend the day readying our condo for tomorrow's arrival of my five dear-ones: daughter, Lena; son-in-law, Larry; Nicole, 15; Zoey, 4-1/2; Bridgette, 8 months. Adrienne washed all the toys, the fridge, the floors. She's wonderful—recommended by Richard. They worked in a hospice together. I even steal some time for book agent searching. I've been away from it for weeks now after sending two queries a week every week between January and May.

Boiling beets to prepare a beet/feta salad. Al will get home about 9:30 p.m., I think. Need to fix something more substantial. He's always hungry.

Went to Dana today to pick up the dye he needs to drink before his CAT scan tomorrow. Tomorrow morning at 8:45 a.m. I have two teeth pulled and a bone graft. Florida family arrives at Logan about 9:30 a.m. They'll rent an SUV, and go grocery shopping. Eventually we'll all be together.

While at Dana, I stop by the Blum Resource Center. They give me a backpack with some stuff that either Zoey or Nicole might enjoy: art pad, markers, a squeeze ball, pipe cleaners. There are materials for children to help them understand cancer. I don't think Lena has discussed it with them, but they must know Al is ill. I already bought Zoey a ball, legos, a jump rope, and play dough, plus plugs for the outlets and guards for the corners of tables. Bridgette is crawling like crazy and pulling herself up. CANNOT WAIT to see them all.

MONDAY, JUNE 27, 2011. Today was the end of a wonderful visit. We visited the Children's Museum, lunched at Barking Crab, and purchased an exercise machine for Al (a gift from our daughters). On their fourth and last day of visiting, Al has to leave early for the six prep appointments, and I need to join him shortly.

Zoey is deeply attached to both of us and is dismayed that she won't see us all day and in fact not again at all before they fly back to Florida. She asks, "How come you guys go to the doctor so much?" I now hug each one goodbye, becoming more and more upset as I move through the five of them, ending with Lena who is already working her magic in the kitchen. This beautiful family—I don't know when I'll see them again. I don't know what's in store for me. I'm scared. I want them to stay.

I run out the front door sobbing, sit down in the driver's seat, and can't see. I can't find my glasses anywhere. I'll need them to fill out forms and take notes during the rest of this demanding day. I'm feeling rushed. After all those dramatic goodbye's, I have to go back upstairs and look for my specs. "They're on your back, Grandma," Nicole says. I wear my glasses on a chain and had thrown the chain behind my neck so the glasses wouldn't get crushed while I clung to my loved ones. I reach behind me, retrieve them, and race back to the car. Okay, I have my glasses now, but I still can't see because of the tears.

Al has six separate appointments today at the clinic—all in preparation for

Transplant. He biked over first thing in the morning. About a twenty-minute ride. He's a rarity—a cancer patient who bikes to the clinic for treatments. Someone dubbed him "the chemo biker." But the biking that brings him such joy is frightening for me. I fear he's been weakened by the pneumonia.

Also, even in the most normal of times, Boston's medical area, arguably the most prominent in the world, is a complete zoo. Every visit requires negotiation of: one heavily trafficked street that connects major parts of the city; narrow streets half blocked with large construction equipment; car doors opening; hordes of personnel bursting out of the trains and rushing across the streets; tons of dashing jaywalkers; taxis discharging wheel-chaired passengers; and, worst of all, very distracted patients and families everywhere. But he needed the bike ride to lift his spirits, to prepare him for the poking, prodding, testing, information-absorbing tasks of the day's appointments.

9:15 A.M. FIRST CLINIC VISIT: Pulmonary Function Test (45-60 min).

11:00 A.M. SECOND VISIT: with Social Worker, Max. He introduces himself by explaining that he is part of the Transplant team and is there to help us and our children with the emotional impact of the procedure. He is wonderful, guiding us to talk about our concerns, our state of mind.

Max asks about Allen's work.

"Business ethics," Al says. "I travel globally and plan to continue working part time."

Max asks about the financial impact of moving to part-time. Do we need to talk about financial support? We say "No, we are okay."

He asks about our family.

"All our kids are in their thirties," we say. "All employed. We're very close to all three of them, in frequent contact."

"What concerns you the most?" he asks us.

I break down when I say, "Isolation. Al loves people. He thrives on interaction. I'm afraid he'll feel cut off and become dispirited."

Max then asks, "Al, have you gone over the statistics with Dr. A?" Max repeats what we already know, but if there's ever a best time to face the statistics, it's now with this emotionally supportive social worker. "There's a fifty percent success rate. Thirty-five percent gain a few more years. Fifteen percent are not successful at all."

Though he doesn't elaborate, I assume that means fifteen percent die during or soon after Transplant.

Dr. A had told us twenty percent are not successful. Or is it fifteen-twenty percent who die during or right after Transplant? I'm not sure I want a clarification. I'll just cling to that fifty percent success rate.

Al said he feels confident due to his age (sixty-five is on the young side for transplant), his generally excellent physical condition, the preparation, the outstanding medical team, and the support of friends and family. Then he breaks down.

"My work is not finished. I have a lot more to do. I may be vulnerable to unrealistically high expectations. Perhaps I should plan for the worst, but hope for the best."

Working for the best outcome is so time consuming, however. I can't say we're doing any planning for the worst.

Max asks, "How did you handle past challenges?"

Al answers:

We've had a gilded life. We've had a steady ship. A superb partnership. The Dutch, who live in an essentially flat nation, say their mountain is a speed bump. That could be a metaphor for our lives. CLL is like a speed bump in an otherwise smooth landscape. Our relationship, our kids all high functioning. We are blessed. We also have strong ties with siblings, nieces, nephews, cousins. Family strength will help.

Al adds:

I wrestle with the burden I am creating. My kids have experienced my four hospitalizations since August 2010. I hate seeing my kids anxious. We travel to the children usually, but the children will have to travel to us now for awhile. This is difficult for them because of where they are in their careers and family obligations. We do have a number of local friends and more people are coming forward. We've been reluctant to depend on anyone.

Max tells us that the most challenging aspect of the post-Transplant period is Graph vs. Host Disease, (GVHD). "The recovery is lengthy. Sometimes couch potatoes do better than active folks like you. As long as they have the remote to click on they're fine. For you, the prolonged recovery may be more challenging, present more adjustments. How will you pass the time?"

Al: *I cannot relate to the concept of "boredom." I'll read. I'll continue to work on projects with my colleagues by phone and email. I might brush up on my French. But isolation is worrisome.*

Max: "You're my boss. Tell me what you need whenever you need it. Yes, your children may certainly email or call me. I'm away on vacation July 9-25, but available until July 8th. Should you have an issue to discuss during my time away, you can page me and another Transplant social worker who will cover for me."

Max ends the session by repeating that he is there to help us, our children, and our grandchildren with the emotional impact of the Transplant—whatever the outcome. We leave that meeting feeling more confident and relaxed, relieved that throughout the process there will be a competent counselor to help us talk through our fears and our kids' emotions. With his encouragement, I give Max's contact information to our children.

Two days later I page Max about some issue and receive no response. I also email and telephone. Two more days go by and I do not hear from him. It is not his vacation time yet, so where is he? I call his department. There is obvious confusion about what to tell me.

"Max no longer works at Dana Farber," they finally say.

"Will we be assigned to a new social worker then?" I ask. More confusion with no definitive answer. I feel a bit adrift.

Kate, back in San Francisco, gets on the phone immediately and tries to straighten out the situation. She locates another social worker with whom we subsequently speak on the phone and occasionally see in the halls or the waiting room. That social worker seems caring too, but somewhat flustered and overworked. We never quite get the level of individual support Max had promised.

Many months later we hear from a friend that Max's wife had cancer and passed away and that he left to work in an organization that sets up housing for families of ill patients in nearby hospitals. That certainly sounds like something he would do, but we have not been able to confirm it. If true, it justifies his sudden departure and erases the unlikely and puzzling scenario that he was suddenly asked to leave Dana.

Meanwhile, on with the six appointments:

12:00. This was supposed to be a lunch break, but there is no time for it. Instead we see Dr. I in infectious disease. There has been some reawakening of red spots on Al's skin. No fever. No fatigue. The virus is resisting the drug. This is ominous and may delay Transplant. He must be as healthy as possible in order for the procedure to be successful. Trying another drug, which they had hoped to avoid because it's hard on the kidneys. *Oy Vey!*

No cafeteria break, but volunteers come around with a sandwich cart. Tuna sandwich on whole wheat isn't too bad. Apples, oranges, and drinks are always available.

1:00. Ninety-minute consultation/teach-in with program RN, Toni, going over more expectations and cautions. "If after Transplant, you have any fever or any other symptoms you don't understand, you call Dr. A at any time of the day or night." I thought, 'He lives a block away, we could just throw stones at his window to wake him up.' July 14 Transplant date not yet confirmed with donor. July 12 is Al's "last-gasp" business meeting—with CERES.

Toni continues to explain. I take notes. If Thursday, July 14th works out, he will be admitted. No one but me and medical personnel will be able to visit for several days. On July 15 they begin to suppress his immune system with chemo, cleaning out and preparing the marrow for maximum receptivity to the donor cells. She names all the drugs. After six days in the hospital, he will be administered the stranger's cells that we hope will save his life. The procedure itself is like any one of the many transfusions he's had over the past thirteen years. Toni repeats what we've heard before about the process–"It's actually somewhat anti-climactic." When the time comes, however, we find it to be anything but. Al will leave the hospital one or two days after Transplant. If all goes to plan, we should see new cell growth, generated by the donor's stem cells, within eleven-twelve days.

HONORING OUR ANONYMOUS DONOR. We give the donor the Hebrew name for Abraham—Abram. "*I just want to give Abram a big hug,*" Al says.

A MONTH AFTER TRANSPLANT, a "chimerian" test will reveal early signs of how successful the Transplant will be. It will indicate the fraction of cell generation attributable to the donor's stem cells versus those attributable to Al's remaining stem cells. It will be a moment in time for "Abram's" cells. Will they muscle out and ultimately overwhelm Al's dysfunctional stem cells? Or will they be slow—or worse, be totally overwhelmed by their assigned duty? At that juncture, eighty-ninety percent of cell production attributable to the donor will be reason for relief; no, for EUPHORIA and JOY! That would mean that the Transplant is among the fifty percent that are successful. The process is Darwinian—new hearty stem cells decimate the dysfunctional ones. It's a story of survival and triumph of the fittest.

POST-TRANSPLANT LIMITATIONS. After one hundred days, we can return to restaurant food—but not IN the restaurant. Absolutely never earlier, and only if all key markers are positive. Al can eventually go to his Tellus office once the risk of serious infection is past. He does not need to wear a mask inside his office, but must once he steps into the hallway. GVHD can be threatening. When the new cells encounter alien tissue, muscle, and other body material, biological combat may ensue, resulting in multiple medical complications. We must report immediately any of the following: skin rash, diarrhea, liver chang-es, temperature. GVHD can show up even years later.

What is under OUR control?

1. Take medicine as instructed.
2. Attend appointments.
3. For urgent matters—page surgeon.
4. For non-urgent—email.
5. Eat no restaurant food for the first three months. Eat only cooked foods.
6. Eat no bakery goods for three months.
7. Even after three months, eat no deli foods. Continue with well-cooked foods.
8. May eat anything frozen, jarred, canned.
9. Small, frequent meals best.
10. May exercise gently at home.
11. Cold weather in itself is not harmful.
12. Close contact with people is always risky.

Many times during the grueling three months post-Transplant, we will repeat to ourselves Toni's metaphor: "The Transplant experience is a marathon, not a sprint."

The day's appointments continue.

3:00. WITH DR. A. About Al's height, Dr. A's broad shoulders are further enlarged by the padding in his beige sports coat, his long neck and narrow face emphasized by a striped tie. Blue, remote, business-like eyes. Toni's words of a few moments ago pop into my head. "It's close contact with people that can be harmful." A few times, Dr. A even puts his head back and sniffs heartily, then looks at us and sort of shrugs his shoulders. I hope it's just allergies. Dr. F joins us.

Both docs are concerned about herpes virus. Need to keep it in remission up to and after Transplant. Steroids, a routine part of Al's medications, can make it more difficult to fight herpes. Herpes reflects and contributes to Al's weakened immune system. It's a sign that despicable CLL continues to assert its murderous self. Without the Transplant, CLL would continue to find new ways to do its hateful mischief. May lower steroids from twenty mg to five mg. Sweats continue in their erratic, idiosyncratic, and sleep-robbing fashion.

May have to return to hospital and resume Foscarnet, the anti-herpes drug we struggled to administer at home. Al is so exasperated at the thought of returning to the hospital, that he throws his keys down on the floor where they splay with a clang. Not in front of docs. Only I witness what I would call a very minor temper tantrum. That's about as much venting as the guy does. He is just so unbelievably steady in the face of so much pressure and uncertainty.

I, of course, am not as sanguine. I still miss Dr. F. who is so soothing and warm and personable and KNOWN. I have to say, though, that Dr. A. strengthens our confidence with his brilliant command of medicine. Someday I'll thank him for directing the team that saves Al's life.

4:00. SIXTH AND FINAL APPOINTMENT OF THE DAY. Lab draw with Melissa. Infusion room. Now testing for infectious diseases, etc. Six vials of blood. FACT: Dana Farber does five hundred stem cell transplants/year. So many . . . but not all successful.

AL SAYS:

> Throughout my thirteen years of disease, only twice have I felt truly debilitated: when I entered the Emergency Room at the San Francisco hospital and just before the last hospitalization for pneumonia when I was continually fearful of coughing during a work situation. Amazingly, even in the most fragile times pre-Transplant, when I'm at the podium, the cough disappears, suppressed by adrenaline, only to return afterwards, as if temporarily denied the opportunity to wreak havoc and now seeking revenge.

We arrive home after this long day of six preparatory appointments. Our darlings have returned to Florida. Under the expert direction of our wonder-woman daughter, Lena, they leave behind:

- A greeting on the front door of our condo unit: an 8-x-10 photo of our three grandgirls sitting on the outside steps holding signs they had made with the optimistic message "SEE YOU SOON."
- Scrubbed condo with toys all put away, sheets and towels neatly washed and folded.
- Long, loving note.
- A memory album filled with fifty photos taken during the four-day visit. That meant that with all that Lena and Larry were doing today, they went to Walgreens and had the photos printed, bought a photo album, and arranged the photos in it.
- A framed 8-x-10 photo of me and my beautiful fifteen-year-old granddaughter—a joy, and one of my favorite photos ever.
- Delicious varied desserts from Finale Restaurant. And in the shiny, scrubbed kitchen, two of Lena's many outstanding nutritious homemade dishes: a green bean casserole and large golden-topped potato/ mushroom au gratin lasagna.

Alas, they also leave behind an unwelcome stillness and silence.

Tuesday, June 28, 2011. You're nobody without a Hickman. Al always likes to take control of every situation—calmly, charmingly with humor. If I enter a restaurant ahead of him, I don't follow the maitre d'. There's no point. Al will look over the room and ask to be seated where perhaps the view is better, we are far from the restrooms, the chairs are more comfortable, we're not next to potentially raucous customers, we're tucked away where we can hear each other. The criteria go on and on. The perfect equation he insists upon is beyond my comprehension. I just stand and wait until he has assessed and decided. He may even move a table and chairs to suit him.

But now, he feels acted upon, feels a loss of power, dictated to. It's back to the hospital again. Unlike the first time when he was shocked at the immediacy of the move without any notice or time to go home and gather what he needed, we're now more used to the routine: "Get into that wheelchair, buddy." Through the maze of catwalks above Boston streets, they push him to Brigham and Women's. I follow behind.

After a long check-in, they push Al across the street to the Shapiro Cardiovascular Center where Al is sedated for a procedure to insert a Hickman Catheter in a vein near his heart. With two ports, the catheter will be used for "fluids in, fluids out" for at least three months. I wait for hours; reading, snacking, dozing, and responding to emails. Finally, I join him downstairs in the bowels of the Center in a scene that reminds me of one of those horror movies where bodies are lined up in permanent comas. But my cheerful husband, now awake says, *"This is a factory. You're nobody without a Hickman."*

I check a list of eighteen items that require attention before Transplant—holding steady for a July 14 check-in date. Al has his own list. We both add items to the list every day. So far, on my list all I can cross off is #4: "Buy large quantity of paper towels."

For now it's back to another hospital room. Al feels fine and refuses to be confined. As with his previous hospitalizations, he informs the nursing staff that he's going for a walk and we take off. They may think it's for a walk around the vast hospital. We have already explored all its public areas, including the "Pike" that includes an excellent visual history of the hospital's major founders, researchers, and physicians who built Brigham and Women's into the world-class institution that it is today.

However, Al insists on heading outside.

I've always believed Al has parking Karma. Downtown Boston, he may go around the block a few times but, before long, he's easing into a spot. Who else but Al then could take a break from his hospitalization, enjoy a long walk, and end up at a picnic on the expansive lawn, the green, flowered quadrangle which spreads out in front of the stately and pompous gray-and-white granite building which serves as the Harvard Medical School? Listening to a recording of Billy Joel singing "The Piano Man"? Someone offers us a hot-fudge sundae? That's a triple play: one of Al's favorite singers, favorite songs and, since childhood, favorite treats. Al protests the offer, which was part of a celebration for post-doctoral students and their families. *"I'm not a Harvard professor or a student. I'm not even a custodian,"* he says. But they insist. So hot-fudge sundae it is . . . with a choice of three flavors of ice cream. Al chooses chocolate.

While we enjoy our treats, a child lets go of a single, red balloon. We watch with envy as it gleefully sways, dances, and rapidly escapes up, up—sucked into the clouds. Freedom—the opposite of what CLL has brought to our lives. My geographer husband says, *"Goodbye, Boston. Hello Portugal."*

6:20 P.M. BACK AT BWH. No more sixteenth floor room with its view of nearly all of Boston like the last time. Room 4C this time. At Brigham and Women's, the rooms are arranged in a circle around a central counter with a walkway in between the rooms and the counter. "Pods" they call them.

Each pod seems to have its own culture and look. The sixteenth floor was casual, but also messy with the corridors leading from the elevator to the pod treated like attic space full of large hospital equipment apparently stored there: wheel chairs, bulky beds, poles with wires dangling. Inside that pod, I could come and go as I pleased, use the community fridge, the microwave, etc. Down here on the fourth floor, things are neater, but also stricter. Hand-washing reminders are everywhere. The microwave is directly outside the room, a mere five steps, but a nurse reprimands me—as she should—for not using the ubiquitous disinfectant soap before returning to the room. Kind of tough to do that, though, carrying two dinner plates.

WEDNESDAY, JUNE 29, 2011. 2:00 p.m. Although it's important that I remain strong and healthy during this time, it's been impossible to adhere to my normal exercise routine: water exercise three-four times per week; Qigong once a week; walking nearly every day. This morning I took my aqua aerobics class for the first time in seven days. I need it emotionally as well as physically. My classmates know I'm struggling and are supportive. At least once when answering their concerned queries about Al's health, I've broken down in someone's arms right in the locker room, emotionally depleted, despairing of a long journey whose end is indeterminate. I've known Sean, the instructor, for about fifteen years. He not only takes us through a rigorous and varied routine, he also stays informed about our challenges. He's comforting. The class lifts my spirits and gives me hope. It's just been difficult to get there when I need it most.

Every day a steady stream of stuff leaves our condo and ends up in the hospital room. After the aqua class, I pack meals and snacks and all the other things Al needs—creams, clean clothes, cell charger. As he continues to work every day, I hunt in his study for specific file folders and other documents. Next I shop for items on the initial eighteen-item list, things he'll need during convalescence: camping chairs we can take to the park when friends visit, gum and spritzers for dry mouth. I also buy a card for Zoey's birthday. She'll be five in a month.

When I arrive at the hospital Al is chatting with a chaplain intern, Sarah. She says, "I've just learned about your experience in the Peace Corps. I had a project in El Salvador." Then she adds, "I understand you've established a close relationship with one of the chaplains here." Later Al says that Sarah doesn't know Richard personally, so how does she know about that close relationship and the Peace Corps? Do the chaplains enter info into Al's file for all to read as they wish? He has shared a lot of info with Richard that he would not share with others.

AL'S LATEST METAPHOR FOR DONOR STEM CELLS:

"They are a SWAT team that rushes into the marrow and overwhelms the enemy—the defective cells. They are Navy Seals."

I also like another one of Nurse Toni's metaphors: "They are microscopic jack hammers. They burrow in, destroy the old foundation, and make way for the imminent arrival of new, flowing, rapidly moving, robust, healthy stem cells that fill up the patient's marrow." This is getting close to the visualizations that I suggested and Al refused shortly after diagnosis. I like these metaphors. Somewhere our donor, whoever, wherever he may be, is quietly going about his business, not aware that he's walking around with our future flowing through his veins. Thank you, Donor.

What happens to old stem cells? They are muscled out as the healthy cells move into the marrow and decimate the old punks that exit the body as waste. Move over, you bastards, we're taking over. You are history. In fact, you are dead and will never be seen or heard from again.

Stem cells are Hermaphrodites. By that I mean, and please excuse the sexism...they have male tendencies toward belligerence and domination mixed with the female capacity for life-producing, life-enhancing behaviors.

Still thinking today about that red balloon. Freed, swaying, dancing all alone, but with such abandon; the way one performs in the kitchen when great music comes on the radio and no one is watching. "I abandon myself to the unknown." It reminds me of when I was taking a yoga class at the Florida YMCA several years ago. At the time, Lena and Larry had invited us to build an apartment above their home there. This, of course, would represent much effort and expense. It also raised many difficult questions. Would we eventually leave our Brookline home? Would they care for us in our final years? Could we get along in the meantime?

But there was the dream of spending more time with them and, of course, having the opportunity to interact more often and in more depth with our granddaughters. We were also drawn to San Francisco where our daughter, Kate, lives, and where we feel more political and lifestyle kinship. But our only grandchildren live in Florida. They are beautiful, bright and charming. Yes, this is a proud grandma writing, but they are! I had become quite envious of friends who lived in the same town as their offspring and saw them often. I missed mine.

With all this churning in my mind during the yoga class, I tried to relax into the various yoga postures. I looked out the floor-to-ceiling windows and absorbed the variety of green foliage: every hue from deep-green, sturdy rubber tree leaves to pale-green, delicate, winding, almost translucent moss. Amid all that green, I saw a deep-red speck. I thought it might be a flower and studied it as I continued stretching. It sat on a branch for a while, solitary. When I was able to identify it as a cardinal, it seemed to beckon. By the time it flew away, I had made up my mind to construct that apartment. It was late 2009. Later my brother-in-law, Keith, told me that birds are harbingers. They deliver messages. They guide and lead us.

By fall 2010 the apartment was finished. A third grandbaby was born September 29th soon after. It's a beautiful apartment with windows on four sides where a tree outside the bedroom cradles us in its branches. The sun reaches out to us, and we can see 360-degree sunsets. It's also a perfect place for the kids to come and play, read, bake, have tea parties. Al sits on the floor with the kids and invents game after amusing game. They adore their Zayde.

During the intense time when we were ordering furniture for the apartment, I visited the local Brookline farmer's market. An artist displayed her wares. One of her themes: beautifully rendered cardinals. I bought a hot plate and a magnet with the cardinal image. I had never seen that artist before and I've never seen her since, but now her cardinals greet me whenever I enter my Florida kitchen. I also sport a St. Louis Cardinals baseball cap that Al gave me—to round out the red bird motif.

For now, though, the Florida apartment sits unoccupied, while we imagine a time when we can return to daily visits with our beloved family in the house beneath it.

Today I make a list of about 75 family and friends and gather their emails to invite them to follow our blog on *Caring Bridge,* the site designed for patients and their families to share information with loved ones. For the next eighteen months, the responses to our postings will be a source of support, sharing, and joy we had not anticipated. *Caring Bridge* will serve as both a social network and a source of therapy for Al and me, a link to our community during uncertain times. In retrospect, it is not an exaggeration to say that the extraordinarily rich interactions via *Caring Bridge* enhanced the prospects of a successful Transplant process.

WEDNESDAY, JUNE 29, 2011. Lena sends a photo of baby Bridgette today looking extremely proud of herself. She pulled her little body up to a standing position for the first time. She turned nine months yesterday.

THURSDAY, JUNE 30, 2011. Another delay. We're slaves not only to the donor's stem cells, but to his schedule as well. He is not available to donate on July 14. New date of July 20. And another disappointment. Al's not coming home today after all. And I had the best night's sleep I've had in ages, believing we'd be sleeping in the same bed again.

Another quick training for me on administering Foscarnet through the irritating Hickman port. I hate and fear this responsibility for which I have no aptitude.

I tote Chinese food into the hospital room for our dinner. Al's fortune: "Stay in touch. Above all with how you feel." Al says he is in touch with how he feels. *That's the PROBLEM,"* he says. *"Not the SOLUTION."*

JULY 2011

With the Transplant moment drawing closer—though exact date still in flux—the month begins with long lists—twenty items each for Al and me. I divide mine with my house-cleaning crew and add an extra day or two to their usual schedule with duties beyond the normal routine:

Crew duties:

- Wash plant leaves;
- Wash all blinds;
- Clean laundry room;

- Lysol all remotes, phones, computers, and glass frames of all photos and art;
- Wash blankets;
- Clean out and vacuum closets.

For me, that leaves this partial list:

Purchases:

- Several large packages of paper towels;
- Sugar-free gum (for anticipated dry mouth);
- Spritzers (for same condition);
- Medic-alert bracelet;
- Lawn chairs for meeting visitors in the park;
- Greeting cards for upcoming family birthdays.

plus

- Hire rug shampoo service.
- Copy and post dietary guidelines.
- Mark all old creams (hand, face, toothpaste) etc. (Al can use only freshly purchased.)
- Copy daily temperature and weight chart.
- Continue to gather 75-100 emails for *Caring Bridge* posting.

I also need to have all upholstery cleaned. Nineteen separate pieces of couches and chairs. The result of calling several different cleaning services: about $1,200. I opt to rent a machine for $250 and do it myself. For two days I drag around the house a heavy, loud machine with two hoses attached. A hand-held apparatus simultaneously applies the soap and sucks it back up. I squeeze the awkward weighty handle and move that thing back and forth, up and down, trying to reach every crevice and every inch of cushion and pillow, back, front, sides. Yes, I feel sorry for myself and for my aching arm. But I'll think positively. Maybe I'm building up some muscle.

STILL MORE ON THAT BINDER. Where did all these instructions come from? From the aforementioned 1-3/4 inches thick BINDER—our revered guide to physical and psychic survival for the next year and a half.

The chaos of Al's out-of-control, invisible lymphocytic cells contrast with the Binder's cover photos—smiling faces of patients and staff—and with the clean, white, smooth Binder itself, carefully and clinically organized into sections: Introduction to the Program; Overview; Your Care Team, Planning and Preparation; Stem Cell Transplant and Collection Methods; Preparing For Transplant; During Transplant—Your Hospital Stay; After Transplant—Going Home; Resources and Support; Contact Information and Patient Care Tools;

Glossary; Your Care Calendar; and Note Pages.[2]

Each divider is covered with colored photos of competent-looking people in white coats talking with patients and families. Gee, everyone looks so content!

I find this particular graphic rather startling: In Section 3 - Page 1, its entitled "Your DF/BWCC Care Team." Encircling a fat center balloon that says "You and Your Family" are two concentric ovals with still smaller circles that identify the titles of those who will participate in the effort to keep Al alive.

From primary care doctor to physical therapist to dietitian to pharmacist, the team includes seventeen people. Fourteen months later when I look at these circles, I see that we have indeed met nearly all of them with two exceptions: we never consulted a psychiatrist together, nor a financial counselor. How grateful we are for every one of these skilled, caring experts! I read THE ENTIRE BINDER twice. I underline. I highlight. I take notes. I copy pages. It's like being at Oberlin College again. I'd prefer to be writing papers on French literature and art history, though.

Among the many graphics, one really grabs me. How often does one ponder what one's stem cells actually look like? Our oxygen-bearing red blood cells, infection-fighting white blood cells, and to-the-rescue clotting platelets—all three of which the "mother" stem cells produce? Working away silently every second? No wonder Al has been challenged with increasing frequency and intensity by episodes of low oxygen and susceptibility to bacterial and viral illnesses. We've never known which or how suddenly or how severely or in what combination the cells will stop performing. It's amazing he's come this far, now more than a decade since diagnosis. I read that red blood cells live for only 120 days and platelets live for only five to nine days. The body's cell factory must remain in high gear from conception until . . . .

With his system failing to generate healthy cells, transfusions have been crucial in keeping him alive. I remember clearly the first time he had one. Blood transfusion. I associated those words with near death, with traffic accidents, but also with the fear of HIV and Hepatitis C transfer. By now he's had dozens—all successful, for a time.

I feel as if I want to bow down and worship graphic depictions of the workings of cell formation and lifecycle, so different one from another in size, texture, shape, and . . . such vibrancy, determination, and skill. They have per-

---

[2] Dana-Farber/Brigham and Women's Cancer Center, *Stem Cell Transplantation,* Fall 2008.

sonality. I'm curious about their color. I Google "stem cell images" and find a page with hundreds of colored drawings and photos. They're magnificent. Some look like bottom-of-the sea creatures, some like they come from outer space. Why does it take a fight for survival like we are experiencing to remind us that life everywhere is so much more interconnected than we realize?

The Binder's Overview chapter ends with this gem: "The stem cell Transplant process can be challenging both physically and mentally for you. The treatment effects of hair loss, skin rash, swelling, weight loss or weight gain, decrease in sexual desire, and other changes to your body can impact how you feel about yourself, as well as your relationship with others. You may feel self-conscious or unattractive as you recover and regain your health. It's important that you communicate how you feel about body image and your sexual feelings with your spouse or partner. Members of your care team can help answer your questions or provide counseling for you and your partner."[3]

Fourteen months after reading these words, I can say to some extent Al did experience all of these effects—with the exception of the final one. Sexual intimacy remained as important a part of our lives as ever.

FRIDAY, JULY 1, 2011. IT MEETS IV. I take photos of Al setting up to give a webinar from the hospital room. In prior weeks, he cancelled or declined all forms of professional engagement—speaking, conference calls, meetings. One remains on his calendar—a webinar for MBA students. He struggles with the decision to cancel this one last link to professional normalcy. In a moment of defiance, he decides to proceed, CLL and hospital setting be damned.

Fifteen paying participants can hear, but not see him and have no idea where he is. The Presidio School of Management in San Francisco hired him months ago. His topic: "Corporate Purpose, Value and Transparency."

When the moderator volunteers to set up a video, Al responds, "I'll pass. The surroundings are less than aesthetic."

It's audio only. We hope the participants, responding to Al's authoritative, knowledgeable voice, imagine him in a large, plush, wood-paneled office. They never see the dangling IV equipment or the heartbeat monitor or the stethoscope.

Privacy does not exist in the hospital, of course. You never know who will come wandering in or at what hour or what they'll say or do. Al's second biggest fear is that a custodian will come in during his presentation and begin clanging trash barrels. His number one fear is that an urgent hospital-wide

---

[3] Ibid.

announcement will suddenly boom from the speakers above his head: "CODE BLUE. All heart personnel report immediately to Floor Seven, Room 721."

Al asks the nurse to put a note on the outside of the door saying, "2:00-4:00 today. Do not disturb." He jokes that the nurses might see that sign and assume he and I had requested some time for intimacy. But he has no control over blaring hospital broadcasts.

Al makes sure I am present so I can quietly shoo away anyone who dares breach the order on the homemade sign. In other words, I have still another duty. I am the all-important bouncer. He settles in with computer and earphones and dials into the meeting. He is sitting upright in a large comfortable, adjustable chair with a high back. It's the only chair in the room. That leaves me with only a bed. I lie down with some reading materials. Al is counting on me to keep my eyes peeled on the door, ready to spring up and hush any intruder. I am alert—or so I think.

AL CONTINUES THE STORY:

3:00 p.m. The moderator, unaware of my physical setting, welcomes me and the students scattered around the U.S. and beyond. Power Points appear on the screen. The session begins.

3:20 p.m. So far, so good. I'm settling into a zone of comfort, even complacency. Participants engage through the chat room. All systems go. I glance to my left to confirm that my gatekeeper is fully operational. There lies my sweet spouse in the bed, the victim of months of exhausting caregiving, fast asleep. I pause mid-PowerPoint for seconds that seem like minutes.

Dainty little snorts escape her lips. Might the sound be picked up by the computer's microphone and be sent over the airwaves? Do I nudge my sleeping beauty or soldier onward, hoping that the feeble sign taped to the door will be sufficient defense against interruptions? With no alert gatekeeper, what will I say to my audience if a stubborn phlebotomist enters the room, insists on an immediate blood draw and refuses to negotiate an alternative time?

My heart trumps my head. I simply cannot interrupt the blissfully resting soul to my left. I gather my wits, clear my throat, and return to the slide presentation, unnerved but determined to complete the webinar against mounting odds of possible embarrassment.

As the minutes pass, my confidence and comfort gradually return. Questions from participants stream in. The moderator deftly intervenes to keep the virtual conversation moving.

I glance at the clock.

4:25 p.m. Time to wrap up with a few closing words, delivered with a mix of verve and relief. Thank you's from participants and the moderator for a job well done. Judith stirs, listening to my parting words. I sign off and slump in my chair as a huge smile sweeps over my face.

The joy, satisfaction, and comedy of the moment overwhelm my exhaustion. Amidst months of anxiety, an hour and a half of professional normalcy—a therapy as powerful as any medicine I have received during the long months of preparation. And there beside me, looking rested and revived, is the love of my life sharing a moment that remains etched in our memories more than a year after Transplant and, undoubtedly, for as long as we live.

SATURDAY, JULY 2, 2011. Al turns sixty-five today. We try to think of something that would make this occasion special. Gee, do they even allow birthday candles in the hospital room? Seems kind of dangerous around all this oxygen and who knows what else? He thinks he might want to skip out and spend a couple of hours at home. So that's what we do. Lunch in a restaurant followed by an hour in our very own bed. When he arrives in the condo, he looks around as if he hasn't seen it before, as if he hasn't lived there for fifteen years. When it's time to return to the hospital, he says the experience was disorienting. Hard to tell if it was the right thing to do.

COUSIN HANS EMAILS AL FROM PARIS: "Happy Birthday! On this birthday of yours, I thought it would be a good time to let you know that you have been a dominant topic of conversation recently at an assortment of meetings and conferences I attended lately. In fact, for a couple of weeks you seemed to be inescapable! In Madrid while working on a sustainable tourism case, the folks at Fundación Banesto told me that they wished they had something like GRI for the sustainable tourism industry. A few days later I was at the Ashden Sustainable Energy Awards in London where GRI was again mentioned as one of the models upon which their criteria was based. The very next day, I was at the European Venture Philanthropy Association in Brussels where GRI came up again, as did your work on Corporation 20/20 as an initiative driving change at the upper reaches of business. To round off the week, I spoke at Sheffield University where GRI was again used in the class of one of the professors and they seem to have sent some students down to work as interns. Finally, I lead a workshop on impact assessment at the Ashoka Changemakers Event last week where 1,200 hot social entrepreneurs from around the world came together, and . . . I was grilled on GRI. (Thank god I knew the answers!)

I know you are going in for a big treatment soon which promises a major improvement, and my thoughts are with you. Carrie had a wonderful time with you and Judith the week before last and brought back lots of amazing tales of your remarkable children . . . and the two of you. Take care dear cousin and very happy birthday!"

AL EMAILS COUSIN HANS:

What an uplifting message at just the right time! Watching GRI flourish is immensely gratifying. And hearing it referenced as a model of 21st C. global governance (my interpretation of the multiple references you report) adds yet another layer of satisfaction.

I can only claim a small piece of the credit. Besides my co-founder Bob Massie (now running for U.S. Senate), my successor, Ernst Ligteringen has brought the organization to levels of influence and impact I never anticipated. Years after I stepped down as head of it, it follows me around like a loyal puppy. Just yesterday, I led a GRI webinar for students at the Presidio School of Management while sitting in a hospital room, which I never disclosed, of course!

Thanks so much for sharing your adventures, and kudos to you for your engagement in so many interesting forums and conferences. I hope you take credit as cousin of the co-founder . . . .

Preparation for the stem cell Transplant continues—now scheduled for week of July 20. It's a grind, but I grit my teeth, listen to all the optimistic forecasts from my medical team and friends, count my blessings for Judith's TLC, and soldier onward. We loved hosting Carrie, as always. Love from Cousin Allen

ALLEN EMAILS HIS INTERNIST, DR. L:

In case you are not current on my journey toward Transplant . . . I contracted Herpes Simplex 1 about three weeks ago, was admitted to BWH for Foscarnet treatment, and discharged a week later on Valtrex oral. Unfortunately, a few new lesions appeared within days, occasioning re-admission and return to Foscarnet for the last four days. Hoping for discharge soon with continuation of the drug on an out-patient basis, perhaps one dosage/day at Dana Farber. Plan is to continue Foscarnet up to and including week of Transplant. Apart from the incarceration at BWH, I'm feeling very well with no electrolyte depletion side effects of the drug. Eventful time—yesterday was Day 1 on Medicare and today is my birthday. Enjoy the weekend. Allen

Dr. L answers Allen "I have been kept up to date. I was so sorry to hear of all of these unexpected bumps in the road. I hope that your next birthday is a lot more celebratory than this one. I know that you care about your wife's writing project, but please do not feel obligated to add extra chapters on your road to successful transplant. I hope that you are feeling better soon and that the warden at the BWH sets you free soon. Best Regards, Dr. L."

DOUG EMAILS HIS DAD: "HAPPY BIRTHDAY, FATHER! I hope my music works as a gift to you. I am in the process of finally getting my financial life together: savings, creating bank accounts, etc. By this time next year, I hopefully will be in a new apartment with a car and a better lifestyle! :) Glad you enjoy the music. More on the way!:) Love, your son"

AL ANSWERS DOUG:

Thanks sooo much for the voicemail, the email, and the musical compositions. Seeing your multiple talents thrive is one of the great gifts of my life. And seeing you stick with music composition as you are doing makes it even more joyful. Just what I need to warm the spirits during these difficult times.

So send me your best vibes and beautiful music and big hugs. We'll talk soon. Lots of love. Dad

SUNDAY, JULY 3, 2011. Email to Allen from Amsterdam friend, Paul. "Happy Birthday. . . Pioneering in yet another field, I see! We send out strong Euro-vibes (which are way more stable than the Euro) and will be hoping that things go well. *Heel veel sterkte,* as they say in Dutch. Kien joins me in sending our love, Paul"

ALLEN EMAILS PAUL:

And thanks to you for remembering my big day (how, I won't ask). Viva Medicare! Viva Social Security! May they both survive the Republican assault. On a more serious note, after thirteen years of managing CLL (the most common adult leukemia), I'm scheduled for a stem cell transplant in three weeks. Lots of preparation squeezes out work and summer holiday, but it's a necessary step after a difficult year of recurrent health setbacks. Send me some positive Euro-vibes and Dutch resilience. Will keep family and friends posted via www.caringbridge.org. Look for an email soon announcing the launch. Hoping the clan is prospering. All the best to everyone. Allen

MONDAY, JULY 4, 2011. Ducked out of the hospital for another long walk today—all the way to Trident Cafe on Newbury Street. The sweet waiter was the same one we met there about 1-1/2 years ago. Peter. Very tall. Very blond. Polite and calm, he sort of bows and gives us a sweet smile each time he leaves our table. Born in Brooklyn to Polish parents, he's majoring in philosophy at UMass/Boston. With our children so far away, it's comforting to meet such a pleasant young person. We enjoyed momos dipped in peanut sauce and fried sweet potatoes dipped in curry mustard. We split a mango tango—orange and mango juice with vanilla ice cream.

Evening. In the hospital room for the eighth night in a row, now waiting to watch the Boston Pops perform their Fourth of July extravaganza. We are disappointed that Lionel Ritchie cancelled four days ago. We were looking forward to "Hello" and "All Night Long" and "Stuck on You." Ritchie's doctor said he needs to care for his vocal chords. We all know doctors make the major decisions about our lives.

Al reacts to the music choices. *"You see what's going on here?"* he says, referring to the Marine band, singers, and songs, *"They're militarizing the holiday. We have Memorial Day. We have Veterans Day. July 4th should be about independence."* He shows me a page in today's *New York Times:* blank on top and on the bottom. In the center is The Declaration of Independence with the signers' signatures. *"That's very powerful,"* he says. *"That's what we should be celebrating."*

After the televised Pops concert, we follow our goodbye routine. Al walks me to the parking garage a block away. He drives the car up and out, then stops on the street for a smooch before I take over the wheel. He walks back to the hospital. I drive home. Twenty minutes later, we check in once more by phone to be sure we both reached our destinations.

TUESDAY, JULY 5, 2011. For me today begins at 4:00 a.m. when I experience a unique and unwelcome warning. While in a deep sleep, I clearly see the shifting bright lights indicating the threat of a migraine. I rarely get migraines because as soon as I see those signs, I pop an Excedrin and go on my way. Never have I been warned while fully asleep. I rouse myself to swallow the usual remedy and so far, so good. But to see those telltale light distortions while sound asleep is somewhat disturbing. Or should I be grateful my subconscious warned me?

Picking up Al soon after eight days in the hospital. Still so much to do to prepare for his re-entry on July 20th. The next day Al shares with me three pamphlets from the chapel that he found helpful: "Finding the Courage to Face a Serious Illness," by Jim Aurer; and "Dealing with Anger," by Louisa Rogers.

From "Hanging Onto Hope Through a Serious Illness," by Rabbi Hirshel Jaffee regarding his own illness, Al reads to me, *"When my physicians noticed how depressed I was in the hospital, they said, 'Be a Rabbi. Go and counsel other patients.'"*

And another passage about keeping your sense of humor. *"One morning when the doctors made their rounds, I said to them, 'I think these antibiotics are doing something to my body.' The docs burst into laughter. I was wearing the*

Frankenstein mask my wife bought me for Halloween."

Al suggests that he might buy a mask to wear the day after his Transplant and ask the docs if perhaps they used the wrong stem cells. I suggested a De Gaulle mask since his surgeon is French.

Al also reads a quote from Aristotle: "*Anybody can become angry. That is easy. But to be angry with the right person and to the right degree and at the right time and for the right purpose and in the right way is not within everybody's power and is not easy.*"

He also enjoyed some lovely poems from *The Song of Solomon*. We vow to read more of those together.

JULY 11, 2011. Now out of the hospital, but hardly off the hook. Back to regular clinic visits instead. The Dana staff is so welcoming, warm, playful, and ready to joke. Given all the hours we spend here, it feels like being part of an extended family. We've wondered more than once if staff is screened for charm and communication skills. Now today we read in the *New York Times* that one medical school is screening applicants for social skills that are increasingly needed for teamwork. They believe that such an approach would help avoid medical errors, even deaths.

The usual blood work today but, damn, also a surprise bone marrow biopsy that Al was not mentally prepared for.

Now for my other daily task (journal writing being one of them): THE BINDER. I've arrived at page 37—Section "After Transplant-Going Home." All about the need to clean bathrooms daily, to clean everything in fact ALL THE TIME—even your plants; outfitting all visitors with masks and gloves; avoiding forbidden (aka "fresh" unless its super-cooked) food. All this, plus managing fatigue and loss of appetite, medications, what to do if you're frustrated or angry, how your life may never really return to the way it was.

The opening paragraph of the Binder Recovery section says "Depending on your physical, social, and emotional adjustment period, it may take a year or more for you to fully recover. When I point this out to Al who always refers to a six-month recovery period, he says, "*I don't want to hear about a year. I'm in good shape (true) and I'll recover in six months.*"

As of today, no more group emails. From now on, we will communicate with family and friends through our blog on *Caring Bridge*. Al sends an email message directing loved ones to the site. Eighteen months later there will have been a total of nearly 3,000 visits to the site. Loving, clever, insightful, these responses buoyed our spirits, comforted us, made us laugh, and we're convinced, contributed to the success of the procedure. Except for the responses to our final posting, which we kept in the main document of our story, we have placed selected responses in the Appendix.

CARING BRIDGE: JULY 11, 2011.
BACKGROUND STORY BY AL

Family, Friends and Colleagues:

Each of you has played a unique role in shaping my life, a life well lived, I like to think. For that I am profoundly grateful.

As many of you know, Thirteen years ago I was diagnosed with chronic lymphocytic leukemia (CLL), the most common adult leukemia. For years the condition remained in the background. I did all that I love to do: visit my three extraordinary kids—Kate, Lena, and Doug, in San Francisco, Jacksonville, and Los Angeles; witness the arrival of three beautiful granddaughters; travel the world from Amsterdam to Johannesburg to Sao Paulo; and pursue a just and sustainable world through transforming business structures and practices. These years have been rich in love, learning, and growing, all made possible by relationships with all of you and, most of all, by my partnership with Judith, the most precious gift in my life.

Meanwhile, CLL quietly threatened to shift from indolence to prominence. That shift has now occurred. My medical team and I have decided to schedule a stem cell Transplant in August 2011. Because of a perfectly matched donor, no other medical complications, and a successful preparatory treatment, the moment is right for this potentially life-changing procedure. As one transplant patient recently observed, 'The day of transplant—Day Zero in medical parlance—is 'my new birthday.''

I invite you to visit this website for regular updates and to post messages if you are moved to do so. All will be deeply appreciated as I climb this mountain and look toward a new chapter as productive and enriching as those now past.

Warmest wishes, Allen

TUESDAY, JULY 12, 2011. Al's last big meeting before Transplant was today. From now on, he claims, his calendar is empty. However, as we are finishing up Clinic appointments, he suddenly announces that he has a telephone conference. I know he's hungry, so we set up his computer and phone in the cafeteria. I get him some lunch and he talks business for almost an hour while under the influence of morphine which they had given him to take the edge off a bone biopsy. He falls asleep in the car and sleeps for 2-1/2 hours at home right through another call he was supposed to be involved in. So much for a clear calendar.

Thursday, July 14, 2011. Duties and Dreams. Every day I continue to dedicate nearly seven hours to ridding Al's body of Herpes Simplex Virus #1. I guess it's not surprising that this activity dominates my night-time dreams.

I'm not a big cat lover, although I have loved a few cats dearly, like our dark-gray cat, Char, in Nicaragua who was born in our house. Our last pet cat was twenty years ago—another kitten whose name I've now forgotten—very sweet. She accompanied us one time on our usual evening dog walk, but never returned. For months as I slept on my stomach I dreamed that she jumped on my back and purred in my ear. I can't remember a cat dream since then. I never dream of fire either. This week I dreamed about both. I was leaving the house in a hurry—probably for a medical appointment—when I glanced down and saw a cat—a cat that belonged to me. Its fur was on fire. There were red and yellow flames. It looked up at me with the indifference only a cat can display. It was not in pain. My appointment was urgent. I left, but I worried about the cat all day.

When I tell my sister, Molly, about the dream, she says that to understand the dream, I should pay attention to the words I use to describe it. "Inflamed." "Couldn't do a lot about it." It becomes obvious that the burning cat dream was my way of working through issues and fears connected to Al's rash. What if they can't get rid of it and can't do the Transplant? What if it comes back?

I also realize that the cat in the dream looked like the first cat my family ever had, Fluffy. When I was twelve, my family moved to the country. Until then we had been living in a cramped second-floor apartment where I shared a small bedroom with three younger sisters. Our new home was probably four times the size inside, with ten times the amount of outdoor space. We immediately acquired two cats, two German Shepherds and a sheep named Dolores (another story).

The houses were far apart, but one day a tomcat showed up from somewhere and pounced on Fluffy. He held her down with his front paws. She meowed loudly as if she were very frightened and in pain. A few months later she gave birth to four scrawny kittens in which she took no interest whatsoever. She did not nurse them. She did not lick them. She did not seem aware of them. My mother said Fluffy was too young to have kittens. We humans tried to save them, but they all died. They say it's good for children to have pets, that they learn how to care for animals, learn about death. The messages I, as a twelve-year-old, took with me were different: do not get pregnant until you are mature enough to care for your baby. AND be sure the boys/men in your life are gentle and respectful. No mean, grabby tomcats. My darling husband meets the criteria I began defining at age twelve based on what I learned from poor, pretty, immature Fluffy.

Al also seems to be having a disturbing, recurring dream this week. He fights and flounders pretty wildly as if he's fighting off someone or maybe a whole group. I touch him gently on the arm and he violently pushes my hand away. He keeps fighting whatever enemies he has conjured up. I keep trying to gently waken him. The second time I try to soothe him, he begins to relax. As I continue to caress him, he stops flailing and begins to breathe normally. He never wakes up during the dreams and does not remember them the next day. One time he did open his eyes, though. He stared at me with a look I've never seen before or since. It was a look of terror and distrust. It was fierce and frightening. He said nothing, but he rolled over and continued to sleep somewhat more peacefully.

Meanwhile, between those time-consuming treatments, we do enjoy ourselves. A delicious dinner at a new restaurant nearby—Café Cognac—including a shared delicate four-cheese tartlette served with a tartarre made of chopped figs, cooked leeks and fennel, and a main dish of fried trout drowned in lemon juice with crisp pumpkin seeds and salty capers.

When I began dating Al, I remember telling my mom that I didn't know what his laugh sounded like. He was very serious, rarely smiled, and seldom laughed. If he did laugh, it was quick and nearly silent. It's so satisfying when he does laugh now and thrilling when I'm the one who contributes to his mirth. This week we've shared several spontaneous laughing sessions that went on and on—the kind where both of us are out of control, chests heaving. Just when you think it's over, you hear the other person gasping and that makes you start up all over again.

It began when I was telling Al about my checkout experiences at Star Market. They have ten registers, but only two of them are manned at any one time. A checkout person can make a difference in my mood. Some are slow so you wonder if they know what they're doing, if they're concentrating, if they might be making mistakes. Some address you in a nasty tone, "Do you want your watermelon bagged separate or what?"

Others are pleasant. A young new cashier found delight in my choice of eye shadow: "Oh, this is lovely!" She even explained what the white was for. I had to buy the white since it was included with the silver I wanted, but I'll probably never use it. I was so delighted to have some kind of personal exchange with a cashier that I felt like running all the way to the other side of the giant place and buying her the same item as a gift. Two middle-aged cashiers have been there for years. Although not chatty, they are professional and efficient. The items just click right by and before I know it they're bagged, I've paid, I'm out the door, I'm ready to cook.

But now I can rarely get one of those good cashiers. Instead, Star Market is firing people and making customers do the work. I don't want to do the work of checking out my own groceries, but I don't want to wait in line for a surly cashier either. So occasionally I try to use the self-checkout. It works fine if all you have to do is scan a barcode and drop the item in a plastic bag. But most of my items are produce. No barcode. Must look up item. Must decide among six different kinds of apples. Macintosh I know. But Gala and Honeycrisp look alike. What the hell are these greens called again?

Then there's the machine talking to me. When I imitate the machine while telling Al about the experience, and then imitate my response—that's what sets off our guffaws. Machine in pert voice trying to sound respectful, but really coming off suspicious: "Please remove unidentified object in bagging area." Me: "The unidentified object is my purse, dammit. Do you mind for gosh sakes? It's heavy. You haven't given me anywhere to put it down. You want me to pay this bill or not?"

In the store this week there were two people kind of off: one special-needs bagger who was talking constantly in a loud voice, and kept repeating *"Bobby and me, boy, we know our job. Bobby and me, we do this job right. Don't we Bobby?"* Bobby said nothing. Another, a customer, well dressed, pushing her cart up and down the aisles talking nonstop in a normal tone and at a normal conversational speed. Elderly. At first I thought she was talking into one of those mini cell phone mikes you put on your lapel. But then I passed her a few times. There was no visible mike and I could see this is something different. *"I'm passing the pasta section now. The deli section is behind me. I wonder where the cheese might be."* She had been moving around for at least twenty minutes, talking the whole while, but her cart did not contain a single item.

When I start talking back to the check-out machine, I guess I sound a little crazy too. When I've really messed up and the machine voice keeps telling me so, one of those efficient experienced cashiers leaves her post to help. She's been "bumped up." She's no longer a regular cashier. She wears a black apron that says "Self Check-Out AMBASSADOR." Because most self-checker customers are more tech savvy than I am and have no need of an AMBASSADOR, most of the time she looks bored. Once she arrives at my elbow, she perks up.

She quickly shuts up that chirpy voice that's been trying to correct my behaviors and whips that machine into place. Punch, punch. Stuff is bagged and I'm done. "How do you do that so fast?" I ask her. "I have all the codes memorized," she says nonchalantly. Then Ms. Ambassador returns to her post and assumes that bored expression. What a waste of a good cashier–and a good mind, for that matter.

Recounting the irritating, mundane realities of everyday life brings us relief from the stress of coping with Transplant preparations. Who would have dreamed that the Self-Check system could be so therapeutic? Thank you Star Market for distracting us from the grueling, day-to-day pressures that have defined our lives for the last many months.

CARING BRIDGE: FRIDAY, JULY 15, 2011
BY JUDITH: "OUR DEAR DONOR"

Dear Family and Friends,

Your messages are treasures. We both return to them many times.

We had a disappointment yesterday, when we received the news that Allen's hospital admission date has been delayed because of some coordination problems on the donor end. We're told this is common. It was unsettling, especially since we don't have a new date yet, but we've rallied. We have no choice.

The donor was selected from a list of hundreds of thousands of volunteers around the world. Our donor matches all twelve markers in Allen's blood. He (we do know it's a he) could be anywhere—as Al says—in Paris, Peoria, or Puno. Friends joke that we'll know the donor's location if Al grows a beret, begins speaking in a mid-western accent, or starts to crave Indian cooking. We can contact him a year after the Transplant if he's willing. For now we call him "Abram."

TUESDAY, JULY 19, 2011. DREAMS CONTINUED. After busy Monday and Tuesday mornings, we take an afternoon nap on our beloved sun porch—sun is peaking through the trees, yet it's not hot out here. We rarely use a fan and certainly never an air conditioner. Through all four seasons, it's just delightful. Waking up to fall colors or snow-covered branches. Falling asleep to spring rains pinging against the windows.

Then everything slowly turns green and stays that way for months. A mini forest in the middle of the city. Playful squirrels. A few birds, including an occasional visit from a hawk. Anyway, Al wakes up and quietly says, "I had a bad dream." He and I were in a car—possibly a rental car, in front of a vacation house, with me in the driver's seat. As we were about to leave, Al realized he forgot something. Several minutes later when he approached the car, he saw that I had moved into the passenger seat. Someone who resembled Brad Pitt was in the driver's seat. Before Al could reach the car, the Brad-like guy took off, apparently with my full cooperation.

Al frantically tried, unsuccessfully, to find a pencil and paper to write down the license plate number. His attempt to memorize the series of letters and numbers also failed. I assured him I was not going to run off with a good-looking younger man, but also asked him if he might be wishing me on someone else? He didn't think so. I asked him if he felt panicked as the car took off and he said he did. To my disappointment, he didn't dwell much on the losing me part. He thought the main point of the dream was his dismay about not capturing the license plate number, that it might have something to do with the fear of not being able to follow all the complex directions following Transplant or managing medicines.

THURSDAY, JULY 21, 2011. Meetings at Dana Farber all morning. Up and down in the elevator. But it's a Hooray! kind of day. Really.

First stop as always—Floor Two for vitals and blood test. There are usually about fifty people in that room, quietly responding when their name is called, disappearing into the vitals "cartels" and moving on for the day's appointments. About ten percent of them are bald and wearing masks. Many of them look exhausted. Today a tall (6' 6' maybe), blond patient, wearing a mask made a point of being loud and boisterous and showoffy, yelling "my main man" when a familiar phlebotomist called his name. Later Al learned the guy had a Transplant just two weeks ago. This was his first return to the clinic since. Good for him. Let him be as loud and boisterous and showoffy as he wants. *That is Hooray #1.*

Hooray #2: Probably thanks to pastries from Clear Flour and Brookline Farmers Market, Al's weight is up to 184 after low of 172. As we move through our appointments, several times there are four or five people in the examining room. Even though there are some anxieties, some straining on our part to understand the complexities of a new trial drug and, in my case, tears at one point, there is also lots of laughter and camaraderie. It feels like a series of parties or like going house to house to visit with neighbors in a village. One certainly gets the feeling they operate as a team here.

First we meet with dermatologist, Dr. C, who says that remaining signs of "rash" are not herpes simplex, but rather residual inflammation, post inflammatory. How come all female dermatologists have perfect skin? What secrets are they not sharing? Stubborn outbreak on Al's neck does not look like herpes, but is CLL inflammation. She takes a biopsy of that area anyway to be sure virus is gone (or rather gone under; it never really goes away). Dr. C sends a photographer in to take photographs of neck and chest. I am relieved that ugly moles are all benign. One especially rough one with multiple parts to it is still blue. Several weeks ago its green/blue color frightened us until Dr. A suggested it might be dye from an arm band. Dr. C said that was the explanation; that the dye had gotten into the mole's crevices. Yuck!

Hooray #3: No skin cancer. Dr. C's advice: use a skin cream with SPF-15 on face every morning. Neutrogena, Dove, Aveeno. Next with Dr. I, Infectious Disease. Born Lebanese, his eyes are intense, but his manner is thoughtful, thorough, calm, and reassuring. We thank him for getting back to email queries almost instantly and asked how he does it. Is Al his only patient? That's how Al feels. Pleased, he chuckles. The original intention was that Nurse Judy and Nurse Al would continue the home therapy of Foscarnet right up until hospital admission, but Dr. I. is concerned about high levels of sodium, so . . .

Hooray #4: Discontinuing home therapy of Foscarnet. In fact, discontinuing Foscarnet altogether. A tremendous relief since the three-hour, two times a day home treatments have left us with very little time to do anything else. Starting a new drug—CNX—that is in Stage Three of a trial. It's a broader anti-viral than Foscarnet and protects the kidneys better. Al will continue it after Transplant. It's a pill twice a week.

Hooray #5: PICC line will be removed on Friday, July 22. No more "Michael Jackson" sleeve. While we are with Dr. I, our new assigned social worker, Tammy, also sticks her head in and we meet her in person for the first time. Kate, who is concerned about our well-being during the long ordeal of recovery, has researched her thoroughly and found a number of excellent articles Tammy has written. Al is pleased that she's a "member of the tribe," as he likes to say. Tammy was raised in Toronto by a mother and grandmother. Tammy is small and has straight blonde hair. She is bouncy and warm and articulate. She has the report on our intake meeting with the now mysteriously dismissed former social worker, Max, and assures us that she is staying at Dana. She has spoken with Kate and knows of Kate's concerns. She has worked in Transplant for fourteen years, at Dana the past five. We figure she must be in her late thirties, although she seems younger. We don't have much time and people are coming and going, but Tammy is able to use the time to reassure us about all the support that is available to us, including her emotional support. As the room is filling up with people and she has others to see, she stands to leave, but first she holds our hands and pats us. I tell her Al would like to meet with her alone before Transplant and she says absolutely. While patting my arm and looking in my eyes, she reassures me, "I'm here for you too, Judith."

Consequently, as the room fills up with more people, I need to head across the tiny room to the box of Kleenex and calm myself down. Sympathy sets me off. Next we head for familiar territory—the infusion room for more blood draws where we are met with open arms and hugs from long-time nurse and friend, Melissa. Richard finds us too and with a second visit from Toni and a surprise hello from Dr. F, it's like old home week. Al absolutely comes alive during conversations with Richard. I feel like we could talk to him for hours every day. He follows our situation and asks questions, but also shares a lot about his own life.

We talk more about adoption, raising teens, what Richard's plans are after his chaplaincy ends August 3, etc. etc. Endless topics. His phone vibrates three times. Twice he excuses himself saying, "I have to get my dad to a special hospital." The third time, he says, "Excuse me, it's Sweden calling." As if this guy isn't busy enough, he and Will are expecting a visit from a Swedish couple with three adopted kids of their own! That means four adults and six kids in his house this weekend. Yet, here he is chatting and joking with us and making arrangements for his dad long distance.

Toni had mentioned that she had one son—a college student—who scares her because he rides a bike without a helmet sometimes, and two children who are special needs. Al and I say to each other afterwards that all these people have complicated lives and obligations yet when we are with them they seem to be 100 percent focused on us. Extraordinary professionals. Extraordinary human beings.

We leave Dana in good spirits, go home for long afternoon naps, visit part of the Museum of Fine Arts' new wing—Art of the Americas—followed by dinner at the museum and an outdoor concert at The Hatch Shell listening to Landmarks Orchestra perform Tschaikovsky.

More hoorays! When we are walking back to our car, a young woman is just getting off her bike. Al and I have our arms around each other and are joking about something. *Final Hooray of the day:* She looks up and says, "You two look so happy. How do you do it?" Al answers, *"Uh, can we get back to you later on that?"*

CARING BRIDGE: Sunday, July 23, 2011
by Judith: "The Wonder of Stem Cells"

We have a date! Hard to get too attached, given previous delays, but we're ready and hopeful that this is it. Tuesday, August 2, hospital admission. Transplant itself on August 8 or 9. Home a few days later to begin recovery period.

About those magic stem cells. With apologies to our medical professional friends for any possible misconception on our part, this is what we understand: stem cells are unique in that they not only reproduce THEMSELVES, but they also produce OTHER cells, specifically red cells, white cells, and platelets. It's like giving birth to your own children, as well as to your nephew, cousin, and neighbor. They create their own community.

After a week of heavy doses of chemo, Al's bone marrow should be sufficiently cleaned out of the bad cells to be receptive to Abram's (our name for the anonymous donor) healthy ones. Once they are infused, they rapidly move through the bloodstream searching for their new home in the bone marrow. Al thinks of the first ones to arrive as little jackhammers, destroying the remnants of the baddies and preparing the way for new arrivals. I think of the stem cells as highly energetic guys and gals giddily tumbling and somersaulting toward their new home, taking a moment to celebrate when they arrive, and then quickly getting down to work. It takes a village.

Visualizing them reinforces our hopes. Our niece, Anna, writes, "When those stem cells get into you they will be soooo happy they will just dance and sing." We invite you to share your own metaphors with us.

Your love and support also reinforce our hopes. Judith

CARING BRIDGE: Tuesday, July 26, 2011, 6:11 p.m.
by Allen: "Metaphors and Root Beer"

Family and Friends:

Reading your postings in the Guestbook leaves me laughing, teary, determined, and, above all, deeply grateful for your compassion and loving support. They nourish my soul and strengthen my psyche for the journey ahead.

The delay until August 2, hopefully the last, has been difficult on the one hand but a blessing on the other by providing an unexpected opportunity to visit friends and family. I'm continuously struck by your appetite for learning the details of the Transplant procedure, evidenced in part by your many charming postings in response to Judith's invitation to share stem cell meta-phors. I share your fascination. I've spent considerable time self-educating—God bless YouTube where one finds an array of stem cell videos, from clever animation to real-world testimonials from former and current recipients. The mystery and marvel of these life-giving creatures is irresistible.

These days I feel terrific—so terrific, in fact, that I sometimes forget what is in store beginning August 2. Knowing the community that stands behind me is an immense source of strength and optimism. Your messages are like a gourmet root beer (my perennial favorite), and your collective embrace is pal-pable. I'm storing both in my marrow where they will participate in the wel-coming party upon arrival of new stem cells. Bring 'em on! Love to all, Allen

---

THURSDAY, JULY 28, 2011. Transplant is just a week away. Into the hospital August 2, procedure August 9. We're frightened, but we're also so full of grati-tude for the support that continues to pour in.

Allen in Yukon Territory, Canada, Summer 1967.

Allen in Yukon Territory, staying warm.

Judith partying in Montreal, Canada, Summer 1967.

Judith's family home designed by her father, John L. Kline, Sr.

Interior of Judith's family home.

Allen's first visit to
Judith's home, 1967.

Just pronounced husband and wife, November 1968.

First married kiss.

Home in La Trinidad, Nicaragua, 1969-1971.

Judith from kitchen window of La Trinidad home.

Allen visiting with La Trinidad neighbors.

Judith with educational nutritional chart in Spanish.

Judith with rural elementary teacher and students.

Back in the states after one-month trip in VW and birth of Kate, fall 1971.

Judith lugging laundry from our Lima, Peru apartment.

In Peru with our two children, 1974-1975.

Al awarded PhD in Geography from Ohio State University, 1976.

Our home in Newton MA, 1979-1996.

Judith in front of Newton home.

Judith teaching French and Spanish in Newton home.

Allen, c. 1995.

Judith, undated.

Allen and Judith, undated.

Our three children as teens.

Allen and Judith with our three children, 1990.

Our apartment building, Amsterdam, 2002-2003.

Judith in Amsterdam apartment kitchen.

View from Amsterdam apartment balcony.

Allen and
his beloved
bicycle.

Into The Netherlands
countryside, May 2003.

C'EST VACHE DE FAIRE TOMBER LE MUR

Remains of the Berlin wall, 2003.

Judith, recently returned to Boston from Amsterdam, 2003.

Allen's new initiative, 2005.

Allen formal business photo, 2005.

Allen introducing guests at his 60th birthday party on Martha's Vineyard, 2006.

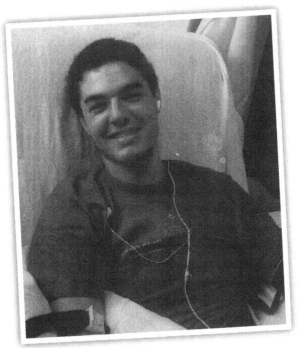

Eli donating stem cells, August 8, 2011—
1-1/2 years before we met him.

Allen post-transplant with mask, gloves, and Judith in front of our condo, September 2011.

Unmasked for photo, October 2012.

Judith cuddling just-released first novel, *The Seventh Etching*, May 2012.

Launch party for *The Seventh Etching*.

Signing books at Book Fair in Florida.

Judith before interview on *The Doug White Show* in Los Angeles, 2012.

Allen, relaxing in San Francisco, August 2012.

Eli and Allen on way to Red Sox/ Yankees game, Boston, August 2013.

38,000 baseball fans cheer Eli and Allen. Electronic board reads "Today we have with us Stem Cell Donor Hero Eli from New Jersey and His Boston Recipient, Allen. Welcome Eli and Allen."

Judith, Allen, and Eli in New York City, December, 2014.

Part IV

Caretaking Galore

August 2, 2011–November 17, 2011

AUGUST 2011

CARING BRIDGE: Tuesday, August 2, 2011
by Judith: "To the Hospital Today"

After a terrific, doctor-approved weekend in Vermont where we enjoyed the company of friends, the gorgeous green, the hills and the streams, plus a visit to Hildene, the summer home of Abraham Lincoln's only surviving son, Robert Todd Lincoln, who died there in 1926 at the age of eighty-three. May we all live at least that long surrounded by beauty. I took a photo of Allen at Hildene; looking, in my opinion, fit, tan, vigorous, and ready to take on the rigors and challenges of the next months.

Outpatient treatment began yesterday. Hospital admission is this afternoon. We soon begin a week in hospital before procedure. Very different from previous hospitalizations. Cannot bring in food. Sealed in. No contact with outside world. I ask if everyone on that floor is a Transplant patient. "Yes." I ask how they are doing. The nurse hesitates. Then she says, "They have all returned after being released." Horrors! This is the specter that will haunt me for an entire year: those patients all around us, unseen and unheard, having endured a Transplant, arriving home full of hope, and then having to return to the hospital. I'm too terrified to ask why.

Caring Bridge continues to play a critical role for us in these grueling times. The caring, clever, and creative responses to our postings not only comfort and amuse us, they are our connection to the world beyond this struggle—a struggle which requires so much of our attention and energy.

Tuesday August 2, 2011. The process of stripping Al of all his immunizations begins. He's as vulnerable as a new-born babe. More so since a newborn has some resistance from its mother. Must open up the marrow and make it welcome for the new guys on the block. Come on in. Make yourselves at home. He will be immune-compromised for an entire year and beyond. On Day 365 they will begin re-immunizing him against polio, measles, small pox, etc.

Wednesday, August 3, 2011. Al's relationship to food. He'll always be Sarah's boy. A decades-long friend of Al's family remembers his mother, Sarah, sitting intently in front of his highchair, barely giving him time to swallow before shoving in another mouthful. Food was king in that household, but it was prepared and served with love and sometimes a few ashes from the cigarette that Sarah balanced in her mouth between tastings.

Al remains a big guy with a big appetite. Three meals a day plus frequent snacks. After his mom died, he missed some of her signature dishes: *tzimmas*, pea soup. He taught himself to make them. Eventually, he began cooking dinner once or twice a week. During the past sixteen years since we became empty nesters, we've become quite proficient at preparing quick, healthy, varied meals.

Ever since the early days of our marriage when I both learned and taught good nutrition, I've tried to make sure our family ate balanced, regular meals. For years, my favorite cookbook was *Mother's in the Kitchen*. Whenever I tried a new recipe, I wrote in the book, "Al likes." Or "Al prefers with nuts." Or "Al finds this too soupy. Find a way to thicken the broth." When the kids were little, I finished teaching at 5:00 and headed for the kitchen. Meal preparation offered a creative outlet. I enjoyed it.

Among the dozens of official visitors today is a nutritionist. But this nutritionist explains that these instructions are NOT about eating healthfully. The idea for now is to eat in order to avoid infection. She gives us FIVE pages of instruction that she says should supplant the food instructions in the BINDER we've been using as a guide until now.

Title: What You Should and Should Not Eat After Transplant.

Column Headings:

> **Food category**
> **Foods permitted**
> **Foods NOT permitted until 100 days after transplant**
> **Foods NEVER permitted**

Two of many challenging examples: list of seven cheeses permitted; eight NOT permitted for 100 days. Not permitted for at least 100 days: raw vegetables, salads. Got it? Me neither. Terribly confusing and time consuming.

When the kids were little, I realized they were snacking a lot on bread. I put the bread in a hard-to-reach spot and replaced it with a colorful bowl full of fresh fruit. For decades that bowl had a place of honor on the kitchen table. Now comes this warning: all cooked or canned fruits okay. Thick-skinned, well-washed fruits okay if not bruised, BUT uncooked thin-skinned fruits NOT acceptable. That NO category means we eliminate apples, peaches, grapes, plums, nectarines, kiwi, berries, etc.

Then there are nine *Food and Grocery Shopping Guidelines* that conclude with "Purchase frozen or refrigerated food items last, and take groceries directly home to refrigerate, freeze, or cook."[1]

---

[1] *Stem Cell Transplantation/Fall 2008.* ©Dana-Farber/Brigham and Women's Cancer Center. "After Transplant-Going Home." Section 8-Page 13.

Next are two pages devoted to "Safe Food Handling." Twenty-three strict instructions along with a chart depicting at what temperature to cook four types of meat, and another chart for determining the minimum length of storage in both the fridge and freezer for meats, fish, eggs, and cheese. Let's see, how many full-time jobs do I have now?

One entire page consists of columns with the headings "Food Category" (ten), "Foods Permitted," and "Foods Not Permitted." The final page is about "Other Nutritional Considerations." For the next three plus months, this is our survival guide. I make copies to take to the supermarket. The original placed in our kitchen drawer, soon becomes a worked-over, wrinkled mess.

I underline passages. "Nothing at room temperature for longer than ten-fifteen minutes." "Avoid tasting food with the same utensil used for stirring." "Do not thaw or marinate food on the counter."

I cover the sheets with notes like: "No frozen berries—they are raw." "Buy milk powder." "Wash dishes from cupboard." "Disinfect sponges with bleach." "Raisins only if cooked." "Absolutely nothing from a deli." "Buy vegetable scrubbers. Scrub everything, even banana peels." "No bakery goods whatsoever."

Later when I treat myself to a pastry from our local European bakery, Clear Flour, I watch as the clerk in a baker's cap takes a dirty $10 bill from the previous customer, makes change from the cash register, and then reaches for the croissant I've ordered. No gloves. No hand washing. It's part of the charm of the place. For Al, the germs she's spreading around could be deadly.

CARING BRIDGE: Thursday, August 4, 2011
by Judith: "Brief Update From the Hospital Room"

Third full day in the hospital for pre-procedure "conditioning." Kill the lingering bad cells, purge the marrow, suppress the immune system to welcome (versus reject) the newcomers a few days from now. After months of anxiety, fears, and tears, we have moved on to impatience, relative calm, and relief, in anticipation of the Transplant date of Monday, August 8. If all goes well, home the next day.

"First unpleasant surprise." Until Monday, Allen is receiving daily doses of chemo for what he calls "the final blowout" of those hateful CLL cells. Actually, more than just daily. Al received a minor unpleasant surprise last night when he learned that until Sunday he'll be wired to the IV line 24/7 for non-stop hydration. Even though he can't go anywhere, the sight of the apparatus at his side is inescapable and somewhat of a downer. "Last night was

the first time I ever slept with a pump," he says. "Not a very cuddly sleeping partner and a real 'drip' to boot."

CARING BRIDGE: SATURDAY, AUGUST 6, 2011
BY JUDITH: "LOSING IT A LITTLE"

Yesterday was the fifth day of treatment and fourth day of hospitalization, all part of "conditioning," for the transplant. One more day (today–Saturday) of chemo, followed by one day (Sunday) of Rituxan, bio drug . . . and then Day Zero—the medical term for Transplant Day (Monday).

We've been pretty brave and cheerful for the most part, with visits and postings shoring us up. Yesterday we were showing the strain—Al from the suffocation of the tiny space, the omnipresent drip, the frequent beep when the pumps finish discharging drugs or simply malfunction, the lingering discomfort of the Hickman in his chest through which therapies are infused. Me from caretaker demands. Both of us from impatience and anxiety.

We check in each morning. "How did you sleep?" he'll ask. "Another long confusing dream." "A nightmare?" "Not really, not this time." "More a Shakespearian tragedy than Stephen King thriller?"

Dana Farber has caretaker support groups galore, from the general "for patients with cancer" to the specific "for Transplant patients" to the dreaded "bereavement." The experience is a throwback to being a nursing mother. Who will nurse my baby if something happens to me?

So, as I did forty years ago, I try to concentrate. Walk slowly. Don't carry too much. Be alert. No slipping. Stay focused. Even so, while backing out of our driveway, I hit a parked car.

Alarming how slowly I was going and yet what a crunch sound there was along with the exchange of blue paint for silver.

Thanks to that great invention, Netflix, we escaped our current situation for a couple of hours and went to Antarctica. Werner Hertzog's Encounters at the End of the World. *Watching a diver explore UNDERNEATH a glacier bigger (for now) than France put our claustrophobia in perspective fast. It's a universe of primordial forms—the first life on earth. Tiny creatures. Lots of violence. One researcher said it was the violence that drove the first amphibians onto the land—the desire to escape and to grow bigger in order to survive. I wondered at what point between that first step/slither onto dry ground and the present, when did stem cells come into being? How many millennia did that take? The tiny saviors are scheduled to arrive Monday eve with infusion about 11:00 p.m. if all goes to plan. Al says they're night owls, just like he is. Let's hope they're as wise.*

CARING BRIDGE: AUGUST 8, 2011
BY ALLEN: "MOVING TOWARD DAY ZERO"

Transplant Day, aka "Day Zero." 2:30 a.m. Red Sox beat the Yankees 3-2. Good sign. A restless night. Body and soul sense a seminal moment is approaching. Somewhere out there my anonymous donor is in the final segment of his immensely generous act as he bids farewell to a fraction of his stem cells that begin their journey to the waiting, anxious recipient. It all borders on the mystical as I sit in my hospital room waiting to greet the new arrivals late tonight . . . always with the caveat "if all goes to plan." Judith and I have planned a quiet welcoming ceremony.

During the past week of medical incarceration, with endless tests and treatments administered by an army of medics, your dazzling stream of metaphors has brought me tremendous comfort, amusement, and optimism. "Pulses of energy," "pain and joy of child birth," "fantastic voyage," "dancing cells" "living plants," "corporate cleansers"—I'm bundling all your images into one, big greeting to welcome the newcomers.

The Transplant is a milestone, but only one, in a long process. The actual "mini-Transplant" (versus the far more demanding standard Transplant) follows the familiar procedures of any blood infusion and lasts less than an hour. Twenty-four hours later, following intensive monitoring, it's time for hospital discharge and the beginning of months of recuperation. Roughly 100 days is a rule of thumb for assessing progress. Monitoring continues; treatments as necessary; restricted diet to block infection; relentless housecleaning; limited visitors.

All these measures are aimed at providing the new cells with the most favorable environment possible for settling in. It's all very Darwinian—the strong cells gradually overtake their weaker counterparts, reproducing themselves while generating the healthy white cells, red cells and platelets that equip the body with life-giving defenses, energy, and clotting.

My heartfelt appreciation for all your messages of love and support. You are members of a precious community that is indispensible to my coping and healing, and to providing indispensible sustenance as the journey continues. Do keep in touch.

FINALLY: MONDAY, AUGUST 8, 2011 AND TUESDAY, AUGUST 9, 2011–
THE NEW DAY ZERO. Al says the whole process is like a James Bond movie.
He can hear the movie theme in his head and wants to ask Doug to write the
screenplay. We receive notice that the stem cell extraction process has been
completed. Then that the cells are en route. Life in a plastic pouch. We figure
that the cells left Germany about 11:00 a.m. our time. They are being flown
from Germany in the trusty hands of a volunteer medical courier.

Six hours later, they arrive at Logan airport. "They're going through customs," we're told. When they arrive at Dana, they'll first go to the lab. Once
approved, they'll be accompanied through the connecting catwalk to Brigham
and Women's Hospital, delivered to our pod and brought into our room by our
terrific nurse, Tracey. Soft of voice, gentle and reverent, Tracey makes us feel
we're blessing her by "allowing" her to share this experience with us.

11:00 P.M. While waiting, Al and I share a small two-person ceremony,
reflecting on what we've experienced, how we feel. Although we speak directly to each other, we recognize that our thoughts are also being directed
to what I call God and what Al calls a Higher Power. I say a prayer. Al gives a
"humanist benediction." I speak of my gratitude to Abram, to the staff at the
donation site in Germany, to the courier, to the DFCI/B&W teams all working diligently and expertly to give Al this chance for a renewed and extended
life. I bless the new stem cells, welcome them, and ask them to do their best
to extend his life so that he might continue his work improving the world,
loving, giving, enjoying.

Al speaks of the many people who contributed to what he is about to receive. He weeps as he talks about the years of work by determined researchers,
a government which funds research and regulates drugs for the public good,
the humility he feels benefitting from all these people. The feeling of standing
gratefully on their shoulders. We kiss through twin blue surgical masks. We
hold hands and wait. I massage Al's arms, head, and back.

MIDNIGHT. The cells have arrived at Dana where they are being given a
final examination. Difficult waiting, but we sure don't want the wrong or infected cells. We wait. The cells are being wheeled through the catwalk to our
pod at Brigham and Women's Hospital.

Quietly, hopefully, Tracey enters the room and holds out the open palm of
her gloved hand for our viewing. "They're here," she says in a reverent whisper.
We stare in awe at a 4"x 5" plastic bag with orange/pink thick liquid inside.
Precious. Life-giving. Carefully chosen with twelve out of twelve markers that
match perfectly. Welcome Abram.

12:45 a.m. Al holds the bag and caresses it, then lies down. Tracey hooks him up and for the next hour and a half the three of us chat and watch the drips pass through a clear cylinder, through long tubes and into the Hickman IV on Al's chest. I take photos and send them to our kids. Tracey has been married twenty years; she asked us how long we have been married. Like many people, she is always curious about long-term marriages and what makes them work. I don't think we were in an analytical, sharing mood at that moment, but hopefully the scene speaks for itself.

I take photos of the bag, the tube, of the nurse hanging up the bag, of Al looking up at the drip anxiously. No need for anxiety. Amidst this profoundly emotional moment, he experiences no physical reaction. Steady pulse, no chills, no shakes, no spike in blood pressure. Abram's little guys are moving in smooth as silk. I imagine them, having been in the body of a nineteen-year-old only hours earlier, saying to each other. "Geez, we had it easy in that other guy. Just moseying along. Everything going swimmingly. A day at the beach. But what the hell is this? We've got our work cut out for us here. Let's get goin' fellas."

After ninety minutes, the infusion is complete. Tracey disconnects the IV. Al cautiously rises from the bed. Freed of all paraphernalia, he says, "I'm taking the first steps of the rest of my life."

2:30 A.M. Al accompanies me the few steps to the exit of the unit. I take a taxi home. After more telephone talking with Al, I'm in bed. After grueling months of preparation, anxiety, and delays, Day Zero is behind us.

4:00 A.M. Talking to Al on the telephone. His window at Brigham and Women's Hospital looks out on the seventh floor of Children's Hospital. He can see into four to five children's rooms. Directly across from him, a small child is sleeping on the broad window sill all curled up on a white blanket. She seems to have created a little nook, a small space all her own. He watches that tiny, motionless figure, wondering how long she has been in the hospital and when she will leave. Just across the narrow alley, a fragile child facing a battle of unknown duration. Al, sixty years older, just passed a major milestone with a sense of renewal. He prays the same blessing will find its way to that little curled figure.

TUESDAY, AUGUST 9:
NOW AND FOREVER "DAY ZERO"

CARING BRIDGE: TUESDAY, AUGUST 9, 11:02 A.M.
BY ALLEN: "NEW CELLS, NEW CHAPTER"

Family and Friends:

Shortly after midnight, the first drop of new stem cells flowed into my anxious body. Harvested in Europe earlier that day and transported across the Atlantic under the watchful eye of a medical courier, the rose-colored cargo began the final leg of its journey from donor "Abram" to recipient Allen. An hour later, the last drop marked the end of the Transplant. I rose from the bed and took the first steps into a new chapter of my life. Described to me by a half dozen members of my medical team as anti-climactic, the process was anything but.

An hour before the process began, Judith and I vetted an array of intense emotions, a mix of awe, profound gratitude, and hope. A superb nurse brought her medical skills, maternalism, and empathy to the bedside. It was, she said, a "privilege" to be present. Home tomorrow, barring any setbacks. The twin challenges of avoiding infection and preventing rejection of the new cells will dominate the days ahead. But for now, it's a day to honor the countless contributions of scientists and patients whose brains and bodies have brought medical science to where it is today. I salute each and every one, and, equally so, Abram for his life-giving gift. Allen

---

TUESDAY, AUGUST 9, 2011. I wake up thinking about a future together—for real. I allow myself that luxury. Then I remember the dream I had last night. For a year or so now I've had the same dream about once a month. I'm with a group of people on vacation and have a weekend romance with a man in his twenties. My age is uncertain, but there is always a clear, if confusing, and tentative mutual attraction. No sex. No nudity. No conversation either. But flirting and maybe a little bit of making out. I've figured it's my subconscious dealing with my own aging, with my own death and, of course, with Al's aging and intensifying disease. The men resemble no one I know and afterwards I don't remember what any of them looks like. Pretty regular young American white guys.

I won't forget the one in last night's dream, though. In contrast to the previous, casual, not really very interesting young guys, he was different—more intense, more serious, darker. He had black thick hair, gorgeous large brown eyes and he was swarthy. There was a clear air of mystery about him. All morning I pondered who he might be or represent. Was he African American? No. Was he Latino? No. Was he Indian? No. Then I knew. He was Israeli. He was Abram. I can't wait to get my man home. I get Al with all his wisdom, charm, and wit and I get Abram's mystery and youth—all in the same bod! Poor Al just gets the same old me!

9:00 A.M. It has now been about seven hours since the Transplant was completed. I call Al. "*I think maybe I won't work today,*" he says. "*Take the day off.*" Gee, if there's any day the guy deserves off, it's today. "To honor what is happening in your body," I suggest. "Yes, that's good." But really I was kind of amazed. I guess he's been working all along every morning before I arrive at the hospital. Now with fresh cells pulsing through his brain, he'll be more fired up than ever. Continued and new initiatives, programs, writings, research, contacts . . . here we come.

In fact, he soon receives an email from a colleague at the Harvard School of Business. "Dear Al, I realize this is perhaps not the best time for you to give this attention, but do you think you could look over this draft and get back to me by noon today with your comments?" Al gets to work.

Al sounds so strong on the phone, though. He imagines the "good guys" having a ball filling in the marrow, chasing out the criminals, energetically and precisely performing their acrobatics. "*It's like 'Cirque de Soleil,'*" he says.

Someone had said "You'll have a quiet morning," but of course that's impossible. "*Compared to what?*" Al asks. "*Coney Island?*" The stream of medical personnel—in ones, and twos and threes and fours—piles in and lingers. I think they are drawn to how articulately he describes what he is experiencing. And of course everyone loves witnessing a miracle. I don't think it ever gets old for them. I'm going to ask Dr. A about that. He'll have a quick, flip answer, but I'll ask.

I email my Qi Gong instructor, Rick. "We so appreciate your keeping us in your thoughts and prayers, your encouraging our intent, and for bringing out the best in us. Transplant went off without a hitch. Plenty of tears of awe and gratitude may have accompanied the procedure, but the body was quite ho/hum: no sweats, no chills, no trembling. No rise in blood pressure or heart rate. That's good. The next marker is in 100 days. Until then the twin evils must be managed: infection and rejection. Bringing our guy home tomorrow. Place has been scrubbed repeatedly. Special foods in fridge. Everything ready. Can't wait."

DAY 1. WEDNESDAY, AUGUST 10, 2011. We leave the hospital; hopefully for the last time. However, except for Sundays, we will now go to the clinic every single day for two weeks straight.

CARING BRIDGE: WEDNESDAY, AUGUST 10, 2011, 8:26 P.M.
BY JUDITH: "HOME TODAY"
First lunch. First nap. First walk outside.
Nourishment. Rest. Exercise. For the newcomers.
Al says he can feel them perfecting their acrobatic moves.
A sweet image, but I hope they've also got some John Wayne qualities:
get rid of the last of the bandits.
  and
keep the twin evils—infection and rejection—out of town.
Love to all. Judith

DAY 2. THURSDAY, AUGUST 11, 2011. First of many days in a row when we must return to Dana Farber. Too early for Graph vs. Host Disease (GVHD), but eventually new cells will look around and think, "Whose liver is that? Whose pancreas? Whose kidney? I don't recognize them. I got rid of those foreign CLL cells. Now I'll attack these organs." That's what we must be alert for. Our savior cells becoming confused. They're warriors. They're masters of search and destroy. They don't rest.

DAY 4. SATURDAY, AUGUST 13, 2011. I put together a five-page list of useful contacts, both for us to keep near the kitchen phone and for our kids, doctors, *Caring Bridge* and computer passwords, homecare assistance if needed, cleaning lady, Dana Care Coordination Department, emotional support, neighbors, friends, my periodontist, food.

While at the gym, I tell my friend, Oakley, how unaccustomed I am to shopping in the manner prescribed in those BINDER pages in my kitchen drawer, how I am feeling overwhelmed at the prospect of facing the harsh light, cold temperature, and overwhelming number of products at Star Market. Oakley says she uses that kind of food all the time, especially in packed school lunches. She goes with me and leads me to the right aisles. We fill the cart. She helps me unload the bags and carry them up to our condo. I'm so relieved. Precious friendship at a difficult time.

House plants are a no-no and one of them has recently grown a threatening spoor. Oakley helps me drag the heavy pot with my twenty-five-year-old bamboo plant down two flights of stairs and place it in the back yard.

For me, the prepared foods are a boon, a welcome respite from relentless scrubbing and cleaning and purchasing, especially at a time when we are in the hospital for hours every day. But Al hates all the prepared foods. Packages of macaroni and cheese? Insulting! Tasteless!

Exasperated, but wanting to help him add needed pounds, wanting him to be happy, I return to cooking fresh foods. This means not just scrubbing, but peeling and chopping. Most of the packaged foods sit in the cupboard.

Just as exhaustion begins to overwhelm me, Kate flies in from California, takes over the kitchen and fills the freezer with her homemade soups and casseroles. Her luminous presence boosts our spirits with hope and comfort. An angel in every respect. Ahh!

We have put our Martha's Vineyard cottage on the market. During Al's medical odyssey, our use of the property diminished drastically. More importantly, both of us—but especially Al—are at risk of insect-bite infections which have sent him to the emergency room. His compromising immune system leaves him vulnerable to bites that would otherwise be unremarkable.

This is an emotional decision for both of us, but especially for Al, whose relationship with the Vineyard dates to his high school years. The sale includes the furniture, but I need to clear the cottage of all our personal items. I'm not ready to leave Al alone for an entire day, so I need to perform that all-day task while Kate is here with him.

I'm much too jittery and stressed to drive there and back. Bus would take too long. Besides, cleaning out is a two-person job and the second person needs to do some heavy lifting, including putting Al's bike on the bike rack. The second person must be a man. He must be a man who is willing to give up an entire day to help me. He must be sympathetic to my distress, but not overly so. I certainly cannot ask the husband of any of my friends. And then I know—Rick, my Qi Gong teacher and dear friend.

Rick agrees to my request and drives me to the Vineyard. Turns out he had a summer love affair here once. For old times' sake, he returns to some of his old hangouts while I rush around like crazy, opening every drawer and closet and cupboard to clear out personal items. Rick packs the car and places the bike on the back. We grab a swim, possibly my last swim ever at Oak Bluffs Inkwell Beach. Rick drives me home. I'm so grateful, so relieved to leave the cottage in saleable condition.

DAY 6. MONDAY, AUGUST 15, 2011. Four appointments.

DAY 7. TUESDAY, AUGUST 16, 2011. Three appointments: 11:00, 12:00, 2:30.

CARING BRIDGE: TUESDAY, AUGUST 16, 2011
BY KATE: "DAY SEVEN"

Third day of my six-day visit. Dad is looking and feeling good. Mom too. The biggest challenge at the moment is the food restrictions, as neither of them is accustomed to processed, single-packaged foods, and that's pretty much all that is allowed. No leftovers that could collect bacteria either. Dad has been craving childhood favorites, so I am going to make some vats of pea soup, brisket, and tzimmis, etc. (thank you, Nana Sarah, Lena and Nadine for all the wonderful recipes!), cook it all very well, then put small micro-waveable containers into the freezer for enjoyment over the weeks to come. Also will set up on-line food delivery so Mom doesn't have to go to grocery store (they've always gone together, and usually Dad carries the heavy stuff, but he's not allowed to go for quite a while).

Spent most of yesterday and now again today at Dana Farber Clinic. Dad has to go every day for various follow-up treatments and monitoring. Met most of the staff that have been giving Dad such fantastic TLC for many years, especially intensively now, of course. Like my parents, I am extremely impressed with the knowledge, intelligence, and sensitivity of every doctor and nurse. People with leukemia fly from all over the world to access these in-stitutions. I heard Sonia Ghandi (wife of former prime minister Rajiv Ghan-di) is in Boston for treatment. And my parents live literally two miles away. Please know, dear friends and family, he is getting superb care here. Dad also does an amazing job himself managing his own care—keeping careful track of every pill, appointment, effect, impact, expectation.

Mom and I went to "caregivers" support group last night led by another wonderful Dana staffer, a social worker assigned to our case, Tammy. She has some good advice for all of us: just take the recovery process one day at a time, try not to fret too much about what might happen weeks or months from now. Just take it as it comes.

Thank you Mindy and Norman for providing such a comfortable place to stay this week and to all of you for your ongoing loving support. Kate

---

DAY 8. WEDNESDAY, AUGUST 17, 2011. Only one appointment! 8:30 a.m.
DAY 9. THURSDAY, AUGUST 18, 2011. Only one 7:30 a.m. appointment.

DAY 10. FRIDAY, AUGUST 19, 2011. Four appointments: 8:30, 12:30, 1:30, 3:30.

DAY 11. SATURDAY, AUGUST 20, 2011. One 8:30 a.m. appointment.

CARING BRIDGE: SATURDAY, AUGUST 20, 2011
BY ALLEN: "DOWNS AND UPS"

Day 11 now and no major setbacks. Kate's cooking, inspired by Lena's cookbook; a continuous stream of heart-warming postings; and coming to grips with the demands of the pharmacy sitting on the kitchen table—all have contributed to my steady progress.

The cycle of preparation-Transplant-recovery is not without its paradoxes. The art and science of suppressing my immune system to avoid rejection of the new stem cells is delicately balanced against the urgency of creating a welcoming environment for generations of healthy white and red cells and platelets spurred by the newcomers as they muscle their way into their new home. Counter intuitively, the more chronic, long-term conditions such as mine, characterized by years of chemotherapy that tax the marrow, create a less hospitable marrow than acute conditions that must be treated immediately. With the help of all of you, I close my eyes and envision in graphic detail the ongoing cell wars that continue as I write this message.

The next two-three weeks are a critical time for "Abram's" cells to take root. The current precipitous drop in white cells, I'm told, is to be expected prior to the rebuilding process. It's alarming but I can only trust my medical team that has seen this process unfold hundreds of times.

First of many attentive visitors arrive bringing cheer and a hint of normalcy. Indoors visitors don masks and gloves; outdoors it's my turn. Loneliness, about which I was warned, has not materialized and I can't imagine it ever will.

With deep appreciation for your continuing support . . . Allen

---

DAY 13. MONDAY, AUGUST 22, 2011. Judith emails Lena: "Normal is 2000-6000. Today Dad tested at 1800! Almost at normal levels. Below 500 is way cause for alarm. Three days ago (Friday) he was at less than 100. At thirty days they test to see which of his cells are old and which are new. Today's excellent levels indicate that new cells must be regenerating. When your Dad returned home after a long clinic day, he fell into my arms and cried with relief/disbelief at the rapid white cell growth, and awe at what feels like a miracle.

Steve M visited that night and we were able to share our joy with him."

DAY 14. TUESDAY, AUGUST 23, 2011. Three afternoon appointments. Nurse Jeanine says "Mr. White, you're grafting! Congratulations!" Abram's cells are digging in like crazy. White cells up to 4100 compared to 1800 yesterday. Can barely feel the lymph nodes under his arms. Goodbye large lymph nodes that have harbored CLL for over a dozen years. May we NEVER hear from you again.

Call from Al receiving final Rituxan—final effort to wipe out mutant/bad white cells that are still floating around. Normal neutrophils are 2000-6400. Al emails our kids: "Neutrophils (white cells) doubled yesterday's figure—now 4100."

DAY 16. THURSDAY, AUGUST 25, 2011. We meet with surgeon for the first time since BEFORE the Transplant sixteen days ago. He guides Al's healing in ways we'll never fully appreciate. We have questions. He sits facing the computer. Doesn't look at us much. He's also sniffling again. Is Al being exposed to cold germs after all we're doing to avoid infections of all kinds?

For the most part, we have been blessed with the most delightful, warm, caring, interactive, affectionate staff at both Dana Farber Cancer Institute (DFCI) and at Brigham and Women's Hospital.

Dr. A is the exception. He sits at a desk and types rapidly, rarely making eye contact. We beg for some confirmation of our understandings and answers to our carefully written down questions. He speaks in an undertone that makes us strain to hear the tidbits of knowledge he shares. A contrast to the smiles, shared laughs, and hugs from female nurses and from Al's long-term oncologist and recent infectious disease doctors (both male) who are also very sympathetic, approachable, and ready to engage.

I remember what happened during the week Kate was here. While she and Al were meeting with Katey, the nurse practitioner who works closely with Dr. A. Katey said to Kate, "Don't worry. We'll take good care of your Dad." Kate began crying and then so did Katey. I understand that not all medical professionals demonstrate the same behaviors and I certainly don't expect tears from our surgeon but the differences here are truly striking.

I must remember daughter Lena's explanation for the discrepancy, something she has observed during many years in the medical field. Surgeons are also afraid of showing too much enthusiasm about progress, lest, in this long affair, something goes wrong, or we become overconfident and become less rigid about following the guidelines. There is always the issue of litigation hanging over their heads too, so they are cautious. "He's doing exactly what he *should be doing,*" Lena says. Her words help me appreciate Dr. A's exceptional skill as a professional and not resent him for what he's not.

In any case our recent leaping for joy over the huge leap in white cells is muted. It's important to remind ourselves that although down from yesterday's 4100, 2800 is still within normal range.

There's confusion about grandchild contact: are their vaccines a threat to Al? How does immune-compromised Zayde manage? He has been stripped of all his childhood immunizations and will not begin getting them until one year after Transplant. "Until then, assume you are vulnerable," Dr. A says. "For one or two years, you will be at HIGH risk for infection. High blood counts do not lower risk of infection. Dietary restrictions until 100-day mark."

Dr. A goes over about seventeen drugs Al has been taking. He eliminates four.

Finally, Al does get in some questions:

Al: "*Is this large growth in white cells expected after only two weeks?*"

Dr. A: "Yes, it's average. Well . . . good."

Al: "*Is this an indication that the new cells have taken root?*"

Dr. A: "We'll know when we stop the treatment whether the high levels are due to the stimulant or indicate grafting. We need more time to see what is contributing to the growth. On Day 30 we'll take blood and begin the analysis. That can take a couple of weeks."

(In other words, no leaping for joy for another month! Doc was equally unimpressed by shrinking lymph nodes that Al had been excited about.)

Al: *Is Graft vs. Host Disease still a risk after six months?*

Dr. A: "Longer. If everything is going well after six months, you can go off the rejection prevention drugs. You're at high risk for infection for one to two years." (I had read it's a risk up to three years after!)

Al: *Do these high levels of whites indicate less risk of infection?*

Dr. A: "No. They have nothing to do with it. Stay with all dietary instructions until Day 100."

Then Al slips in something personal and gets a response:

Al: *Judith calculated that Day 100 falls on our anniversary, November 17.*

Dr. A stops typing for a moment and actually glances at us. "Well if all goes well, you can get restaurant food for that day." Then he warns us, "You still can't go INTO a restaurant and eat there."

'OK. We'll behave ourselves,' I think but do not say.

Al: "*So the message is, 'Stay the course.'*"

Dr. A: "Yes, 'Stay the course.' And then some praise, a little excitement as

Dr. A. stands up to take his leave. "Doing great," he adds, "Very happy."

And then over his shoulder as he rushes out, some real emotion, although spoken quietly, so we barely catch it. "I'm delighted you're doing so well. I love it."

But, in spite of the general lack of confirmation, Al is celebrating and relieved for several reasons:

1. His next appointment is Wednesday. "*A whole week off!*" he says. "*I never thought I'd hear that.*"

2. "*I can take a full shower.*" For over three weeks, he's had the Hickman to contend with. Every morning I've attempted in my fumbling, impatient, and untrained way to cover all the paraphernalia with Press-n-Seal, awkwardly cutting off the excess with nail scissors. After that, Al tapes all around the seal and he still has to be careful not to get the area wet.

3. With the Hickman gone and the soreness that plagued him because of it, he is sleeping much better AND sleeping all night in our bed. Waking up next to him . . . it's wonderful.

4. Delicious being able to hold each other chest to chest. "*One more rebirth,*" Al says.

DAY 17. THURSDAY, AUGUST 2, 2011. Why did God give females the superior sense of smell? This is why: while men are out hunting in the open spaces, women need to be able to protect the nest by identifying the location of a foul and possibly threatening odor—especially one that has been worsening for days.

In this case, with my nose to the ground I determine the odor is coming from under the refrigerator. Al had thought it was coming from outside. I also think I know what is causing it and I am pissed. Already clean living, we've made a triple effort since way before the Transplant. We had rugs cleaned. We took books off shelves and cleaned behind them. I dragged a rented upholstery cleaner all over the condo. We doubled the cleaning crew visits. We stored up and frequently use the Lysol swipes and Swiffer wraps our modern daughters introduced us to. Our son-in-law helped us pull appliances away from the walls and clean behind them.

Now with only about one-quarter of an inch between the bottom of the fridge and the floor, I can't see much with a flashlight. But I sure can smell something that is making me gag. Why did God give man superior muscles and facility with tools? So he can roll the 300-pound refrigerator away from the wall and say to the woman, "*Bring a flashlight, a pair of pliers, a coat hanger, and three pieces of wood.*"

Once he has the fridge propped up, Al begins poking around. I am alarmed. He may be exposed to God-knows-what under there, something I am sure has been dead for days. We consider asking the thirty-something guy upstairs to help with this unpleasant and possibly threatening task. I can hear that guy pounding above us—probably preparing for Hurricane Irene—and he has already taken all of the buildings' trash barrels inside to protect them from the storm. I don't want to bother him.

So Al and I don masks and gloves and soldier on (or at least Al does.) "*I see your critter,*" he finally announces, swinging the coat hanger back and forth to root it out. When I see the mouse's dried-up tail poking out, I shriek, cover my face, and back away fast. Is this an instinctual or a learned response? I remember my mother leaping onto a chair and frantically screaming, "Jack! Jack!" whenever something scurried nearby.

"*Do you want to do it?*" Al asked. I really am not capable of it and I feel so guilty refusing to take over. Once he has transferred the thing to a garbage bag, I do bravely carry the garbage bag down two flights of stairs to the basement where the trash barrels are handy, but also stinking—oh that olfactory sense again.

Now with an apple-cinnamon scented candle burning away the remaining smell and trying to forget the unpleasantness, on to preparing for Irene: dozens of candles, candle holders, flashlights, batteries, radio, fridge temp at lowest setting, fill bathtubs with water. I already had stockpiled five gallons of bottled water before Transplant.

CARING BRIDGE: Saturday, August 27, 2011
by Judith: "Mr. White, You're Engrafting. Congratulations!"

The welcome, caring words in the title were spoken last Monday by a nurse reading Al's blood levels. In three days, his neutrophils (a white cell indicator) had moved from a frightening low of 100 (called "bottoming out") to 1800, then to 4100 the day after that. Normal is between 2000 and 6000. Most recent count was 2800—well within normal range.

Nurses pronounced the trend as an early sign that Abram's cells are settling in. The surgeon–our behind-the-scenes Wizard of Oz, Al calls him—was less effusive, reserving judgment until an upcoming milestone on Day 30, September 8. At that time, using a technique developed only five years ago— the chimerian test, named after the mythological multi-species creature—the medical team will be able to determine which white blood cells are progeny of the new, versus old, dysfunctional stem cells. We're hopeful, while anticipating another emotional moment in our journey toward normalcy.

We have a routine. For daylight hours, I pack ice and lemonade and we head with our guests to the park, two blocks away, Al in mask and gloves as a protective measure. Evening visits are more restrictive. Then the burden is on the guest to wash hands and don mask and gloves. No eating or drinking.

As I write at 9:05 a.m., it is eerily still and quiet. Our plan is to take a long walk before furious Irene arrives and we, along with the rest of the East Coast, must hunker down.

With love and gratitude to all on what for us is Day 18.

DAY 19. SUNDAY, AUGUST 28, 2011. Keep waking up, reading, and going back to sleep. Finally, hunger drives us out of bed at 10:30 a.m. Lots of rain and heavy winds, but I don't see any tree limbs down. Storm passed to the west. Oh well, my Jacuzzi tub leaked out all the saved water overnight. Terrible destruction from Hurricane Irene in Vermont, though.

DAY 20. MONDAY, AUGUST 29, 2011. Second grocery delivery. Oh, is that a relief. Instead of doing the shopping which I detest, I can dedicate time to my favorite parts of food: planning meals, cooking, and putting groceries away, while avoiding the dreaded shopping and lugging up the stairs.

DAY 21. TUESDAY, AUGUST 30, 2011. Fourth day of predicted nausea, cramping, and diarrhea. Fatigue. Not eating well. Doesn't feel like seeing visitors or walking very far from the house. Distressing, but the team had warned us of these post-Transplant symptoms, which makes their emergence more tolerable. Surprises are what we fear most.

Meanwhile, I've been diagnosed with a fungus. My dermatologist says we should not be intimate and perhaps should not be sleeping in the same bed. That would be awful after so many nights apart. We're really enjoying falling asleep in each other's arms and waking up to each other. I write the Nurse Practitioner:

"Dear Katey, Allen and I look forward to meeting with you tomorrow.

I need some advice. My dermatologist diagnosed what I thought was a rash as a fungus. She's put me on a twice-a-day anti-yeast and anti-fungal, Econazole. She said I should not get close to Al for a month. Do you agree that we should abstain for a month? Not even sleep in the same bed?

My dermatologist thought there was an unlikely possibility that it might be a staph infection, but will have those lab results this weekend and will adjust medication as necessary. I've also had a wart on the bottom of my foot for years. Dermatologist said Al could get that too. "Wear socks or he could catch the wart virus and be walking around with warts all over the bottom of his feet." Al has a previously scheduled meeting with his dermatologist, Dr. C, tomorrow, so we'll also discuss these issues with her, but we wanted your opinion about how to proceed. Thanks, Katey. Judith"

Al's dermatologist thinks my skin irritation will disappear in two weeks and that we can relax about it after that. She also pooh-poohs the wart warnings.

Katey makes the time even shorter: "Once you get the lab report that it is not staph, I wouldn't worry about intimate touching. We don't want to take all your fun away from you."

Al says the judgments by three women about how dangerous my skin condition might be range from the prissy to the understated, quietly sensual to fiery temptress, and that the advice depends more on who is delivering it than on the medical condition itself.

However, these days, given his stomach cramps, Al just wants tummy rubs.

Five days later: I'm on an antibiotic. It's neither staph nor fungus. Still have the rash, but it's improving. I dreamed, though, or perhaps it really happened, that I was scratching the rash and then scratched my eye. I woke up frightened and cleaned out my eye.

TODAY'S ERRANDS: Dermatologist appointment, optician to repair Al's glasses.

Two days ago we both got out of bed at the same time. I returned first and felt my knee hit something, looked down to see his glasses in the middle of the bed minus a lens. Now they are okay. Then to pharmacy for my skin condition. Next: deliver eight pairs of shoes to Goodwill. When Al plopped that size 14 clodhopper on my coffee table on October 30, 1966, it never occurred to me that someday I'd be plodding down Commonwealth Avenue in Boston, carrying four pairs of those enormous things (plus four pairs of my 9-1/2's— quite a bit lighter) in a trash bag on my back Santa style. The shoes were just accumulating all over the house. I brought four pairs back from the Vineyard cottage and had him sit down while I showed him every pair of shoes. Size 14 is not easy to find in regular stores—where did they all come from? He had to make a decision: give away or keep.

Finally to Star Market to pick up odds and ends that I had not ordered or could not get through Peapod.

Then roasted a Kosher chicken with yellow potatoes and carrots which Al loved. Al has had nausea and diarrhea for four days. Trying to fix things he can eat and really likes. Previous night: fettuccini with swordfish, bits of ham, corn and green beans, onions, cheese, olive oil. He loved it.

After dinner we practice a little Qi Gong with a DVD Rick gave me and then look at photos from Kate's fortieth BD party, and watch YouTube performances by ten-year-old singer, Jackie Evancho.

We end the evening's entertainment with an incredible performance of "Hallelujah" by K.D. Lang, wearing a long priest-like black dress, barefoot. Enormous audience exclaiming throughout, bursting into enthusiastic shouts often, but there's a sudden hush as she approaches the final stanza. They all know what's coming and they do not want to miss a note. When the song comes to its dramatic end, the audience explodes. During the entire minutes-long, on-your-feet applause, K.D. bows humbly, hangs her head low for long periods, finally rises to face the audience, eyes closed, her palms together in front of her in prayer pose, smiling with gentle appreciation for her still shouting, adoring audience.

As we get into bed, me on a hospital sheet because of my rash, Al says, "*It could be a long day tomorrow. I may need to be hydrated.*"

"I'd like to go to a water aerobics class at 3:30 if possible," I say.

Al rolls his eyes and shakes his head back and forth. I think he must be in more pain or thinking of something really disturbing.

"What is it?" I ask him.

"*I'm so sick of hearing about your gym schedule,*" he explains.

About that gym: with the exception of ping-pong, I hate participating in any sport that involves chasing, hitting, catching, kicking, or throwing a ball. I get a lot of exercise, though—walking, dancing, swimming, and recently from Qi Gong, Tai Chi. For seventeen years we lived within view of a lake. I rode my bicycle to the lake beach and swam there all summer. For winter swimming, I joined a Marriott Hotel pool.

When we moved to our condo in 1996, I did not know what I would do about my need to swim. I soon discovered a gym only three blocks away—one with a large indoor pool and lots of classes. In addition to swimming regularly, I used to dance there several times a week and performed with a group at the Celtics pre-game show. The gym also has an outdoor, rooftop pool. Walking there is part of my routine. I'm delighted. Through the years, in addition to providing me with a way to maintain weight and manage arthritis, the gym has become a source of many friendships. I'm open about my fears and burdens connected to Al's Transplant. The instructors and fellow members are part of my support group. They ask how Al's doing, how I'm doing. They embrace me.

Not only that, I've honored his pre-marital request that I never get fat. I wore a size 8 or 10 then. In four decades, yes, I've expanded some, but I am not overweight. He takes delight in my appearance, comments often, admires my clothes.

So, given all that and the lovely evening we had just shared, when he reacts as if in pain and says, *"I'm so sick of hearing about your gym schedule,"* I am shocked and extremely hurt. "Too fucking bad," I shout.

I had thought we were just working together to plan our day. What was going on? Could he be jealous that I'm free to get out more? That he has so little freedom to determine HIS schedule? He can't ride his bike or play basketball? Given how unpetty and generous he is, that explanation seemed unlikely. We rarely quarrel. I sleep badly.

I know I'll have to be the one to bring up the nastiness and at a time when he's not nauseous. Not easy to find such a time these days. Al is non-confrontational and will just let it pass even if it's bothering him. I think that for starters I will offer to give him a written schedule of my classes. The next day, after a morning at the clinic and a great aqua aerobics class, we take a walk and I ask him about it. It is, in fact, pretty simple and straightforward. As often happens, he has the same solution that occurred to me. *"Why don't you just give me a written schedule?"* He meant exactly what he said. He didn't want to hear about my gym schedule every day. With everything he has to remember in order to care for himself, he does not want to try to remember MY schedule. He is totally supportive of my taking some time for myself to exercise. I type up the schedule. He posts it above his desk. Irritation overcome.

Sadly, we cannot attend Kate's fortieth birthday party in San Francisco, "40@40," where she exhibits forty pieces of her art work. Most of her friends and colleagues have no idea she is so talented in that area. She also displays the pink baby book in which I painstakingly recorded every new development of my first, chubby, green-eyed, intense, smart baby girl. Photos too. The party is a success.

FIRST CLINIC APPOINTMENT IN SEVERAL WEEKS. Most viruses are transmitted through hands. WASH. WASH.

Public events? No. Flu season is ramping up. Very dangerous for Al. His immune system is still "piss poor" and will be for a long time.

Challenges:

a. Blurred vision. Dry eye. Will start drops.
b. Hip pain caused from lateral movement. Now gone.
c. Tremors. So bad he's having trouble writing. I hate seeing him with

tremors. It makes him seem so diminished when he's really otherwise not. Decreasing prednisone (steroid); will decrease some of the other approximately fourteen drugs too.

d. No GI problems.

e. No mouth symptoms.

f. No new rash.

g. Energy level down. Sleeping more.

h. Dry mouth may be sign of Graph vs. Host. Too early for GVHD, but all transplant patients experience it to some degree.

DAY 23. WEDNESDAY, AUGUST 31, 2011. Another visit with Al's DFCI dermatologist, Dr. C. He has spots in front of each ear and on forehead. "Possibly pre-cancer," she says. Puffy. Possibly from pre-Transplant conditioning. Needs a biopsy. Right one can be treated with liquid nitrogen, but left must be surgically removed. Platelets must be above a certain level before that procedure can take place. Meanwhile, I worry about a new cancer on his temple, bearing down on his brain.

SEPTEMBER 2011

DAY 25. FRIDAY, SEPTEMBER 2, 2011. BILLY RUBEN MISBEHAVES. Appointment with Nurse Practitioner, Katey. For days Al's been sitting with his head hanging, saying little. Reminds me when my Dad sat in that same position toward the end of his life. It was a shock to see my dynamic, interactive, teasing Dad in that position. Now it's my husband.

BAD: Sixth day of cramping, diarrhea, and nausea. Started nausea meds yesterday. Twenty-thirty percent better. Interesting. How do you measure improved nausea? When Al was a teen, he regularly stopped by Smithfield's ice cream shop in Worcester. In those days, they thought chocolate contributed to acne. Faced with the choice of aggravating his teenage breakout or giving up his beloved hot-fudge sundaes altogether, he compromised. He asked them to reduce the fudge by fifty percent. The waiter looked partly amused, partly confused, and proceeded to scoop what appeared to be a normal serving of hot fudge.

Diarrhea persists. Less frequent, less urgent, follows eating. Last night two whole hours of cramping. Not getting worse at least. Sleeps flat on stomach. Up three times to urinate. Eating and drinking modest amounts. Still losing weight. Drinking half-gallon of water/day. No fever. Again—symptoms are expected, not alarming, but making life miserable—temporarily, we hope.

GOOD: White count 4700; hematocrit 28.2; platelets 179. Less than one month after Transplant, these levels are nearly normal. Bilirubin, a measure of liver function, still low, though I just learned how to spell bilirubin. I've always thought it must be named after the person who first identified it—the imagined Billy Ruben. Sounds like it could be a childhood friend of Al's from Worcester, MA. Mouth—no thrush, but dry. Possibly less-yellow skin. Liver better. Apparently heading in right direction. Restart acyclovir—an anti-viral, to keep herpes from returning.

Al says to Katey, "*Judith went to a restaurant last night for the first time in a month.*" Katey looks at Al with narrowed eyes and asks, "Did you have a good time?" "No," he answered, "*She didn't go with me. She went with a girlfriend. Was that a trick question?*" Katey answers, "Yes. Some patients sneak into restaurants. We have to catch them."

DAY 26. SATURDAY, SEPTEMBER 3, 2011. Judith emails sister, Martha. "Forgot to answer your question about how I'm doing. Pretty good, I'd say. Lots of support from my kids, my sisters, friends, *Caring Bridge*. Girlfriends are taking me to a movie or restaurant occasionally. Will go to my French conversation group. Still there's a lot of extra work. Al has always been helpful around the house. Now there's no way he can take out the garbage or wash dirty clothes. He's too tired to do much cooking and, of course, we can neither eat out nor bring food in. Plus lots of dietary changes which are a real challenge.

I miss the rich life we've always shared. But we can take walks every day and he's hoping to begin riding his bike soon. I hate seeing him limited, knowing he has so much more to give, but I'm confident those times will come again. So there it is. Thanks for asking."

CARING BRIDGE: SUNDAY, SEPTEMBER 4, 2011
BY ALLEN: "ROUGH PATCH"

Family and Friends:

I hope the conclusion of your summer was full of pleasure. Here in Boston, we were fortunate to have been spared Irene's fury which brought such destruction to parts of NJ, CT, NY state and the sweet state of VT.

Now Day 27 post-Transplant, ending a week of predicted discomfort. I felt like I needed a stomach transplant as the confluence of multiple meds and continuing engrafting of the new stem cells wreaked havoc on my digestive system. Unfortunately, it overlapped to some degree with visiting sisters Lisa and Betty, so we were unable to spend as much time with them as we would have liked. In spite of these gastrointestinal (GI my docs like to say)

challenges, my key blood markers have been consistently strong. I'm counting on a better week ahead.

We have fallen into a routine, with days of the week blurred by sameness. Morning breakfast and meds, work a few hours, lunch, nap, work another few hours, dinner, second meds, (often) a Netflix movie, check the Red Sox score, off to bed. Always the news junkie, I watch/read about the horrors in Somalia, the heroism in Libya, and the human rights abuses in China—and my Transplant recovery is quickly put in perspective.

A breakthrough this week—Judith and dear friend TC went for dinner and to the cinema to see THE HELP. Her first restaurant/movie outing in a month. It was healing for me to think of her temporary reprieve from caregiving. Her patience and tenderness, and meticulous management of the oppressively restrictive diet, have been extraordinary. At the same time, daughters Lena and Kate, send a steady stream of advice and encouragement, all of which boosts our spirits just when the grind of recovery starts to take its toll.

Day 30 is the next milestone, a time when tests will reveal the balance between cell production attributable to donor Abram vs. those attributable to the old-timers. We're told it will take two weeks, though, to analyze and share the results. That will bring us to approximately September 22. Please join me in an energetic cheer to encourage an A+ performance by Abram at this pivotal moment.

I again thank each of you for your love and support. Allen

DAY 30! THURSDAY, SEPTEMBER 8, 2011. Weekly clinic. Doctors quietly congratulate Al on arriving at Day 30—a significant marker. He's had challenges for sure, but NO INFECTIONS, no fever. They take blood as they always do, but today lots of it in order to test for new cell/old cell ratio. They're hoping for 80-85 percent new. Should know on September 29 (Bridgette's first birthday). The process is called "checking chimeras." Of course we had to ask Dr. A to spell that word. He throws out lots of rapid medical terms while we lean forward and try to grab whatever we can. But he willingly obliged with this one—"chimeras." I think he likes the sound of it. So do we.

Diarrhea and cramps gone. Nausea still hanging around. Al's in better spirits and has a better appetite. Twenty pounds underweight. 168 and should be

188. A friend brought him yummy chocolate croissants from Trader Joe's that are 350 calories each.

His voice is croaky and dry, though, and he has thrush. Thrush—such a pretty word compared to some of the side effects Al has endured. Not a pretty little singing bird, though, this thrush refers to white spots in mouth and on tongue. Long before Transplant, I bought him brightly colored spritzer bottles for this anticipated condition—dark blue, light green, and lavender—now placed around the house. Just bought him sugarless gum too which stimulates saliva. There is medicine to counteract thrush. He's been on the medicine for long periods before for other conditions. He has to rinse his mouth with it thoroughly and then swallow it. The taste is so revolting, he gags every time and moans. He has asked the team to come up with an alternative. Not sure there is a good one.

With Dr. A who opens our meeting by saying to Al, "You sound like you have a cold." He then turns and points at me accusingly as if to say, "If he does have a cold, it's your fault. You're not taking good enough care of him, are you?" I find the gesture very offensive amidst weeks of unrelenting caregiving. Downright obnoxious in fact. However, he was more pleasant and interactive than ever before thanks perhaps to vacationing recently in Nevada. Interesting observation in any case since Dr. A ALWAYS sounds like HE has a cold.

Al has a rash on his back and stomach—all over his trunk and also on his arm. It is not herpes, thank God. He'll have that basal cell spot on his temple surgically removed next week. Not fun, but actually a good sign since his strong platelet count is a green light to proceed with the surgery. More promising results thanks to Abram's gift.

So three issues to deal with:

1. GI stuff improving. Need option to CMX. Another anti-viral. However, Dr. I joined us and said he would like Al to try another round of CMX because there really are no good alternatives.
2. Rash—not huge, but more than last time.
3. Liver numbers are still up as they have been for a couple of weeks.

The symptoms of Graft vs. Host Disease are 1) GI problems; 2) rash; 3) high liver counts. He's had all three, but they're not willing to diagnose him with GVHD yet. Fifty-fifty chance he'll get it. If they do, what is the cure I ask, fearing another hospitalization. But, no, it's treated with a topical steroid. Slight fever today, 99.2. First time in weeks over 99.

Platelets are at 129. Good. Neutrophils are 3700. Good. Hematocrit 24. Not good. He's anemic right now. Not quite bad enough to transfuse, though.

Skype with Lena and grandkids for the first time. So wonderful to see them all. Bridgette walking all through the house—not even one year old yet. Zoey bouncy and chatty as always. Teen Nicole smiling shyly, sharing tidbits about school and *Les Miz* rehearsals.

They take us upstairs via the bouncing computer and then through every room in our apartment. We haven't been there since March—six months now and God knows when we'll return. I may go by myself, but not before Day 100 on November 17.

After we say goodbye I cry and cry, missing all of them, wishing I could participle more fully in their lives, their friendships, their activities in Florida. I had begun to build a life there, make friends, attend meetings with reading and writing groups. Now it's all on hold. Yes, I feel sorry for myself.

DAY 31. FRIDAY, SEPTEMBER 9, 2011. Al seems barely able to move. He just sits and stares or stands and stares, sometimes with his head hanging forward.

"What is it?" I ask.

"*I feel listless,*" he says.

"You mean low energy?"

"*Yes.*"

He answers as if even pushing out that one word takes too much effort. Later in the day, when he seems so despondent, I ask him what it feels like.

"*Like my body is a battleground with the cells staking out their territory and fighting.*"

He seems to get better as the day goes on. He's so thin, though. With puffy circles under his eyes, he looks eighty years old. When Kate was here, she commented on how she misses his thick, black eyelashes—the ones she inherited. They'll come back.

In an attempt to add weight, I make a frappe (Massachusetts lingo for shake with real ice cream) out of chocolate ice cream and coconut cream, but he doesn't drink much. And that's a drink he has adored since childhood.

We are planning to bake muffins or kugel and go to the waterfront. Spectacular fall day.

DAY 33. SUNDAY, SEPTEMBER 11, 2011. Tenth anniversary of 9/11. We have our own little commemoration ceremony over breakfast, reading stories about how victims' families have rebuilt their lives, sharing memories of that morning. One of the most memorable 9/11-related stories I experienced was in a documentary on the life of Kate Taylor, sister to James Taylor. Kate and another of her four brothers, Livingston, performed for a group at Ground

Zero to commemorate the fifth anniversary of the attack. This time siblings of the victims were invited. What better duo to perform for that occasion than the Kate Taylor/Livingston Taylor siblings from a family that experienced a lot of loss and grief themselves, including the death of their oldest brother. Kate's husband was also gravely ill at that time.

When they got the request to perform that very day, they were on their way home to Martha's Vineyard from Boston. Instead they detoured to NYC. As they arrived, the standing crowd was completely silent except for the calling out of the name of a mourned brother or sister. Alison Lessing. Sibyl de Santos. Jonah Jackson. The names just kept coming as the crowd remained silent. Then Kate and Livingston climbed up on a small podium above the crowd and with a breeze blowing their hair, they performed a duet version of Liv's song, "There You Are Again"—a sweet, sad song about missing someone who is no longer there. My family of six siblings lost our youngest brother at age 43. The whole scene was so powerful and poignant. I learned about that performance watching a movie about Kate's life in our local Coolidge Corner theater. Both Kate and Liv were present at the showing.

Later I bought the album with Liv performing that song. Al and I listen to it this morning:

"There you are again
Til I forget to close the door
And the heartache's in and I'm damned I'm sure
To each day miss you more
When I think I can't endure
There's a whisper in the wind
There you are again"[2]

What gifts these spectacular fall days are. We're reaching beyond Coolidge Corner now for our walks. Yesterday along the Boston Harbor Walk. Today to our old haunt around Crystal Lake in Newton Center. We park in front of the house that was ours for seventeen years. I don't miss it. But today is a reminiscing day. The current owner, a photographer, works alone in the front and side yards, still wearing the white ponytail he wore at closing fifteen years ago. He must be at least mid-sixties, but he just keeps going slowly, trimming, cutting, raking.

The peach tree and raspberry bushes we planted and enjoyed are gone. A fir tree that was little more than a seedling when I used its branches for holiday

---

[2] Taylor, Livingston. "There You Are Again," Chesky Records. January 24, 2006.

decorating once, now reaches to the second story. The legendary copper beach that is double the height of the house and reaches all the way across Beacon Street. We were told that all copper beeches were brought from England in the late seventeen hundreds and that the tree was written up after Eleanor Roosevelt stopped by to admire it. Neighbors told us it was the oldest and largest copper beach this side of the Mississippi. One friend said the double, entwined trunks remind her of Al's and my relationship. Our Kate named the tree Rodriga and wrote about it for a school assignment. Every fall I would repeatedly walk into our bedroom thinking I had left all the lights on, but the light was coming from the sun's reflecting on Rodriga's copper and golden leaves.

After we moved, a friend called to tell us that a massive branch of Rodriga's had fallen on Beacon Street blocking morning traffic. It hardly left a gap. There were still plenty of large branches left. But today we could see a very large gap on the other side—about one-fifth of the tree missing perhaps. Still produces plenty of leaves and debris for the current owners. When we told Kate later about the gap, I was afraid she would be sad, but she responded in her optimistic way, "Still not bad for a 200+-year-old tree."

We pass by the official local swimming area I bicycled to every summer. In her late twenties, a friend of ours was arrested at one of the lake's parks along with a bunch of young teens. They were swimming near a clearly marked "No swimming allowed" sign. The defiance persists. Today about a dozen swimmers enjoy themselves at that same spot, having ignored the same sign. Year-round, in every season, we walked our dog, Sheba, around the lake. Now we sort of plod along from bench to bench. The changes are a reminder that life goes on. An addition. Fresh paint. A house removed to enlarge a public park. All the kids we knew on the street have probably graduated from college by now. In fact they're probably parents.

More reminiscing on the way home.

Me: "What was the name of the lawyer who handled the house sale?"

Al: "*Bob Smart.*"

Me: "I see a train stopped just a block away from Beacon Street. What's the name of that stop?"

Al: "*Beaconsfield.*"

Me: "Al, you know everything."

Al: "*Well, I do need to bone up on my astro-physics a little bit.*"

I know he's feeling better when that delightful wit returns.

When we arrive home, we just sit in the car, neither of us ready to summon the strength to pull ourselves up from the Honda's low seats. After a few minutes we begin laughing at our lazy selves. Al calls us a couple of *"Alta Kakas."* Thinking of this journal, I ask him, "How do you spell that?" *"Oh, we yids don't worry about spelling,"* he answers.

When we arrive home, I prepare a high-calorie kugel, following the recipe in the *Jewish Home Cookbook* Sarah White gave me years ago when I became her daughter-in-law. Kugel came out golden perfect. Al gained five pounds at one sitting, or so it seems.

DAY 34. MONDAY, SEPTEMBER 12, 2011. I come home from aqua aerobics and Qi Gong classes and notice a glue trap beside the fridge.

"Did you see another mouse?" I ask.

"Yes, in my study. I called management to send an extermination service."

I have a dream about rats.

DAY 35. WEDNESDAY, SEPTEMBER 14, 2011. Weight at 173. Going up! Temp at 98.2 Good. Hematocrit 22.3. Low. Contributing to fatigue. He falls asleep all over the house. I tiptoe up to see if he's still breathing. Just as you do with a newborn. So far, yes, he's always breathing.

Katey needs to talk with Dr. A. about levels. He processes all the facts in that extraordinary medical brain of his in order to arrive at a diagnosis and, hopefully, a solution. Once Al ran into him on the street near our two homes. Instantly, as if he were reading a computer screen in front of him, Dr. A began going over Al's drugs . . . and even the dosages. "Let's see, you're on X mg. of Y drug and . . . " He continued like that through the whole list by memory. Brilliant guy!

CARING BRIDGE: THURSDAY, SEPTEMBER 15, 2011
BY JUDITH: "BALANCE"

Balance: "A harmonious arrangement or relation of parts or elements within a whole"

Is life all about balance? Balanced diet. Work/life balance. Credit/debit. I keep thinking of that metal equipment on the playground of my elementary school. In the Midwest, we called it a teeter totter. My Worcester boy calls it a seesaw. I see now that it was preparing us for adulthood. Up and down. Down and up. The thrill of being high up with legs dangling. The fear that your "friend" might leap off without warning and send you crashing down. The satisfaction of forming a perfect horizontal line with a compatible partner.

Balance: A state of equilibrium.

That is what we strive for in recovery.

- *Al is taking both immune suppressants AND immune boosters.*
- *An anti-viral drug was causing all the GI upset last week but what drug can effectively replace it?*
- *And another: shall we exercise . . . or just nap?*

That said, we've had a wonderful week beginning with doctors' muted but sincere congratulations on having reached that marker —Day 30 (September 8)—with no infections, no re-hospitalization. We expect the new cell/old cell analysis report in another week. Best scenario would be 80-85 percent of cell counts attributable to the newcomers.

As the GI problems disappeared, our guy returned with more energy, focus, productivity and that wonderful wit that sends me laughing multiple times a day. He cautiously, but joyfully rode his bike to the clinic. He gained five pounds in less than a week. Fifteen more to go.

We've taken terrific walks, moving beyond our immediate neighborhood—along the harbor and in our old haunts around Crystal Lake, Newton. Next we'll experiment with day trips, maybe to nearby Rockport and other New England gems.

This is the time when the second evil twin—rejection—lurks as a threat to continued progress. Graft vs. Host Disease. GVHD. We are going to the clinic only once or twice a week, but must be vigilant for signs in between and act quickly. We must encourage, cajole, and support Abram's cells in every way possible. Your continued good vibes will help.

Frequent skyping, texting, emailing, phone calling with our children and grandchildren, visits from friends, your clever postings and ongoing encouragement—give us a sense of normalcy and boost the healing. Send us your balance stories if you wish. We love knowing what's happening in your lives. Thank you all.

DAY 38. SATURDAY, SEPTEMBER 17, 2011. Al and I had agreed to talk twice a month—on the first and the 15th—about how we're doing. Still in bed, I point out to Allen this morning that the 15th was two days ago. We are overdue. I take charge and set the agenda: Food, Money, Sex.

FOOD. We're doing much better. Al is pleased. And he thinks his improving taste buds are helping.

MONEY. So far we've been able to manage with Al's reduced salary, some extra cash from two classes he taught (including the webinar I slept through when I was supposed to be guarding the hospital room door), and my Social

Security check. Then this: a drug he must have—Mepron—is not covered by Medicare. We have to reach into savings to pay the $511 dollars a month perhaps for a whole year. Also, I recently began dealing again with my own health challenges, including hearing loss which has been especially irritating for Al when it takes effort to project his voice. It's creating tension between us when we need tighter, clearer communication than perhaps any other time in our marriage. I need to do something about it. Hearing aids may cost $4,000 and that's with a discount from an audiologist friend. Must also come from savings. (Later—these alarm bells were premature. Mepron was needed for only one month. Only needed one hearing aid, which cost $1,800.)

SEX. More touchy subject, so to speak. His physical ups and downs, my continuing struggles with rashes, both of our energy levels taxed by the slow healing process coupled with medications. We discuss, adjust, find a middle ground with which we are comfortable, at least for now, with the expectation and hope of a return to the rich sex life we've had for decades.

SATURDAY EVENING. First visit TO someone's house. Met with Norman and Mindy on their patio. Much like taking visitors to the park. Al wears the mask and gloves. No one else needs to. As if he's been liberated from months of isolation, Al talks and talks. After almost two hours, I suggest we leave. He ignores me. I turn the conversation to Mindy and Norman's lives and to Elizabeth Warren's declaration to run for the U.S. Senate from Massachusetts. Allen suddenly gets up and heads for the back door. Mindy and Norman look at me in alarm. Our hosts both yell, "*You can pee in the grass, you know!*" but Al is gone.

Inside someone else's home for the first time in five weeks. I think Mindy and Norman are pretty concerned since, never dreaming he'd be in there, they made no effort to give the bathroom an extra scrub. They don't want to be the ones responsible for infecting him. Al exits shortly. More talking. Finally after 2-1/2 hours—by far our longest visit with anyone yet —we walk home, thankful to our dear friends for their warm welcome, patience with the lopsided conversation, and reassurance that they are available any time we need help.

DAY 41. TUESDAY, SEPTEMBER 9, 2011. Exterminator shows up. I'm not there when he arrives, so Al's the one to ask him to remove his shoes before entering the apartment and to put on the mask. He's already wearing gloves. They're not the spanking clean ones we pull unused out of the dozens of glove boxes around the house. His are plastic, light-blue ones with dark smudges that make me terribly nervous. He wears them to protect himself, not us, and who knows how many times he has worn them in how many houses, cleaning up after who knows how many rodents.

It quickly becomes apparent that our exterminator adores his profession. He even looks like and behaves somewhat like a mouse. A small, pointed nose. Darting, jumpy movements. Searching for secret crevices and openings. I first meet him when he's sitting cross-legged on the tile in front of our kitchen sink. He explains that he's patching around the pipes. His tool of choice: mouse glue traps which he rips apart and slaps against the wall.

A proud professional, he is disparaging of the former exterminator whose work is still in evidence from four years ago. "These boxes were placed quickly for the convenience of the worker, not where they could do the job effectively." But he knows his enemy and he's willing to crouch, twist, lie down, or do whatever it takes to counter it.

Al is impressed with his knowledge and thoroughness, notwithstanding the disgusting nature of the creatures he pursues. He chatters constantly—educating us. "See, they like to run along the baseboards. They don't want to be seen. And they love closets," he says, pointing gleefully to what he calls 'poop.' "Very nasty stuff. Shaped kind of like a football. Do you want to see it?" he asks holding out a blue index finger for my inspection. He appears utterly crestfallen when I decline the opportunity.

Finally, after promising to return for free any time for the next thirty days, he is gone. I grab a container of Lysol wipes and try to retrace his every step, cleaning every doorknob and cupboard handle and surface.

BUT a week later—no more mice. Just a roach caught in one of the glue traps. An improvement! Never thought a dead roach would be so welcome.

Another problem that requires an expert: the toilet in Al's bathroom has been running for months. Al finally arranged for a plumber to visit this morning. When the plumber arrives, I meet him downstairs to warn him about the routine: shoes off, hands washed, mask and gloves. I don't really get much farther than the shoes off, when he says, "Can't take off my shoes. Against insurance regulations." But he does have a suggestion: "I could put on booties." "You mean over the shoes?" "Yes." "Well, okay."

It gets worse, though. Pointing to everything he is wearing, he informs me, "I just pulled up a toilet. It was a mess. I'm covered with bacteria and feces." Good grief! Thank goodness we are still downstairs in the building's foyer. He says they have suits that cover their whole bodies, but we would need a new appointment so he could arrange that. I thank him, say goodbye and run upstairs to change my socks. Hard work keeping infection out of here while maintaining a well functioning household. Meanwhile, drip, drip.

I call the plumbing company owner and ask if they can send someone in the special suit. I also ask him not to bill us since the guy never even came upstairs. We've used the company for years. The owner is unpleasant, in fact, downright nasty. "You should have informed us that you have special needs." All I originally asked was that the guy remove his shoes. That's special needs? Plus, Transplant or no Transplant, should a plumber "covered with bacteria and feces" really be wandering from house to house? I'll use this plumber until the job is completed, but never again.

DAY 42. WEDNESDAY, SEPTEMBER 21, 2011. Clinic day and what a day! With Katey. Al's rash continues. Hanging around. Rash on back, on stomach. "Looking like GVHD," Katey says. But she, like the rest of the staff, is reluctant to say for sure. Avoiding treatment? What is there about the treatment that is so bad? That re-hospitalization possibility hangs over our thoughts like an ominous cloud. That would really bring Al down psychologically. Liver good/normal. Thank goodness. Platelets are at 82,000. They want a count of 100,000 before Al can have the basal cell on his temple removed. I love those temples, the way my lips fit perfectly in their slightly concave space. I want the basal cell GONE. Get going platelets. MULTIPLY!

We ask for the results of the chimerism test that shows the proportion of cells generated by donor v. cells generated by Al's old, defective stem cells. We are talking to Katey and Dr. I when Toni bursts in with a little yellow sticky. I read "pb-98 percent; CD3-100 percent; grans 95 percent." I don't understand the letters, but I sure like the numbers. "This is unusually high," Toni says. "There are virtually none of your own cells left!" This is roughly the equivalent of a gold medal in the battle of the new-versus-old stem cells. A stunningly successful outcome.

Then she cautions, "But they [Al's punk cells] could return. This is a marathon, not a sprint." Al is in the bathroom during all this. We greet him with the thrilling news. The room empties out. We close the door and fall weeping into each other's arms, the words, "There are virtually none of your own cells left" ringing in our ears like Christmas bells.

Because Al had to get a line removed from his arm we head across the waiting room to Melissa who has been his transfusion nurse for years. Al says she knows him so well she can read his emotions even when he's wearing a mask.

"*We have some good news,*" Al says quietly.

"Are you going to make me cry?" Melissa asks.

When she hears the words *"95 percent,"* she does cry with us and hugs us both. Al and then me.

Melissa says, "It's so sci-fi. You're a whole new man."

I say, "Do you think I'll still like him?"

She says, "Maybe you'll like him better."

No sign of GI problems. No more thrush.

On the other hand—there is always another side—he has a rash covering his whole body—everywhere except on his face and neck. They're reasonably sure that it's Graph vs. Host Disease. They're taking no chances. The disease can be serious. Our Binder defines it as "A condition whereby your transplanted stem cells (graft) view tissues in your body (host) as foreign, and attack them." He's starting on a steroid. Whites and platelets (82,000) are down somewhat, which is typical of GVHD, but his liver is normal. Kidneys too. Early intervention is the way to go. Need to watch for lesions. Fifty percent of transplant patients get GVHD.

Later Al explains to me what the CD3 cells are. Sometimes they're called killer cells because they attack infections. Those are the ones that are 100 percent new. Go, Abram baby, go!

AL TEXTS OUR KIDS:

Donor Abram is kicking ass. 95+percent of my cell production is thanks to Abram's stem cells. A major marker. My team is delighted. Onward....

The phone is ringing when we walk into the house. I pick up and am treated to a rich husky few lines of *"Amazing Grace.* How sweet it is." It's Lena putting on her best contralto voice, responding to the good news. Contralto? She sounds like a full gospel choir.

What else is happening in kids' lives? From Doug today: "Hey folks!!! Had an amazing night tonight! Had the read-through [my screenplay] with the cast. It was awe inspiring and magical. First time experiencing something like this, and not the last. Just the beginning. It was totally professional, everybody loves the final draft, everyone was in character and bringing their game as actors, and the cast is really stunning. I have assembled an amazing cast and crew for this project! Wait 'til you see the film!!!!! I can't wait to start filming. Begins in less than three weeks. Stay tuned. I have rehearsals with everyone next week and honestly, this film is going to be stunning and leave audiences gasping for breath. The finale we have created is truly brilliant and shocking. The film is at once hilarious and shocking and thought provoking. It is now called "THE CAMERA NEVER LIES." It is a dark comedy/thriller and will be made for the budget of $4,500. Stay tuned . . . Me"

AL RESPONDS TO DOUG:

Excellent. I'm thrilled the read-through went so well. What a joy it must be to see your work come to life. I had my own good news this morning. Tests show that my donor Abram's stem cells are now producing 95+ percent of the cells in my body—an Oscar-level performance. Even 80 percent is considered strong, so this was above and beyond. You and I—kicking butt in our own ways:) Dad

Eight visitors this week. We feel blessed with all this attention. The companionship not only makes us feel cared for, it gives us a chance to focus on the lives of others.

CARING BRIDGE: THURSDAY, SEPTEMBER 22, 2011
BY ALLEN: "CHIMERA, ABRAM, AND ME"

Chimera: (1) (a) a fire-breathing she-monster in Greek mythology having a lion's head, a goat's body, and a serpent's tail; (b) an imaginary monster compounded of incongruous parts; (2) an individual, organ, or part consisting of tissues of diverse genetic constitution; (3) a test to determine the status of engrafting of donor stem cells after transplant.

The Day 30 "chimera test" results are in. By all indications, donor Abram has the same fire as the mythological she-monster. At this milestone, another intensely emotional moment for us second only to the moment of Transplant. It is clear that Abram has been busy kicking butt. 95+ percent of my cell production is attributable to the new stem cells. 80-85 percent is the norm for defining success. We are blessed. "Your results are as good as it gets," said Nurse Toni. "Its Sci-Fi," said Nurse Melissa, awestruck even after dealing with hundreds of Transplant patients. Daughter Lena, upon hearing news, broke into a throaty 'Amazing Grace' on the phone from Florida.

It's now Day 44 and our hope for steady progress continues. At these times, we must remind ourselves that recovery from Transplant is, as my team regularly reminds us, "a marathon, not a sprint." Even with the recent good news, symptoms of GVHD have appeared in the form of skin discoloration—an unpleasant but common occurrence as the recipient's body slowly adjusts to the arrival of new cells. And the severe restrictions on human contact, travel, and diet remain unchanged until at least Day 100 in mid November.

So we must dig deep, cheer Abram onward, and muster the patience required to reach the 100 day marker and beyond. We found some relief from our grandchild deprivation with a recent Skype call to Jacksonville. Our three beautiful granddaughters Nicole, Zoey, and Bridgette + Lena and Larry + two dogs + two cats paraded across the jittery screen during a joyful, chaotic visit. Kate and Doug are in close touch sharing our triumphs and challenges from the West Coast—as are you from around the world.

Hoping all is well with each and every one of you who belong to this extraordinary community. Do keep in touch. Love to all, Allen

---

DAY 48. TUESDAY, SEPTEMBER 27, 2011. Plumber returns today—the one we prefer this time, Erik. All prepared to suit up. Downstairs in the vestibule, he steps into a thick, white one-piece plastic suit that covers his whole body, including booties that cover his shoes and a hood that cover his whole head. He looks as if he's prepared to take off into space. Two jobs are over quickly, but he does have to go to his truck once, which means removing the suit and putting it back on again. He is totally good natured about the dress/undress/redress.

I enjoy breakfast with our decades-long friend, Roberto today. When I tell him about this journal to which I've given the working title of "Stem Cells–a Romance," he promises to read it when it's published. He wants to know about sex, he says, and about how our routines and lives are changed by what we're going through. I'll address the latter.

HOW OUR MUNDANE DAILY ROUTINES CHANGE:

GROCERY SHOPPING. As if Al's appetite isn't enormous under the most normal of times, now I have to "feed the steroid" too. Until now we've had a smooth weekly system at Trader Joe's. We arrive together, head for different sides of the store, meet in the middle for a quick check to avoid duplicates, and head for check-out. Efficient. Quick. A metaphor for our partnership.

No more. Kate set up Peapod, a home delivery grocery service. I use it for months. Wonderful. I live for the delivery. I watch from our second-floor condo as the driver consults our list, lifts items out of the cooler, grabs others and arrives at our doorstep sometimes with our entire week's order dangling from plastic bags held in both hands. He can hold five full bags in each hand. Extra cost per week: about $20 for delivery and tip. Worth every penny. Only challenge: I'm not very versant in sizes and weights. I need to be buying small quantities, but I bought a giant bag of potato chips and tub butter and yogurt in containers twice the size I buy normal times.

TRASH AND RECYCLING. Was always Al's job. Out the back door of our condo. Down two flights of steep, winding stairs carrying heavy bags. Through the basement. Prop open the back door. Open bins and receptacles. Throw in.

Reverse. Now? Al cannot be near trash for many months. This has now shifted into my column—with the ever-present need to use the green hand disinfectant afterwards.

LAUNDRY. Except for my delicates, which I wash separately, Al has always washed and dried. I fold and put away. Now he cannot come in contact with dirty clothes. So we've reversed roles: now I wash and dry. He folds.

ORGANIZING VISITS. We can have one or two people at a time, only healthy close friends at first. They just call and show up. Lots of them. Wonderful visits in the park. Blessed with gorgeous crisp fall weather.

CARING BRIDGE UPDATES. We both post when we feel there is something to share.

RIDES TO CLINIC. I accompany Al for the first few months. Daily for two weeks. Twice a week for a long time.

EXERCISE. For Al. Must give up beloved bicycle for a while. We take walks. He uses the elliptical that Kate and Lena purchased for us. When scheduling of medical appointments allows, I can continue my water and Qi Gong exercises where I also absorb much needed support from both my instructors and fellow exercisers.

CAREGIVER SHOULD I NEED TO BE AWAY. Never materialized.

BACTERIA BATTLE. Hand-sanitizer in every room.

DAY 49. WEDNESDAY, SEPTEMBER 28, 2011. Al emails to three kids and two of their spouses:

> *Kids: I want to share with you my pride and delight in connection with the stream of professional accomplishments you have brought to my attention. I also want each of you to know about the others' activities to fully appreciate the breadth of talent represented in our little family . . . .*

> *Kate—for being honored at two upcoming events: by the San Francisco Business Times "Women of Influence" Luncheon, for contribution to wise urban land development in her role as ED of the Urban Institute/Northern CA; and as Co-founder of SF City Car Share at its Tenth Birthday Celebration.*

> *Maureen—for successful launch of Futtner and Associates PR/communications company in service to small business and non-profits in the Bay Area . . . "PR for the People."*

> *Lena—for high praise and vote of confidence by National Health Care Review in connection with a new project assignment in Jacksonville.*

> *Larry—for a promotion and raise, and an A-Class presentation to the CEO and other colleagues of his firm, Biomet.*

> *Doug—for his boldness and determination in taking initial steps as Ex-*

ecutive Producer of a full-length film, tentatively titled "The Camera Never Lies."

Kudos and love to all of you, Dad

178.5 pounds. Half-way to desired twenty-lb. post-T weight gain. Normal weight: 190. Labs good. Rash gone. No GI problems. No return of Herpes. 80 mg of Prednisone working, although giving him insomnia and making him hyperactive. Nice thing about his not sleeping is I wake up in the morning to find the clean clothes all folded and the dishwasher emptied out. One evening I went to bed after he had spent an hour and a half trying to open the battery compartment on the elliptical. He had eleven different "tools" laid out and showed no sign of stopping the attempt—twisting, pushing, grinding away at the screws. With the batteries still hidden and elusive, I went to bed.

I ask Katey about possible November trips for me to D.C. for a board meeting in early November and to Florida for Thanksgiving. Katey is not encouraging. "Can't tell what state he'll be in. Wait until 100-day mark. If we give the okay at that point, buy flight insurance."

OCTOBER 2011

DAY 55. MONDAY, OCTOBER 3, 2011. Last Friday, my darling had another little operation. Removal of a basal cell. It was barely visible on his temple. He had one removed before on his nose, so he knew the routine. We got up at 6:00 for the 8:00 appointment. At Faulkner Hospital. Local anesthetic. They cut off the offending skin, then we waited for thirty minutes while they analyzed it. They kept cutting and examining until they could see that there was only healthy tissue left. During the four-hour ordeal, I parked myself in the waiting room and stretched out in the large, comfy chairs with leg rests. Got lots of reading done at least.

Al joined me twice while waiting for the results. Finally I went into the operating room. I was upset to see the incision—first horizontal from very near the outside of his left eye then vertical all the way down to his ear. Neat stitches, but there must have been fifteen-twenty of them.

Today he awoke with puffiness and redness around that left eye. Not too bad. He told me that during the operation he could smell the cauterization of the skin—just before they put in the stitches. What a beating his skin has taken—the struggle with herpes virus, then the rash from GVHD, and now this.

However, still on steroids, Al is high energy, sleeping less than six hours a night, getting up often, and barely taking naps. On the other hand, by Sunday, having awakened very early four mornings in a row, I was exhausted and determined to sleep late. I did and was able to rally.

We have another of our monthly chats—with me initiating as always. Al is thrilled with the way the meals have evolved. Trying to use as little pre-prepared foods as possible and still follow the protocol. He is very non-confrontational and mentioned softly that we had had a couple of spats. One was after a delicious fish dinner I prepared. The Binder forbids the use of our wooden cutting board. We have three thin plastic cutting boards. We try to use only one of those per meal and put each one in the dishwasher immediately after use. But if I'm fixing dinner and want to serve a hot meal, I don't always get to clean up right away. I found that Al was using the dirty cutting board on which I had cut raw fish and vegetables before cooking them. I was alarmed and asked him to please take some responsibility for changing cutting boards. To Al, that was a "spat."

The second spat occurred when I returned from the gym on Saturday and found a note on the kitchen counter: "half-n-half for tomorrow." It feels so inhospitable to both of us to not offer our guests anything to drink or eat. Pam and Paul were returning for the second time the following day. We enjoy them both so much and are grateful for their taking the time to keep us company. We are blessed with many guests and, increasingly, Al's colleagues are coming to the house too. It's Day 55 and it's getting too cold and rainy to meet friends in the park. We state clearly in our "Visits with Allen" information sheet which we pre-send visitors that inside we don't serve food or drink.

Too much work and too much risk of infection and too difficult for them while wearing masks. It also keeps the visits down to a manageable length. Last week we had eight visitors. So spat #2: I was not happy when I saw that "half-n-half" note which seemed to indicate that I should buy cream and serve coffee tomorrow—along with the rustic strawberry tart from Clear Flour Bakery we already bought, but which Al can't eat since it's from a bakery. I was irritated. "We are not serving coffee," I said. "Too much work. Too much exposure. Impossible to sip wearing masks. We are continuing to follow the protocol. I need to put my energy into serving you healthy foods. I can't be worrying about serving guests yet."

We're both disappointed. We've always loved having company and serving brunches and dinners, but I need to set limits—both to protect Al's health and to protect my time and energy. So we agreed to keep the tart frozen and give it as a gift to someone, and nix the coffee.

However, we decided to venture into a daring attempt to keep our guests at least a little hydrated. We told the Raskins they were part of that experiment—our first guests to be offered lemonade with a straw. Al prepared an ice bucket and I added a lemon to each plastic cup. Our good-sport friends were able to stick the straw up under the mask and sip. More challenging and irritating than you might think.

Since I am able to return to facing my own health challenges, I made an appointment with an audiologist friend, Judy C. Today I got a hearing aid on trial. Below is the poem I wrote shortly afterwards. When I sent it to Judy, who has been in this business for about fifty years, she said it made her cry. She shared it with an award-winning poet friend of hers and hung a framed version of it on her office wall.

I HEAR MY OWN WHISPERS

When I left the office
        with the device,
        I was like a child again—
        the way they always look
up when a plane flies overhead.
No plane, but a flock of birds
        in a low tree.
        It felt like they were welcoming me
        but maybe my presence alarmed them
or they were just discussing dinner.
In any case they produced chatter
        and clatter I hadn't remembered.

My steps on the pavement sounded like
those NPR interviews taking you on
        an aural tour of a long-dead author.
        "And NOW we're approaching his study."
        followed by only step . . . step . . . step.
        Tension and curiosity build as the steps stop,
        the doorknob turns and the door creaks open.

Arriving home I had to turn down the radio.
Preparing rice, I was amazed at the

sound of water boiling. Who knew?

Why is Al making such an effort to speak loudly?
    He's not, he said. That's his normal speaking voice.
    He's stronger than I thought.

And do I always whisper to myself?
    I could hear my voice coming back to me.
    How long have I been sharing revealing thoughts
    out loud and to whom?

Maybe now the next time I see her, Nicole
    will come through more clearly
    when she chooses
    to give me a peek
    into her adolescent world.

And maybe now
    I'll be able to decipher those
    breathy, excited phrases spoken
    in my ear when Kindergartner Zoey
    shares a quick, confidential thought
    before she darts away.

DAY 57. WEDNESDAY, OCTOBER 5, 2011. I began "writing" the above poem in my head in bed during the night. When we arrive at Dana Farber early the next morning, I head for the computers provided for patient and family use. While I'm transferring the poem from my mind to computer file, I receive an email addressed to Al with cc to me: "Excellent letter in the *Boston Globe* today." I have the Globe with me, grab it, abandon my poem for a moment and take the paper to Al.

Sitting in the waiting area of the clinic is always a downer.

Even though the Yawkey Center has been open less than a year and is spanking new space full of windows that open to sun and sky, one cannot escape the masked people, most in far worse shape than my sweetheart. Some barely walking. Some in wheelchairs. Some who cannot hold up their heads. Others who are being fed by their caretakers. Bright, hopeful scarves and new caps cover scalps and we all know why: thanks to chemotherapy, there is not a single hair left on their heads. One sees adults of all ages and youth too, but fortunately not children. They are cared for elsewhere.

So I know that seeing his letter in print—and the lead letter too, among five addressing the same topic—will give him a needed pickup. Indeed, he is pleased. Here it is:

OCTOBER 5, 2011. LETTERS TO THE EDITOR (THE BOSTON GLOBE)
ELIZABETH WARREN'S IRE

Her tone may be provocative, but social-contract pitch is a nod to civility.

JEFF JACOBY ("Entrepreneurs don't deserve the professor's ire, » Op-ed, Sept. 28) sees ire toward business and undue exalting of the public sector in Elizabeth Warren's remarks on the social contract. I hear passion, fairness, and profound belief in indispensability of the pubic goods only government can and must produce.

During the last two decades, I have interacted with hundreds of socially responsible business leaders from large and small companies. The vast majority would have no objection to Warren's core message: Companies need the stability, services, and infrastructure that government provides every day; government needs a healthy private sector as the primary engine of job and wealth creation; and a social contract needs partnership and mutual respect from both, along with an informed and active citizenry to serve as the ultimate arbiter of whether each side is upholding its end of the bargain.

Warren's tone may be provocative to some. But her injection of the centuries-old concept of the social contract to reframe the current debates over the relationship between government and business brings much-needed civility to the vitriolic language that is contaminating current political discourse.

ALLEN L. WHITE, Boston

The writer is a Fellow at Boston's Tellus Institute

CLINIC VISIT. Al has worn glasses since he was eighteen months old. He was cross-eyed until he had an operation at age ten. His glasses are the first thing he reaches for when he gets out of bed each morning. He travels with an extra pair. So when after an examination, the doctor pronounced, "No eye impairment," I felt more alarmed than relieved. I hadn't known —or had I suppressed the fear—that eye function might have been affected by . . . what? The new stem cells? The drugs?

Al asks, *"How about my I.Q.? Has that been impaired yet?"*

"Your CBC (Complete Blood Counts—a collection of markers) is ridiculous . . . and I mean that in a good way."

Prednisone: Still experiencing insomnia from that darn, but necessary steroid.

"*Can I lower the dose?*" Al asks.

"No," comes the swift answer. "Can't move that quickly."

Chimera test. It was the positive results of that test that we celebrated on Day 30 by falling sobbing into each other's arms in the doctor's office after all the personnel had exited and we were alone. The same test will be administered on Day 90 or Day 100, at six months, nine months, and twelve months. High chimerism is good, but sometimes disease remains. CLL is slow-moving. It's a tortoise-and-hare situation. Abram has time to look at a CLL cell and think "You're a mutant. You don't belong here. You're history. Zap." Al will also have regular CAT scans to examine the condition of lymph nodes.

CARING BRIDGE: WEDNESDAY, OCTOBER 5, 2011
BY JUDITH: "A BLACK EYE YET LOOKING GREAT"

A black eye isn't really black, is it? I've never seen one up close . . . until now. I think Al has one. It's deep pink above the slightly drooping lid. Puffy underneath. It does not interfere with his vision he says, and adds, "I still have the same I.Q." No, I did not sock my beloved. It's the result of a skin removal operation last Friday. Removing a small cancerous growth resulted in a trail of stitches that begins horizontally just at his outer eye and turns vertical ending halfway down his cheek to the middle of his ear. Results are a kind of an Al Capone look, as in Ken Burns' recent series on Prohibition.

Nurse Judy has been called back into duty to perform home-care skills to dress the wound. Writer turned medic each morning. I'm not very good at it, but Al is patient with my impatience and we get the job done, leaving a bulky patch and gobs of tape. It still flops a little under his glasses. During our walks, the children stare more than ever. They've been asking, "Mommy, why is that man wearing that mask?" Now with the patch added, they may wonder if he's trying out his Halloween costume. He sometimes flips his mask up for a moment to say: "See, I have a real face." Amidst all the costuming, his good looks shine through.

Sometimes the real nurses, much as we admire them, give instructions that sound as if they've been carved on stone tablets—Moses like. Al, not being much of a believer, frequently challenges these commandments. After the skin op, the nurse told us he could not exercise for two weeks. Al was despondent. He's getting stronger in part because of his biking and daily elliptical regimen. He even played hoops by himself last week on a neighborhood court.

Two weeks without exercise would set him back, he felt, physically and emo-
tionally. He called the surgeon to double check. She responded ten minutes
later on a Saturday. "No exercise for only three days." A big difference. Mood
lifted. Muscles back in action.

More good news: stitches come out tomorrow after only a week. Also:
when he goes into remission—our hope and prayer, of course—there should
be fewer such episodes thanks to Abram's stem cells building a new and better
immune system with plenty of "killer T-cells" to assault any dysfunctional
ones that appear.

Honestly though, even with the above, Al looks SO GOOD. And I don't
think this is just a love-is-blind thing. He's gaining weight. He's energetic. He's
re-engaging with the writing, organizing, and advocacy work he loves. He has
more color than he's had in the last five years. Sometimes he looks downright
ruddy.

Thank you for letting us share all of this—it means so much to both of us.
Love, Judith

DAY 61. SUNDAY, OCTOBER 9, 2011. Since the Transplant, Allen's emotions are so near the surface—just behind his eyes at all times, ready to spill
over. The first time I saw him cry, we had been dating just a few months. We
were struggling to talk tentatively about our feelings for one another—a new
experience for him. Suddenly we both felt overwhelmed. We held each other
and just cried. At that moment I understood how appropriate the "falling" in
"falling in love" is. *Ask.com* gives these definitions of "fall":

1. to drop;
2. to decline;
3. to lose position;
4. to be overthrown;
5. to pass into a specified condition;
6. to die in combat.

In other words, to lose control, possibly even lose your life. No wonder
we cried. We were terrified. Many years later when he received word that his
father had died after a struggle with lung cancer, Al broke down totally and
sobbed. "I just want to kiss his face," he kept saying.

During these past months, dealing with a stem cell Transplant: the decision, the preparation, the fear; having faced his own mortality; missing travel
and children yet experiencing profound gratitude every day for a multitude

of blessings, Al has never cried so much. He cried when we got the news that Abram's stem cells had arrived at the clinic and during the 45 minutes while we waited for them to be inspected and approved before they were delivered to his hospital room. He cried at a meeting with our wonderful chaplain, Richard, also attended by Kate, both trying to help him make the decision whether to cancel an important meeting—and possibly his last engagement before Transplant—in Washington, D.C. He made the trip and his family held its collective breath. He cried when we got the positive news from the chimera testing.

Now, 61 days after transplant, he cries nearly every day. I find him bent over the newspaper reacting to an article. I walk into the TV room and there he is with his head hanging, box of Kleenex in front of him, having seen an upsetting news report. A researcher who dedicated his life to studying stem cells dies. Steve Jobs dies. The baby of our nephew and his wife is a month away from being born when its heart stops. Upon learning that upsetting news, we both sob. Al's emotions have become emotionally taut by the whole transplant odyssey and sharpened by the daily dose of steroids.

Since Chaplain Richard is so busy with new job and family, we are pretty brokenhearted that we don't see him anymore. Two books of poems he gave Al wait on the entrance bureau ready to be returned. But a meeting with Roberto in the park offered Al the kind of male-with-male sharing that is rare for most men, I think, and certainly for Al. I am so grateful for that.

AL SENDS ME A TEXT MESSAGE:

Sitting on a dock by the Charles River. Napped. Snacked. New York Times blew into the water. Life is good. Home at 3:30.

After eating three slices of French toast, two blueberry blintzes, and about six potato blintzes—all of which he fixed—Al had ridden his bike down Memorial Drive, past MIT, across the River on Longfellow Bridge, turned west along the Esplanade until he came to the Arthur Fielder statue, and then approached the dock where he spotted one remaining Adirondack chair, waiting just for him. Wearing his mask and gloves as he always does when he's outside, he slept while the water lapped against the dock and the first section of the Times flew away. He rode home, happy, grateful for another beautiful fall day.

While Al is biking, I am lunching at Panera with Andy E whose husband, Paul, has lymphoma. Paul is back in the hospital for the second time as his medical teams try to raise his depleted white cells and platelets to a level where it is safe for him to have a Stem Cell Transplant. Paul is a soft-spoken, handsome, sweet and quietly brilliant MD who has dedicated years to educating the public and government officials about the health effects of climate change.

His cancer journey often brings him to the clinic at the same as Al. They share anxieties and family stories. Andy always greets friends with a huge burst of affection, calling us "*Sweetheart.*" She hugs me and we hold hands as we walk the half block to the restaurant. Paul's cancer is more aggressive than Al's and, because of complications with an ulcer in his esophagus, he's not eating. Andy says, "It's so hard to plan." And "I'm frustrated, impatient and frightened." How well I understand. How sad and scared I am for them both.

DAY 62. WEDNESDAY, OCTOBER 12, 2011. Clinic with Katey, "You are the Norma Ray of Brookline." By that comparison, she means Al is full throttle, high energy, zealous, and triumphant. Down to 60 mg of Prednisone from 80. Taking several twenty-thirty minute naps per day. He shares his emotional pinnacle this week: shooting hoops. Yet his body always seems on guard. Can feel exhausted mentally and physically. Steroids still keeping him up at night. Katey reassures: "All this is normal, Allen."

Down to 170 lbs. Liver function mixed bag. Bilirubin up a little. Pink rash on back and belly. Not absorbing enough protein. Skin dry.

CARING BRIDGE: FRIDAY, OCTOBER 14, 2011
BY ALLEN: "WEEP, EAT, SLEEP"

WEEP. It was the third visit to my local basketball court for light exercise. During the first two, the ball and hoop just couldn't get along. This time was different. Shot after shot found its way through the net. Then something happened that I'd never experienced in fifty+ years of playing the game: I began weeping in the middle of the court—uncontrollably, profusely, mask and all. I stopped. I embraced my torso where I most easily connect with the new stem cells. I savored the moment. Donor Abram and I were making shots.

I've been doing a lot of weeping lately, triggered by circumstances that would never have resulted in quite such emotion pre-Transplant: news of a family success or loss; watching a French movie on the Algerian liberation movement; discussing spirituality with a visiting friend. Describing the situation to my nurse practitioner, she said: "We see that among Transplant patients, in part owing to steroid treatment which tends to raise one's emotional pitch and keep it elevated, contrary to the usual peaks and troughs of everyday life." OK. But surely the immense sense of blessing and wonder that fills my days is the raw material that unleashes the steroid effect. So I just let it flow, knowing it's part of the recovery process that continues apace.

EAT. Day 66. I'm in a phase where "Is it time to eat?" is no longer the ques-

*tion; now it's always time to eat. I eat every hour, sometimes more. It's part-
ly those steroids and partly the process of rebounding from a twenty-pound
weight loss. Thanks to Judith's wizardry, the grind of a bland diet of packaged
and processed food has morphed into a burst of culinary creativity that keeps
my bottomless appetite satisfied, all within the strict dietary restrictions that
remain unchanged. Roasted chicken and vegetables, salmon in cream sauce,
turkey burger loaded with multiple dressings. All cooked to the point where
any lurking bacteria have no chance of survival. It's no longer just the "safe"
diet my medical team demands; it's safe, healthy, and delectable. Another
indication of our journey back to normalcy.*

*SLEEP. I'm writing this message at 4:30 a.m. Yup—blame the steroid
effect, in part. But add a mind racing with ideas about how to change the
world, imagining where we will travel when I'm able, and anticipating visits
by family, friends, and colleagues the following week. So, for now, it's five
hours/night of sleep and barely any fatigue during the day as I continue to
work more than half time—at home, of course. The days fly by. The concept of
time has new meaning. So much to do in life, so little time to do it—surely the
perspective of most who, like me, have faced the grim prospect of a curtailed
future and have returned to hopefulness in the warm embrace of people like
you.*

Weep, eat, sleep—l'chaim! Allen

DAY 68. SUNDAY, OCTOBER 16, 2011. Al wide awake, of course, still on
the steroid high. I would have enjoyed lounging in bed, looking out on the
trees that remain steadfastly green resisting autumn even as the breezes intensify and their leaves drop. But how could anyone resist his stories and enthusi-
asms, accompanied by tears? He's thrilling right now to a new post from Kate
on *Caring Bridge*—that community builder of candor and confessions—and
looking forward to talking to Zoey about making three out of the six goals that
won her team's Saturday soccer match—and the kid is only five!

DAY 69. MONDAY, OCTOBER 17, 2011. Clinic visit. Request to doc: Can
Al fly to D.C. to speak on November 9th or 10th? That's one week before Day
100." Answer, "No."

Has some throat rawness. Weight still low. 174 pounds. He's eating and
eating. It's hard to keep enough food in the house, prepared. He's begun baking. Sister-in-law Molly's recipe for Magic Cookie Bars. Sister Betty's recipe
for chocolate-chip cookies with a pound of butter. Trader Joe's terrific brownie

truffle mix. After the first delicious batch—just the right balance of cakey and gooey, rich chocolate flavor, I read about a recent blind brownie taste contest. One hundred mixes. Trader Joe's brownie truffle mix was the clear winner.

Energy still artificially high-pitched. There will be a dip when he comes off Prednisone. At that time, he may experience a slump that could last two weeks or so. Right now the weeping seems extreme.

DAY 77. TUESDAY, OCTOBER 25, 2011. OVERDOSE. Usually now, 2-1/2 months after Transplant, clinic visits are on Wednesdays and they're getting shorter: blood taken upon arrival; meet with P.A. or surgeon to discuss blood report and make necessary drug adjustments; quick look at the chest and back to determine how rash is doing (still there and may be an indication of GVHD, but not getting any worse).

Yesterday, however, was a Monday and involved a long day with extra tests. In addition to the usual above, Al also needed to have a cat scan in the morning and a bone marrow biopsy in the afternoon. I wanted to attend my once-a-week medical Qi Gong class in the morning, so Al said he would come home for lunch and then we could return to the clinic together.

When I got a message from him saying he wasn't coming home after all at midday and I should meet him on the eighth floor to attend the appointment with the surgeon at 1:00, I took a taxi to the clinic. I arrived on the eighth floor first. Al was still on the sixth. When he showed up, he had just been administered morphine for the biopsy and was starting to get drowsy.

I usually accompany Al to everything, but he does not like me to be there for the biopsy. It's so intrusive. He has to lie down, trousers lowered, while the nurse goes through his hip, boring through flesh and muscle and into the bone to extract marrow. He's had the procedure dozens of times over the past ten years or so. It used to be extremely painful. Now the discomfort is substantially reduced. They administer morphine to relax him, then apply a slender (but noisy) drill. He barely feels it. But he does feel the after-effects of the morphine—usually for an hour or two. So I always drive afterwards. For some reason, today they give him a double dose.

When we go in for the appointment with the surgeon, I explain to Dr. A that the morphine has taken effect, but that I, on the other hand, am wide awake and will take notes as usual. My new hearing aid helps enormously in these situations since both Dr. A and Dr. I are soft-spoken—Dr. I because he's a gentle, understated person and Dr. A, I suspect, because speaking softly and in medical jargon seems to be a way to assert power.

Katey had told us that Dr. A was turning forty this week. I put together a card and leave it on his desk for him to find before the "official" appointment begins. "Pour notre cher chirugien." It's a beautiful photograph of Boston's Public Garden. Inside that card, I tuck a postcard of Isle St. Luis in Paris. I write: "Two cities. Two homelands. We're glad you're on our side of the pond. Bonne anniversaire. Judith and Allen." And we really ARE glad he's in Boston because, notwithstanding his sometimes off-putting manner and our limited success to engage him with humor, he's absolutely brilliant at what he does and Al is thriving under his care.

Dr. A is somewhat touched and seems more relaxed than usual. During these check-ins, he never stops typing and only occasionally turns to make eye contact. Rapid click, click, click that goes on for twenty minutes. Afterwards, I ask Al, "What do you think he's writing all the time?" Al says he's probably writing, *"Here's that wise-ass patient again."* "And his intrusive, irritating wife," I add. Al said he probably adds a P.S. to every report of our visits: *"I sure hope this Transplant works because I don't want to have to go through another one with these people."* Clackety, clack, clack.

Dr. A says he wants Al to have a flu shot. The team had put that off, waiting to see how he was doing. Dr. A says he thinks we need to go up to the tenth floor for the shot. The moment we leave the doctor's office and begin moving through the waiting area, Al collapses in a chair and falls sound asleep. It's the morphine. I determine that we can get the shot on the eighth floor where we are, but that it would take between thirty and sixty minutes to prepare. A staff member suggests he get the shot at his regular appointment on Wednesday, but I explain that we aren't coming on Wednesday this week because everything that is usually planned for Wednesdays had already been accomplished today.

Furthermore, I am determined to wait it out today because in the next ten days, we are expecting company from California, Ohio, and Maine. That means that before our next appointment, Al could be exposed to germs from the West, Midwest, and Northeast. Dr. A brushes by with his long strides and goes down to the lobby exit in the elevator. It's 5:00 p.m. The clinic is empty-ing out. But Al can sleep there as well as at home and I have reading material. I prop his long legs on a chair and pull over another chair for my own legs and settle in for the long haul. I can see a low sun through those big Yawkey windows. Looking for a little escapism, I open the entertainment section of the *Boston Globe*. There on the first page are three related photos with these captions:

"Top: The tables at Firebrand Saints are made out of recycled truck hoods. Above left: Erin Dunham and Bob McCloskey enjoy drinks at the bar. Above right: a *mojito.*" The up-close stemmed glass and sweet liquid fill the entire frame. Although this activity was taking place just across the river in Cambridge, to me it was so far from what I was experiencing at that moment, it might as well have been on Mars.

After a few minutes a nurse appears and tries to shake Al's shoulders. No reaction whatsoever. I explain that he's sleeping off morphine. She says she needs to know if he is allergic to eggs. No, he's not, I tell her. More sleeping/reading/waiting. Another nurse—a diminutive one—comes to get him and leads him to the office for the shot. I feel I should probably accompany them, but I would have to gather up my large purse (packed for the long day), his extremely heavy briefcase with his computer inside, our jackets, etc. I know the shot won't take long, so I watch him sway away with the little nurse supporting him. They disappear.

Pretty soon he's back, slowly placing one foot in front of the other zombie-like and accompanied by his usual nurse—loving, attentive, and authoritative Melissa. "I'm getting him a wheelchair," she says. She sits him down in the thing and he immediately falls back to sleep. Unfortunately, Al and I have had a mix-up. When he said he was going to pick me up at home at midday, I assumed he meant in the car, but no, he had ridden his bike to the clinic that morning. The car is still parked at home. The bike is chained somewhere in front of the clinic and obviously he is in no shape to ride it home. Although the walk home is only twenty-five minutes, we could never have handled the bike on foot either. That means I have to get a taxi at rush hour.

Melissa takes Al down in the elevator and parks him, sound asleep, near the clinic exit. I call for a taxi at the front desk. The dispatcher says, "It will be a few minutes," in a tone that makes me think he means possibly hours, not minutes. When a taxi pulls up in front, I rouse Al, grab all our stuff and open the back door of the taxi. "Going to the airport?" the driver asks. "Wilkerson?" Whoops, not our taxi.

I sit Al down on a wooden bench outside with his briefcase and computer beside him, and walk half a block to a busy street to try my luck at hailing a cab. Every minute or so I turn around to look to make sure he hasn't fallen over or that the briefcase hasn't been stolen. That scene remains unchanged, thank goodness. However, no luck with hailing. Al's Texas sister calls. She's in Brookline for a high school reunion. Boy, could I use some help right now. But she sounds giddy. I can tell she's been partying. I'm on my own.

I am trying to call a taxi on my cell when a taxi pulls up at the Yawkey entrance. I ask no questions. I just open the door and say, "*I need to get a patient to Brookline.*" The driver looks over dubiously at Al asleep on the bench and asks, "*Is that the patient?*"

Once again, I grab our stuff and hold onto Al while he sleepwalks. I tuck him into the back seat. Ten minutes later I pay the taxi and rouse Al again. Believing that his muscles, even when he's only half conscious, are a lot stronger than mine at full alert, I stick the handle of his weighty briefcase in his hand and we climb out of the taxi. I then sort of push him up the stairs ahead of me to our second-floor condo. I look way up at my almost 6'3", 172-pound guy ploddingly placing one large foot after another on those stairs, and hope he doesn't fall backwards on top of me. I fear two crushed skulls and mangled bodies sprawled at the bottom of the staircase. Even that probably would not awaken him. I also hope he doesn't drop and bounce the briefcase that contains his computer—his entire work life. Now THAT just might wake him up.

Once safely in the condo, I lead him to his study and sit him in his favorite chair—again with his feet raised. When he was twenty-two and in the Peace Corps right after we were married, we would spontaneously visit other PC couples in other parts of Nicaragua and they us—no phones. Friends would look up and see us coming and panic. What am I going to feed Al White? He had a reputation—deserved—for being ravenous at all times and it wasn't always easy to get one's hands on a meal spontaneously. No supermarkets in the campo. No car. Not a lot of variety at the little outdoor markets with unpredictable hours.

Since he's been on steroids for the past month, he's back to his twenty-two-year-old appetite, eating three large meals a day plus constant snacking. He bakes himself brownies and cookies and apple bread. I keep a supply of cheeses and deviled eggs for easy grabbing. After a day at the clinic, I know he will wake up starving. It is now 6:30 p.m. But while I cook I keep checking on him trying to be certain in the dark that he is still breathing. I worry about the interaction of all the drugs he takes daily combined with today's morphine and flu shot. Fortunately, his study is near the kitchen so I can go back and forth easily. Another 2-1/2 hours pass. I wake him up. I feed him.

The next day he's back to sleeping five hours a night and working six or seven hours a day. Because of the puncture from the biopsy, he can't bathe or shower for twenty-four hours. When he does finally shower on Wednesday morning, he discovers a little round Band-Aid on his upper arm. "*What's this from?*" he asks me. He has no memory of getting the flu shot. No memory of arriving home either. Just as well.

We have a small neighborhood dry cleaner run by an appealing couple from Colombia. She is lovely. He is straight-faced, but extremely witty. We always speak Spanish with them. He and Al have very funny exchanges and they are both fond of Al. When Al was working from his Boston office, he would go to that dry cleaner at least twice a month. They call Al *el rey* and me *la reina*. The king and queen. If I go myself, they always inquire about him, "*¿Dónde está el rey? ¿Qué hace?*" When they learned three months ago that the reason he wasn't coming was because he was recovering from an operation, they were very concerned. Now, without the need for clean, boxed dress shirts, we haven't been seeing them very often.

Yesterday Al took a load of clothes and stood, masked and gloved, of course, just outside their door. When they saw him, he motioned for them to come out and pick up the clothes. They were so glad to see him and rushed out, counted out the items while he waited on the sidewalk, and returned to him with the pink pick-up slip. When Al started walking home, he had one of his weeping attacks. "*It's a combination of experiencing something so very normal —taking your clothes to the dry cleaners—and my worry about Paul E,*" he explains.

DAY 78. WEDNESDAY, OCTOBER 26, 2011. Al calls from clinic, weeping with joy and relief. Bone marrow biopsy excellent. PLUS they did another chimera test. We didn't realize they had done one. Virtually 100 percent Abram!!! This is fabulous. CLL is barely traceable. The medical term for remaining CLL is appropriately "Fragments." Within a small margin of error, it's possible they may not even exist at all. The amount of CLL is tiny. Barely decipherable. Another milestone. Joy and wonder once again.

Later, Al tells daughter, Kate:

Katey nearly pinwheeled into the room, ebullient, breathless. "You are way ahead of the game, way in advance of the usual schedule. You are virtually 100 percent new cells."

He further told Kate that Abram has completed a search-and-destroy mission and added that Katey demonstrates such caring and giving. Last week we gave Katey a box of Trader Joe's Fudge Brownie Truffle Mix. Now her two boys say, "Mom, we want more of Allen's brownies."

LATER AL TEXTS OUR KIDS:

Excellent news today from recent tests . . . Abram has virtually wiped out old stem cells and purged the marrow . . . more blessings, more weeps."

Apparently, this level of success can be achieved by the five-six month point, but these tests were conducted on Day 70! I like to joke that I'm married to a nineteen-year-old—Abram's age we were told—but it's beginning to feel that's true. How will I ever keep up?

AL EMAILS KATEY:

- *I'll stay with 60 mg Prednisone unless I hear otherwise, correct?*
- *I've been a bit erratic with Troche. I'll return to regular dose unless you indicate otherwise. It's been a few weeks since I've had signs of thrush, but I know prevention is important.*
- *Looking ahead (which I know you don't like to do until Day 100), I'm feeling pressure from FL grandkids re: XMAS visit. If I continue to steadily recover, is a visit (via car—I assume air travel is out of the question) to FL during XMAS plausible, with necessary diet/lodging restrictions? It would bring me in close contact with fifteen-, five- and one-year-olds, though I could mitigate that somewhat with a mask and time limitations.*

Thanks so much for your enthusiasm and empathy in sharing the very encouraging bone marrow results. I had no idea a second chimera was in process. Was that a last-minute decision or was it on schedule for last week? Allen

Katey answers: "Hi, Allen–I spoke with Dr. A. He would indeed like you to stay at 60 mg. Your tac level was a bit low yesterday so, assuming that you took it at the similar time as you usually do, i.e., the evening before, let's have you increase from 3.0 mg to 3.5 mg. Sometimes the troches can affect the tac levels so as long as you haven't missed all/most of the doses I think we should still proceed with the increase. The chimerism test was planned, by the way.

I leave all questions regarding fun/rules to Dr. A. :)

Take care," Katey

CARING BRIDGE: FRIDAY, OCTOBER 28, 2011
BY ALLEN: "THE MANY FLAVORS OF CARING"

During the Boston Marathon, thousands of spectators line the 26-mile course, holding out water and oranges to passing runners in a collective offering of encouragement and caring. When my nurse, Toni, recently commented that Transplant recovery is "a marathon, not a sprint," I was reminded of how my community of loved ones has brought me a continuous offering of compassion and encouragement throughout the journey of preparation, procedure, and recovery. How easy it can be to forget the role of caring in our lives. It is a phenomenon so pervasive, so basic, and often so subtle that we must force ourselves to ponder its beauty, variety, and critical role in sustaining well-being through life's most difficult times.

– Nurse Practitioner Katey. Enters the exam room this week with more

than her usual positive energy to deliver the news: the second chimerism test (that measures progress of engrafting Donor Abram's stem cells in my bone marrow) has increased from 95 percent to "virtually 100 percent" as the source of white and red cells measurable in my blood. In other words, my old stem cells are history. Further, the marrow is virtually free of lymphocytes— those unwanted mutant cells from the pre- Transplant period. It was not just the substance of the news, but the joy, the empathy . . . the caring with which it was delivered. We stared at each other, reflecting on the news in a moment that mixed awe, mystery, and profound gratitude.

*– **Visiting friends Kina and John from San Francisco.** The earlier email from John reads "We'll be on the East Coast in October and hope to visit with you." I reply: "Of course—please do. And what brings you to the East Coast?" John's reply: "You." Three days of intense sharing about grandkids, work, and retirement plans, politics, reminiscing about our 43-year friendship that began in the Peace Corps in Nicaragua.*

*– **Visiting sister/sister-in law Molly.** A four-day cooking blitz produces an array of dishes and desserts fit for a king, not to mention dozens of hours of conversation with sister Judith as both partake in a shared passion—storytelling. I drift in and out of the conversation, absorbing the joy Judith feels from the unique role Molly plays in her in life.*

*– **Sister Betty.** Recalling the emotional moments I recently experienced on the basketball court when I felt Donor Abram guiding my shots into the hoop. Betty shares an extraordinary video of another hoops dream story equally replete with emotion. http://www.youtube.com/watch?v=cZtU676jA_k.*

*– **Our kids.** Stoking my soul with pride and a sense of intergenerational continuity. Doug shares his latest keyboard composition (www.youtube. com/douglaswhitemusic); Kate shares her awards as "Woman of Influence" in Northern CA real estate (http://www.ulisf.org/news/ulisf-ed-honored-as-2011-2012-woman-of-influence/)and as Co-Founder of SF CityShare on its tenth anniversary; Lena shares pictures of the three grandkids immersed in a pumpkin patch, high school homecoming, and weekly soccer games. All eliciting acute impatience on my part to break out of travel restrictions and smother each one with hugs.*

*– **My neighborhood Guatemalan hardware shopkeeper.** Inquires about my mask, leading to a conversation about stem cells that challenges my rusty Spanish as my friend's face transitions from anxiety to understanding to optimism when he listens to my report of steady recovery. Then with a warm Latin smile, he says, "I hope this little air purifier you are buying helps make*

you even better."

– My friend, colleague, and fellow world traveler, Bob Massie. For fifteen years in airports and hospitals, and through phone calls and emails, a source of inspiration and commiseration based on a shared passion for politics and social change, reinforced by the common experience of both having lived through the Transplant experience (liver, in Bob's case).

To all of the above and countless others, the caring all of you bring to me is precious beyond measure. My caring cup runneth over.

Warm wishes, Allen

NOVEMBER 2011

DAY 90. **MONDAY, NOVEMBER 7, 2011.** This has been a game of firsts. After the one-hour Transplant procedure, Al stood up, began walking, and said, "I'm taking the first steps into the rest of my life." Soon after he arrived home, the first guests began showing up. We began to see that the isolation and loneliness we had feared were not going to happen. Then came the first time he rode his bike, the first time he played hoops.

This past week—nearly three months after Transplant—we experienced another first. The woman Al refers to as his Queen Caretaker—me—left him alone for three days, two nights. What a long way we've come from my checking on him every few minutes to make sure he's breathing.

As usual, guests and colleagues showed up to keep him company.

AL TEXTED:

Lenny just left after two hours . . . pure pleasure. Writing, religion, kids . . . the full gamut. And a thxgiving invite to boot.

We talked both evenings. I'm accustomed to traveling with him, often tagging along when he's attending a conference or has a speaking engagement. He makes the reservations, prints out the boarding passes, checks us in, lifts the bags overhead, figures out the on-ground transportation, etc. This time, with some guidance, I was on my own. But I managed. To D.C., back where we met. Many years later, there's a subway now. I like to exit at the George Washington University stop and pass the apartment where Al lived during our rocky courtship. Then I walk up New Hampshire to Dupont Circle—my old stomping grounds from decades ago.

DAY 91. TUESDAY, NOVEMBER 8, 2011. Surprise letter from Dana: possibility of a virtual trans-Atlantic hug.

"Dear Mr. White:

Some patients who have received stem cells from an unrelated donor like to communicate with their donors after the Transplant. The guidelines on page 2 of this letter provide details on the process, should you choose to communicate with your donor. These guidelines have been put in place by the National Marrow Donor Program and have been designed to protect the rights and privacy of patients as well as of donors.

During the first year after Transplant, you may communicate anonymously, through cards and letters sent through and screened by the Transplant and Donor Centers. No direct contact with your donor is allowed during this period."

"GUIDELINES:

Within the first year, you MAY correspond anonymously. You MAY NOT include any identifying information; no names or initials, no schools, no places you receive care, no photographs, no geographical references, no references to weather or sports teams.

YOU MAY discuss emotions and feelings, your health, your family, employment—all in general terms. (For example, you may say that you're a baseball fan, but NOT that your favorite team won the World Series twice in four seasons, after an eight-year hiatus.)!

All correspondence will be screened by both the Search Team and the Donor Center."

It is Al's dream and deepest desire to someday meet his donor, to embrace him, to look him in the eye, to deliver his heartfelt thanks. Although his presence looms large, for now "Abram's" identity must remain a mystery. Al writes him for the first time—anonymously, as required.

November 14, 2011

Dear Donor:

It is my great pleasure to send this brief note of deepest gratitude for your generous stem cell donation. The Transplant occurred in early August and my recovery—now approaching the 100-day milestone—is proceeding ahead of schedule with very promising results thus far.

The Transplant occurred after thirteen years of managing adult leukemia with various therapies. About one year ago, my medical team determined that it was time to search for a donor and proceed with a Transplant, the only treatment with the possibility of achieving long-term remission of, and possi-

ble cure for, the disease. In the spring of this year, the registry identified you as a perfect match.   The news brought immense joy to me, my wife, three children and three grandchildren.

Your gift brings the hope of many more years of precious time with family and friends, and for continuing my professional work in the field of sustainable development.

It would be a privilege to hear from you if you are so inclined, and perhaps to meet you in person sometime after the one-year post-Transplant marker has passed.

With best wishes,

Recipient of your stem cell donation

CARING BRIDGE: TUESDAY, NOVEMBER 8, 2011
BY JUDITH: WELCOME SIGNS

At first I couldn't believe it. I kept counting the days on the calendar. A significant marker —Day 100—falls on our anniversary, November 17. I asked Al why, beyond being just a coincidence, that fact should feel so significant. He immediately answered, "A Transplant renews a life. An anniversary is like the rebirth of a marriage."

We have lots of questions for the surgeon who we've been warned, is conservative. He's also brilliant and we'll continue to be obedient. We know we have to be cautious for many more months, but we are indulging in some dreams of travel. Dates are tentatively appearing on our calendars. New York? Florida? West Coast? A Conference in Quito? Another in Amsterdam? Reschedule that speech in Spain he was forced to cancel last June? And eventually, if he's willing, meet Abram wherever he is—in Germany? Israel?

Al will report after Day 100. Thank you, dear ones, for staying with us.

DAY 100. THURSDAY, NOVEMBER 17, 2011. Day 100 Magic. YES, DAY 100—a big Transplant marker AND our forty-third wedding anniversary. One hundred days ago, we were obsessed with limiting Al's contact with bacteria. Bacteria on an apple, on the kitchen counters, in the butter, on the sponges and the towels, on plants, in the air. Clean. Scrub. Wash. Mask. Glove. Buy an air filter. Replace the filter. We read that bacteria can collect on skin under rings. So we removed our gold wedding bands. They've been waiting patiently side by side in my black enamel jewelry box, resting on red velvet.

Forty-three years ago, because I was working at the Washington, D.C. Public Welfare Department, I had access to discounts at stores reserved for government employees. We picked out our wedding rings in a bare-bones basement. Mine was a quarter-inch brushed gold now worn down to a smooth shine. His was a simple thin band. I never got a proposal. I never got an engagement ring. But that $13 brushed gold band has served me well.

So tonight we celebrated. Takeout!!! The first time in 100 days that we can eat a meal not prepared in our own kitchen. But from where? There are probably seventy-five restaurants within walking distance. We chose Rani—a high-end Indian restaurant. After telling the pleased owner our story—that we had honored HIS restaurant by making it our first choice—we headed home with a large bag of rice, chicken khurchan, chicken kholapuri, mango lassie, mango chutney, and three sauces.

Then we got out the rings. Wedding vows. The last time I was at a family reunion—last June—before Transplant, my sister The Reverend Martha Kline, and I were discussing wedding vows. In 1968, Al and I eschewed anything traditional and wrote our own vows. I regret so much that I lost them. I have absolutely no idea what we said to each other. Martha, who is not a traditionalist by any means, said, "Actually I think the traditional vows really stand the test of time. They pretty much sum up everything you need to say to each other."

I asked Martha to send me the traditional vows, wondering if we should say them this time. "Al, I give myself to you to be your wife. I promise to love and sustain you in marriage, from this day forward, in sickness and in health, in plenty and in want, in joy and in sorrow, as long as we both shall live."

"Pretty simple, but ring so true, I think," Martha added. "Particularly now for you two—you have done so much to love and sustain him during this very difficult time and I love how he appreciates you on the *Caring Bridge* site."

But we're still too untraditional, I guess. Instead of those vows, I read two blessings Martha sent:

"May the God of Sarah and Abraham, who watches over all the families of the earth, continue to bless your family in peace and steadfast love."

And another that Martha says is from Martha and Charlie and all our family: "We rejoice to celebrate with you the renewal of your marriage covenant. We celebrate the delight you have found in each other and thank you for the model you provide to all of us."

Then, as I put the ring on Al's finger, I say, "Al, I look forward to continuing to be your spouse. I return to you this ring in love, admiration, and gratitude for the caring, delightful, and always interesting life companion you are to me.

May we share many more years together of joy, exploration, and laughter."

Al returns my ring with words about the coincidence of the renewal of his health with the renewal of our marriage and about his gratitude for my devotion and attention of the past demanding 100 days.

He gives me three gifts. The first is actually from my sister, Molly, who gave him money to return to *Brookline Booksmith* and purchase a scarf I had admired when she was visiting. I had forgotten about it. Multicolored, feminine, warm, and lovely. I am so pleased. The second gift is a bag of chocolate truffles. Al and I each take one, relishing the melting of the outer chocolate followed by the pop of the creamy truffle inside reaching all our taste buds. The third present is a response to a day I exhausted myself peeling and chopping and slicing mounds of raw white and sweet potatoes and carrots, in order to prepare a double batch of a roasted chicken dish that, I hoped, would last several days. To make that preparation task easier in the future, Al gives me a cute little white chopper that will do that work for me.

I give Al the present of my assistance should he want to move from baking cookies, brownies and cakes from mixes to baking from scratch, baking having become a new hobby that will probably last at least until he's off steroids.

CARING BRIDGE: THURSDAY, NOVEMBER 17, 2011
BY ALLEN: "DAY 100"

At last...Day 100 post-Transplant, coincident with our forty-third wedding anniversary. Identified at the outset as a major milestone, we awaited the verdict of my medical team. Have I progressed to the point where dietary, human contact, and travel restrictions would ease? Or would the semi-quarantine remain in place for several more months?

The words flow like a fine French Merlot from our usually reserved French chief surgeon. With new blood lab and CT-Scan results in front of him, he exudes: "Excellent . . . excellent . . . I'm pleased, very pleased." And minutes later, Nurse Toni delivers the news—with the exception of eating inside restaurants—virtually all dietary restrictions are lifted. Travel by car anywhere is allowed. Mingling maskless with small groups of healthy folks is permitted with this continuing caution: "Remember, your immune system remains primitive, like a baby's. You must remain vigilant."

As Judith and I absorb the news, we ask for clarification and repetition, to be certain our understanding is accurate. Our heads spinning with liberation and possibility, and waves of raw emotion displacing the anxiety we felt in the days leading up to these meetings. We were hoping for the best, but we had planned for the worst. Instead, our hoping for the best is matched by receiving the best of news. We are blessed.

The intensity of Day 100 is rendered even more poignant by a letter that arrived three days earlier from a Stem Cell Transplant Coordinator at the clinic. I am now free to write anonymously to Donor Abram and Abram, in turn, may (or may not) choose to reply anonymously. After one year, if both parties consent, personal, direct contact—including in person—become possible. In a short note, I opened a line of communication with my clinic and Abram's clinic as intermediaries. My mind drifts across the Atlantic to my unidentified donor living in an unknown European city, hoping that he will reciprocate. And that one day I'll embrace him as cherished soul and cell mate.

Amidst the joy and gratitude associated with Day 100 is the shadow of a painful loss of an extraordinary human being. Paul E—friend, colleague, fellow traveler in the race for a sustainable future, and member of this Caring Bridge community—passed away just days ago after a battle with lymphoma. Paul and I crossed paths numerous times during the last two years at our clinic, providing mutual support in our shared struggle to conquer the beast threatening our lives. For a glimpse of his life, intellect, and impact on the world, see the "New York Times" at: http://www.nytimes.com/2011/11/15/health/dr-paul-epstein-public-health-expert-dies-at-67.html?_r=1

Day 100. New chapter. New hope. New inspiration. In this Thanksgiving season, my heartfelt thanks to all of you for helping Judith and me reach this marker with the strength and expectation that many more milestones lie ahead.

Love to all, Allen

Part V

Normal with Caution
November 2011–November 2013

NOVEMBER 2011

DAY 101. **FRIDAY, NOVEMBER 18, 2011.** I email our offspring:
"Hello dear ones, I just returned from a walk around Crystal Lake with friend, Sarah. It was fast paced and it's quite brisk outside. As I turned my key in the door, I was thinking 'Hmm, I'm kind of hungry. I wonder what we've got for snacks!!!' Did that gorgeous basket just appear on the kitchen counter at that moment when I had that thought? It certainly felt that way. I would have been happy to uncover a potato chip. Instead, I had a choice of dozens of yummies. Love you all. Mom"

The accompanying card says, "Happy Anniversary and Day 100, dear parents! You are both such an inspiration to us all. Lots of love, Kate, Morna, Lena, Larry, Doug, Nicole, Zoey and Bridge."

AL EMAILS THE GROUP:

Arrived moments ago. Gorgeous. All the things I love—cashews, cheese, cookies, etc. With my steroid-fueled appetite, it will be consumed within hours. It's been the best anniversary ever . . . and all of you made it even better. Much love, Dad/Zayde

DAY 102. SATURDAY, NOVEMBER 19, 2011. Slurpy Machine at Cumberland Farms. The tale of "firsts" continues. Last night our first dinner party out—at the home of Lenny and Linda, Mindy and Norman. Shabbat with chicken, salmon, veggies, Al's latkes and sour cream, pasta, Linda's homemade *challah*. Apple crisp for dessert. Red wine which I drank. Became tipsy quickly as I always do. Al sat way at the end of the table wearing a mask when he wasn't eating. Lots of conversation centered on Lenny's novel, climate change, birthing experiences—and donating stem cells.

Lenny and Linda's twenty-four-year-old son, Jonathan, donated at Dana almost a year ago. It was fascinating for us to hear every detail of that experience—more complicated and demanding than we had thought. For five days Jonathan went to the clinic and was given a shot to enhance the production of his stem cells. He was sore. Felt fluey. The day of the donation, his parents accompanied him. The blood was drawn in small amounts. The stem cells were separated in a centrifuge device that Jonathan said sounded like a slurpy machine at Cumberland Farms. His blood minus stem cells was returned to his arm. Perhaps eight different times. The clinic still calls regularly to check in with Jonathan and see how he's doing. No problems. No side effects.

How did he happen to donate? He was in a bar in Israel with some pals. He had been drinking and was leaving to meet up with more friends when some people at a "Gift of Life" table approached him about donating his stem cells. He had no idea what that meant, but agreed to a cheek swab and signed a form. It was over in minutes and he barely remembered it until he received a call from Dana eighteen months later. They thought he was a match. Would he please come in for more testing? He followed through on the whole process, but never thought much about the recipient until meeting Al. Now Jonathan realizes how profound the effect of his donation was. For the first time, he's thinking about the recipient, a sixty-four-year-old man, hoping his donation helped.

Al wakes up this morning a little disoriented. The evening was pretty intense for him. But it's wonderful to be making travel plans together again—all by car since public transportation of any kind remains prohibited.

It seems to me that Al's considerable intellectual prowess is stronger than it's been for several years. His recall of names and facts and situations is so far out in front of mine. I ask him about it. He's always modest, but he said it makes some sense because there are more and healthier red blood cells fueling his brain function. Sometimes in the past, CLL has exhausted the oxygen flow to his brain leaving him foggy, although even then it didn't seem to interfere much with his analytical thinking. But now that brain is roaring. Look out world. A game changer is back and he's out to make a difference.

DAY 105. TUESDAY, NOVEMBER 22, 2011. Al emails Kate.

Hi, Lilly—A short article by Daddy appears in this newsletter. A colleague, John Fullerton, founded Capital Institute after years on Wall St. and eventual disillusionment with the culture and greed. He's now a leading voice for radical reform of finance. We are planning lunch with him in Greenwich, CT on December 9 on our way home from New Haven (I'm speaking at Yale) and NYC (a meeting of www.ratingsustainability.org) at headquarters of Bloomberg.

Ahhhhh . . . freedom. We shall overcome. D

DAY 109. SATURDAY, NOVEMBER 26, 2011. Allen emails Carrie.

Dearest Cousine: Wonderful to hear from you. Yes, Judith is in FL until Weds, our first time apart (except for her recent two nights in Washington for a board meeting) in six months. I packed my schedule with friends and family, including Txgiving with twenty-five people at a neighbor's place.

Yesterday was Worcester day. I "introduced" donor Abram to his family at the B'nai Brith cemetery where my folks and paternal grand folks are buried. A simple ceremony on a beautiful November day—placing stones on the gravestone, caressing the engraved English/Hebrew letters, feeling the power of bloodlines and ancestry, as you did at the Wailing Wall, as I read the birth dates of Wolf (1883) and Sarah (1881).

We have planned our first trips—to Yale U. for presentations—then on to NYC for two nights for a business meeting. By car, of course—no planes or trains for several more months. Barring any setback, a drive to FL for XMAS with stops along the way to see friends.

So you get the picture—I feel strong, focused. Just biked along the Charles to the harbor on a glorious sixty-degree day. At times I pause, ponder, and reflect on just how blessed I am, wrapping my crossed arms around my torso to embrace Abram and the magic of my new, emergent immune system.

Sounds like neither of you is slowing down—my head is spinning reading about your travels. I remember those days.

Much love, Al

DAY 117. THURSDAY, NOVEMBER 24, 2011. 2:30 A.M. Conversation in bed. Al wide awake from steroids and reading. Judith falling back asleep even with the light on.

A: *Do you love me?*

J: I love you, Al.

A: *Why do you love me?*

J: Turning toward him: Because you are sweet and handsome.

J: Getting warmed up now: and because you are so smart and know so much. Because your conversations are so interesting. Because of your moral fiber.

Judith, feeling she has delivered the goods, falls back asleep.

A: Silence.

Judith rouses herself to open her eyes and sees Al staring straight ahead.

J: What are you thinking?

A: *About my moral fiber. Isn't that something you get by eating Grape-nuts?*

J: Wide awake now, laughs out loud, probably disrupting the sleep of neighbors.

DECEMBER 2011

CARING BRIDGE: DAY 114. THURSDAY, DECEMBER 1, 2011
BY JUDITH: "FAREWELL CARING BRIDGE . . . FOR NOW"

Before the procedure, when tensions and fears were high, one of my many weepy moments was out of concern that my husband, who thrives on interaction with people, would suffer from isolation. The isolation never happened. Thanks to your loving attentiveness, the texts, calls, cards, and visits began immediately and have never stopped. When Kate set up Caring Bridge *in July, we could not have imagined how integral a part of Al's healing it would become, how we would read and reread all your clever and heart-felt postings, how much they would make us smile, laugh, and cry.*

There are significant markers ahead: six months (February 9, 2012), a year (August 9, 2012). We're feeling confident as we march, slowly and steadily, toward normalcy while never forgetting the intricate human body is not a robot and always subject to setbacks. But we're weary of so much focus on us and look forward to hearing more about your lives. What might we have missed?

There's a tune in my head: "Time to Say Goodbye." I hear Andrea Bocelli and Sarah Brightman singing it. We'll keep this site active and communicate again in February, the next milestone . . . or sooner if there is strong reason to do so.

Until then, dear Caring Bridge *community, stay healthy and safe. Never will we take for granted the thrill of knowing we can now visit with you in person—in the flesh— all over the world.*

DAY 136. FRIDAY, DECEMBER 23, 2011. First time we've taken such a long car trip in decades. A little hard on our backs, but we're staying two nights in mossy, mysterious Savannah. We take a walking tour and learn about the early presence of Jews in this city. First documented arrival is 1733 from London, most of Spanish and Portuguese background, most likely expelled from Spain and Portugal during the Inquisition. Right down the street from our B & B is a Reform temple. The front is in a mysterious, Gothic style. The addition in the back is modern.

We read there's a Hanukkah party. We imagine all the families partying, feasting, singing, lighting candles. All the cute kids. We hover outside like lost waifs since Al is not yet allowed crowds. A woman steps outside and introduces herself. Barbara Feldstein, a long-term Savannah resident. We have a lengthy, delightful, informative chat on the sidewalk by the light of the gas-lit street lamps. She used to work at our B & B and knows the owners. She tells us there are 300+ families involved with the Temple. We even learn some local gossip when we ask about one of our favorite restaurants, The French Café, which has furniture piled against the front door behind a sign, "Renovating. Will reopen January 1." That's awfully soon, given the mess. But, unfortunately, Barbara's not sure it will open at all. The owners are divorcing.

DAY 137. SATURDAY, DECEMBER 24, 2011. In Jacksonville after a four-day drive from Boston. SURPRISE! Grandgirls did not know we were coming. Lena orchestrated the whole scene while she, we, and Larry coordinated to get the girls out of the house and hide our car. They thought they were playing a treasure hunt game—searching for reindeer—but the rhyming hints brought them to the dining room where, next to the Christmas tree, Grandma and Zayde were sitting quietly wearing . . . what else? Reindeer hats. I'll never forget the looks on their faces when they came upon us. Brief shock and disbelief followed by joy and tears all around.

That evening—Christmas Eve—we exchange ugly Christmas sweaters. Kate reacts to a photo of us: "Those sweaters are pretty darn ugly, but my parents are awfully cute! So glad you made it safe and sound, and great to hear all about Savannah. Happy Hanukkah and Merry Xmas!"

Al responds to Kate: *Yup—nastiest sweater I've ever worn. But you can't kill Zayde's good looks.*

DAY 138. SUNDAY, DECEMBER 25, 2011. Christmas Day. Wonderful gift exchange yesterday—all in two hours. Zoey is tops in number of gifts received. Bridgette focuses on wrapping and ribbons and grabbing others' gifts. Nicole is thrilled with a super high-end Nikon camera (she has a terrific eye for great pics) and sheet music for Adele, the British pop star. I spend a little time working with her, reviving her sight reading from two years of piano lessons years ago. Soon she just takes off with it. She has fantastic recall and is progressing rapidly toward mastering an Adele hit.

JANUARY 2012

DAY 146. **Monday, January 2, 2012.** Judith sends New Year email love letters to Dana staff. Each email begins: "Just a quick note from the elated spouse of one of your patients—Allen White. We drove to Florida to surprise our three granddaughters on Christmas Eve. There was shock followed by joy and tears. Since our arrival, there have been many wonderful times with them, opening presents, building sand castles on the beach (yes, it was 75 degrees this past weekend), reading, and dancing. There was a time when I believe Allen feared he might not see them again."

First to Melissa, Al's principal infusion nurse for almost a decade:

Dear Melissa,

I have no doubt that your loving attention, wisdom, good sense, and humor have contributed enormously to Allen's healing.

Thank you, dear Melissa, from our entire family.

Wishing you and yours a healthy and rewarding 2012. Judith

Melissa responds:

Hi there, Judith!

And Happy New year to both you and Allen! Your kind words mean so much! I am so glad you both got to enjoy some much-needed time with your family! I know how important the grandbabies (and your children for that matter) mean to you. It has been an absolute pleasure to care for Allen. Thank you again for taking the time to think of me! 2012 is going to be a great year! Melissa

To Toni, Transplant Nurse Coordinator:

Dear Toni,

I have no doubt that your thoughtful attention, wisdom, good sense, and professionalism have contributed enormously to Allen's healing.

Do you have a sixth sense about matches? I suspect so, since so far, Allen's donor seems to have been plucked from heaven.

I send you the gratitude of an entire extended family.

Wishing you and yours a healthy and rewarding 2012. Judith

To Katey, Nurse Practitioner—second in command after Dr. A:

Dear Katey,

What a pleasure for us both to have benefited from your care both at the very beginning, immediately after Allen's diagnosis, AND again thirteen years later throughout pre- and post-Transplant. I have no doubt that your thoughtful attention, wisdom, good sense, and professionalism have contributed enormously to Allen's healing.

From the bottom of our hearts, I send the gratitude of our entire extended family. Judith

To Dr. A, Chief Transplant Surgeon:

Dear Dr. A,

We'll drive back in time for Allen's next Dana appointment on Wednesday, January 18. As we look ahead to a new year full of promise and hope, I want to thank you for the enormous role you, as Chief Transplant Surgeon, have played and continue to play in Allen's healing. We are grateful for your dedication, discipline, determination, and brilliant coordination of all the factors that have contributed to his steadily improving condition.

Please accept the gratitude of our entire family.

Wishing you and yours a healthy and rewarding 2012. Judith

Dr. A responds:

Judith,

What a heart-warming email. It is very much an honor to be a small part of the joy which Allen is spreading around him. Your gratitude is much appreciated but hardly needed, imagining your trip is thanks aplenty. Happy New Year to you and yours and thanks again for emailing. Dr. A

To Dr. F, former main Doc/oncologist who managed Al's CLL for a decade before shift to Dr. A:

Dear Dr. F,

For the many pre-Transplant years during which you guided Allen through multiple treatments and decisions, for your wisdom and knowledge, for your calm reassuring manner, I send the gratitude of an entire extended family.

Wishing you and yours a healthy and rewarding 2012.

Dr. F responds:

Dear Judith,

Thank you for your kind note. I am glad to hear that Allen is doing well. Happy New Year and best wishes to the whole family. Dr. F

Al's work continues. The excerpt below from the Corporation 20/20 website (www.corporation2020.org) captures the ideas that motivate his passion for transforming the role of business in society.

Dear Colleagues:

A decade ago Charles Handy, among the most incisive contemporary observers of the modern corporation and a keynoter at the first Corporation 20/20 Summit, asked the most fundamental of all questions to those working in the field of corporate purpose and redesign: "What's a business for?"

His response remains as relevant today as it was when first offered: "To

turn shareholders' needs into a purpose is to be guilty of a logical confusion, to mistake a necessary condition for a sufficient one. We need to eat to live; food is a necessary condition of life. But if we lived mainly to eat, making food a sufficient or sole purpose of life, we would become gross. The purpose of a business is not to make a profit. Full stop. It is to make a profit so that business can do something more or better. That 'something' becomes the real justification for a business."

Since its inception, Corporation 20/20 has defined that "something" as "harnessing private interests to serve the public interest." Reflecting on the social, political, and economic turbulence during 2011, this public interest purpose provides a valuable lens through which to observe citizen demands for change in corporate conduct in both financial and "real economy" organizations. Growing wealth disparities between managers and workers, regressive taxes, privatizing gains while socializing losses, "too big to fail," hyper-leveraged organizations linked to financial destabilization and dislocation—these are among the many, linked conditions that are bringing unprecedented scrutiny to the purpose and design of corporations.

But for all the volatility and hardship during 2011, it was not entirely devoid of hope. New corporate charter laws in California. Signs—however weak—of taming socially damaging risk-taking on the part of financial institutions. The rise of social networking innovation as a powerful instrument of citizen empowerment and movements building. These discrete measures fall short of urgently needed systemic change but, nonetheless, are glimpses of the possible.

In early 2011, U.N. Secretary General Ban Ki-moon offered this challenge: "We need a revolution. Revolutionary thinking. Revolutionary action. It is easy to mouth the words 'sustainable development,' but to make it happen we have to be prepared to make major changes—in our lifestyles, our economic models, our social organization, and our political life."

2011 set the table. 2012 has the potential to accelerate the "revolution" toward the new corporation agenda. With your participation, Corporation 20/20 will continue to play a vital role in the corporate dimension of this Great Transition.

Here's to a healthy, prosperous, and purposeful New Year.
Allen

January 3, 2012. Charles Handy responds from his home in Britain:
Dear Allen,

Thank you for quoting me in your last message. I follow your discussions with interest and am only sad that I have not been able to join you all once again, but I do wish you a very successful year ahead in your important work. I sense that the general view of the role of business is gradually changing, and some of that must be due to you.

Best Wishes, Charles

FEBRUARY 2012

DAY 203.

CARING BRIDGE: TUESDAY, FEBRUARY 28, 2012, 7:59 A.M.
BY ALLEN: "SIX MONTHS OF BLESSINGS"

Dear Family and Friends: I hope this finds you well.

This is the six-month, post-Transplant update I promised three months ago. It will be short because, well, joyfully there is very little to report. I never dreamed normalcy could be so exciting. Not a day goes by without contemplating the dark days pre- and post-Transplant and the blessings of a smooth recovery that, so far, has proceeded without a serious hitch.

Monthly visits to my clinic. Working about two-thirds time, split between office and home. Back to theater and movies, restaurants and socializing. The major restriction that remains in place—air, train, and metro travel—is prohibited, probably for another five-six months. Thoughts of all those germy passengers packed into a closed space sends shivers down the spines of my medical team. It likely will be one year post-Transplant—August 2012—before the public transportation travel restriction is lifted. For now, it's car and bike only. A slow, ten-day RT, 2,000 mile road trip to Jacksonville, FL to see the grandkids turned out to be a liberating, if tiring, excursion,

To all of you who have visited, phoned, texted, and emailed during the last few months, my deepest appreciation. I cherish every communication. Each provides nourishment to the heart and soul of a grateful survivor. Next stop—the one-year milestone.

Warmest wishes,

MARCH 2012
The Prednisone Dance

DAY 212. FRIDAY, MARCH 9, 2012. Clinic meeting with Katey. Exactly seven months after procedure. Blood work fine. Problems: very swollen feet and legs; eyes dry—probably GVHD; athlete's foot pretty much gone; pink rash on torso which Katey says is GVHD. Eyes two-thirds better; have been bothering him for two months. Less tearing. Less stickiness. Swelling from toes up to knees began two weeks ago. Prednisone was 10 mg. Dropped it. Then the problems began.

Remedies: Eat protein. Use compression stockings.

Symptoms of GVHD better controlled with the steroid, but negative effects associated with its use too. May have to continue for a long time. Bones soft. Balance of drugs and dosages of those drugs is both an art and a science. Constant vigilance and decision-making. Emotional. Examples of crying. Hyper hands trembling. Al appears so old.

DAY 222. MONDAY, MARCH 19, 2012. Meeting with Dr. A re eyes, rash, edema—better since he's on steroids. Continue with appointment with ophthalmologist. Need baseline. Dr. A: "Looking good. Taper off steroids. Fourday dosages: 30 mg - 30 mg - 30 mg - 10 mg. Then repeat: 30 mg - 30 mg - 30 mg - 10 mg. Eventually 10 mg only."

Challenge of long-term use of steroid: cumulative toxicity. Dr. A suggests ultrasound on right leg to be sure there is no clot. Donor's cells reaching tissues. Must have bone density test plus ultrasound. Avoid sun, avoid sickness. Any change in skin, eyes, nausea, legs? Note them. Blood sugar is highest it has been. Keep log of blood sugar before breakfast plus one hour before meals or two hours after.

APRIL 2012
Keeping CVS in Business

DAY 256. MONDAY, APRIL 23, 2012. Clinic with Dr. A who walks to work. On our way to our appointment, we drive by him crossing the street on foot.

DAMN BACK. Lower back pain has struck with a vengeance. Watching Al struggle to get out of bed is the worst. It takes a long time. He crawls out. The pain that began about one month ago was originally distributed on the right side. Now it's still on that side, but is more focused. Three days ago he began taking Percocet. Ibuprofen before that was marginally effective. Main effect of Percocet (one tablet at night) is drowsiness. No pain on left side of spine. Lidocaine patch—no side effects. Better than Percocet. Probably a strain. Possibly from exercising on the elliptical. An MRI revealed a compression fracture. In addition, a disc was rubbing a nerve.

Skin looks good. Urinating often but okay. Swollen legs almost gone. Blood counts good. Whites have improved. Platelets have improved. No sniffles, no sore throat. Kidneys good. Magnesium slightly low.

Dr. A in unusually exuberant utterance: "Everything looks great! YOU look great!" Lowering steroid. Continue with glucose test two or three times more to keep an eye on blood sugar. Should get better because tapering steroid.

With Dr. L at Harvard Vanguard. Back problem is probably an aggravated disc. It's moving into one area and that's a good sign. Al has very tight hamstrings. Try physical therapy. Deep tissue massage good. Acupuncture too. Pain control while body heals itself. After trying about six different doctors and remedies, Al has ten appointments with a chiropractor. He does daily back exercises. Finally after seven months the pain lessens.

JULY/AUGUST 2012
The Joy of Travel?

We've already been blessed with travels to Florida, New Haven, New York City, Montreal, and Vermont by car but, alas, still no plane travel allowed. Of course, we want the world. Specifically, we want quite desperately to go to Paris, for two reasons: one joyful, one deeply upsetting. Al's talented artist sister, Betty, is fulfilling a life-long dream with an exhibit this summer at the *Galerie Théo de Seine*. We are missing the opening—*le vernissage*—of the exhibit and are forced to share the excitement of this triumph from afar.

However, our beloved, beautiful, and dynamic cousin, Carrie, is hospitalized at the *Hôtel Dieu de Paris* having been diagnosed with stage-four uterine cancer. We communicate by email, through her blog, and with her husband, Hans. Al Skypes with Carrie once, but she is weak and must preserve energy. We want to visit, to hold her hand for a few minutes during those few hours each day when she can summon the energy to interact with visitors. She has steadfastly supported both of us with her numerous, upbeat postings on *Caring Bridge*. We had a wonderful visit from her in January. Now we cannot get to Paris to be with her during this harrowing medical threat.

As for lifting the international air travel ban, Dr. A insists on caution. In discussing the possibility of flying to Florida and Paris, he responds: "Well, here's my view. The medicine in Florida falls short of Boston, but at least it is in the U.S. where I can manage your care if something goes wrong. Paris is the opposite—world-class medicine but, well, it's France. Managing your care in the event of a medical setback abroad is very complicated. I know from personal experience. So remain domestic, for now."

So we fly West. A delicious, exploratory trip for both fun and business. Of course, it's always the people one visits or encounters that make trips memorable. With sister, Martha, and brother-in-law, Charlie, on Guemes Island, Anacortes, WA; to Vancouver, lunch with Kina and John, dinner with Mike Lazarus and family; Seattle, dinner with Kortens; San Francisco with Kate and Maureen and cousins, Betty, Nat, Nina; Los Angeles with Doug. Martha, and Charlie; Kate and Maureen organize book events in Guemes and San Francisco where I speak, read from, and sign my recently published first novel. I'm delighted with their efforts on behalf of *The Seventh Etching* and pleased with the attendance and the enthusiastic response to my work.

Berkeley cousins give us framed gifts. Al's is a painting of a broad-winged turquoise phoenix rising toward a bright orange sun. Mine is the number 2012905743. I don't know what the number refers to. To my delight, Nat and Nina explain that it's the Library of Congress Control Number for *The Seventh Etching.*

We stay three nights in each place, with the exception of San Francisco where we rent a roomy apartment. For nine days, we immerse ourselves in Noe Valley, The Mission, Downtown. It is a triumphant return to a city where eighteen months ago we rushed Al to the hospital in an ambulance, with plunging red cell counts. Now, in contrast, he organizes and moderates a workshop on the Future of Finance, hosted by Business for Social Responsibility. Another indicator of a return to normalcy, doing the work about which he feels so passionate.

CARING BRIDGE: AUGUST 9, 2012, 5:50 A.M.
BY ALLEN: "DAY 365!"
REFLECTIONS ON ROSE-COLORED CARGO
    Family, Friends, Colleagues:
    Exactly one year ago today, August 9, 2011, I wrote:

"Shortly after midnight, the first drop of new stem cells flowed into my anxious body. Harvested in Europe earlier that day and transported across the Atlantic under the watchful eye of a medical courier, the rose-colored cargo began the final leg of its journey from donor 'Abram' to recipient Allen. An hour later, the last drop marked the end of the transplant. I rose from the bed and took the first steps into a new chapter of my life . . . for now, it's a day to honor the countless contributions of scientists and patients whose brains and bodies have brought medical science to where it is today. I salute each and every one, and, equally so, Abram for his life-giving gift."

Fast forward to ten days ago, July 30, 2012, my chief doctor's email, upon reviewing the results of a critical bone marrow biopsy, reads: "Marrow is negative for CLL! Congrats and happy tidings."

In short, no detectable residual disease in the marrow. That report, coupled with regular monitoring showing all my cell production is attributable to my donor's stem cells, comprises a diagnosis for which every Transplant recipient prays.

I write today at a moment in deep reflection, pondering the events and meaning of this last, momentous year. Dietary restrictions, visitation restrictions, public events restrictions have passed as I have returned to a life and lifestyle that was a distant vision one year ago. Today, not long after a Florida visit in June with daughter Lena and family, Judith and I are on the West Coast enjoying the company of kids Kate and Doug, and numerous relatives and colleagues. My energy and health now restored thanks to that "rose-colored cargo" infused a year ago. To Judith's delight and amazement, even my formerly thinning white hair, miraculously, is returning to a thickness and darkness I've not seen for many, many years. "De-aging" we call it.

Adding to this good news was the arrival two months ago of a message from the still anonymous donor in response to my outreach. His humble words of generosity and encouragement upon learning of my steady recovery, and his opening the door to possible direct communication in the coming months, triggered a flood of grateful emotions. I hope to meet him someday soon.

While the year's journey has been one of continuous blessings, it has not been without pain. The loss of a dear friend and a cousin to cancer, together with the ongoing struggle of a second cousin battling cancer, are stark reminders of life's fragility and my own extraordinarily good fortune. We—all of us—have to do more to defeat this beast.

So onward into Year Two and, hopefully, a future of continued good health. To all of you in my caring community, your visits and communica-

tions throughout the past year have been my sustenance for which I am pro-
foundly and forever grateful. I would not be where I am today without you.
Warmest wishes, Allen

MONDAY, AUGUST 20, 2012. 3:30 p.m. and Al awaits a hip x-ray. Because the suppression of the immune system in preparation for Transplant elimi-nates all the protection of his childhood vaccinations, Al receives five shots, just like an infant. New birthday. New round of vaccinations. More to follow in a few months.

TUESDAY, AUGUST 28, 2012. **Al emails Dr. A.**

The lumbar discomfort disappeared in early August four months after onset. But within a week after that (which is about two weeks ago), pain in the right hip began which I reported to Melissa Cochran, leading to the ultra sound and hip x-ray you have reviewed (Melissa reported "looks good"—do you agree?). Leg swelling reappeared about the time hip pain appeared and remains at a moderate level.

Separately, this morning, I had an MRI for the cyst detected on the pan-creas by an earlier CAT-scan. Please advise if there is anything of concern in today's MRI.

So, at this point, I'm inclined to deal with the hip pain with PT and chi-ropractor and see where we are on September 17 when I see you. If pain intensifies, I'll certainly let you know. OK?

3:30 and waiting for a hip x-ray. Received five baby shots; few more in two months.

ON MRIs. A TORTUOUS QUALITY. Once, perhaps fifteen years ago, my doctor told me I had a spot on my liver they couldn't identify and I should have an MRI. I thought an MRI would be a variant of an x-ray. When I arrived, I was told to get into what looked like an iron lung or a surround-sound white plastic coffin. I refused. "Didn't anyone explain to you what to expect?" the technician asked. No. No one had prepared me. "We suggest people arrive with a family member or friend who can support them. Or bring earphones and listen to music. You can reschedule." I never had the procedure. No one has ever mentioned the liver spot since, but probably they've never looked at my liver since either.

With national health care expenses soaring and as supporters of President Obama's attempts to lower those costs, Allen and I are beginning to question the necessity of tests.

I recently questioned the necessity of a simple urine test for my kidney function, for example. This was after mildly ambiguous results from a blood test and a CAT-scan that had determined my kidneys looked normal. The nurse replied defensively, "The doctor would not order it unless it were necessary."

Al emails Dr. A asking if this MRI for his pancreas is really necessary. He gets a terse one-word answer back: "Yes."

Thursday, August 30. 2012. Although Al had had at least two previous MRI's before today's, he seemed to take them in stride. One more necessary medical procedure like scores of others, maybe hundreds of others over the past fourteen years. But today he arrives home, sits down to lunch, and says,

"Boy these MRI's are stressful. Not painful, but you're placed on this—not a bed, but a horizontal platform no wider than your body. The platform slides into a 360-degree machine. You're in a narrow tunnel. If you open your eyes, which I did once and not again, you're looking at a roof, only inches away from your nose. If you suffer from claustrophobia, I don't see how you can endure this procedure.

"And you're in there for forty-five minutes during which you are bombarded with intense noise. Grinding, beating, pumping sounds laced with a stream of instructions voiced by the technician: 'Breathe steadily. Hold your breath. Breathe normally. Breathe through your nose. Breathe through your mouth. Remain still. Do not move.'

And all this with an IV stuck in your arm so they can monitor the body part they are zooming in on. In this case my pancreas, which was found recently to have a cyst. All in all it has a tortuous quality to it.

The problem is the machine can handle only one body part at a time. There's no full body scan. You need a separate MRI for each body part. Here I am slender, strong state of mind, patient, calm, being treated at one of the best care facilities by one of the best trained staff in the entire world . . . and I was unnerved. What happens to people who are lacking any of those positive characteristics?

The noise alone is enough to terrify you. I need a nap."

I join Al for the nap, but quickly became alarmed when I feel how hot he is. I want him to take his temperature immediately, but he wants to sleep. Finally, an hour later he takes it. 101. Not good. He's also had swollen ankles for weeks. No rash, though. We were told over a year ago that any time he has a temperature he should call Dr. A immediately. We've never made an emergency, off-hours call to his medical team. Al does not want to bother them this time either. Instead of calling, he emails Dr. A and Katey.

By the time he goes to bed, he has no more fever. None when he wakes up either. He thinks it might be a reaction to the large restaurant meal he ate yesterday morning, but he attributes a lot of bodily reactions to food. I'm watchful.

Thursday, August 30, 2012–8:00 p.m. Allen White emails Dr. A and Katey. Subject: Checking in—temperature and hip pain

I started feeling warm mid-afternoon and just recorded a 101-degree temperature (8 p.m. Thursday). Slight throat congestion, no coughing or mucus.

Left hip pain continues, requiring assistance of cane for walking. Right hip pain virtually disappeared after two weeks; lumbar pain also disappeared about three weeks ago.

FRIDAY, AUGUST 31, 2012. Katey calls after reading the email. Chastising. "Protocol requires you call Dr. A anytime you have a fever. Protocol is there out of love. Get yourself to the clinic."

On the same day, Al receives what I believe is the longest email he's ever gotten from Dr. A and it includes a threat:

"Allen, you will hear or have already heard from Katey about coming in today. Just for the record:

1. Fevers get me a page, as do other significant acute changes.
2. Concerns of semi-urgent nature (e.g., significant new hip pain) get us an email or message.
3. Questions about non-urgent stuff (meaning that it can wait a few weeks) best left for clinic visits.
4. After last night's email, Katey and I toyed with the idea of sending you to a Maoist re-education camp high in the mountains of Outer Mongolia. You will be quizzed today on #1-3 above, if you can't answer correctly pack your bags for the East. Dr. A"

Because Al, who has three degrees in geography, carries a world map in his brain and can instantly visualize the location of any country on the planet, he found the Outer Mongolia reference intriguing but the Maoist education camp not his cup of tea. Going forward, though, I think he'll remember the threat and take fevers more seriously.

FRIDAY, AUGUST 31, 2012. Al responds:

My appreciation for a reminder of the protocol, especially #1. I must guard against complacency and react to acute conditions appropriately. Your/Katey's excellent care is to blame for such complacency and neglectfulness on my part. As to Outer Mongolia, it's not exactly the Paris or Amsterdam I had in mind when I restart international travel . . . As always, AW

FRIDAY, AUGUST 31, 2012. Al emails Dr. A and Katey.
Re: Checking in—temperature and hip pain update:
temperature has returned to normal;
no cough or congestion;
moderate night sweats last night (first sweats in eighteen months);
foot swelling decreasing.
I wonder if I experienced mild food poisoning? AW

SEPTEMBER 2012

TUESDAY, SEPTEMBER 4, 2012. I wake up to stop Al from shaking and jerking—a sign that he's having a nightmare. When I pat repeatedly, he wakes up and tells me he had the same bad dream three times in a row. He was on a college campus. A pack of wild dogs had already killed one domestic dog and were approaching another one. Al was torn between trying to protect the dog and worrying that the wild dogs would attack Al himself. He had awakened earlier, but when he went back to sleep, the dream continued. He thinks it's disease and death threatening people he loves (Carrie) and himself.

Part of this dream actually happened to us years ago—in Columbus, though. The ID collar of our gentle dog, Sula, had fallen off and we hadn't yet replaced it when she ran off for a run on the Ohio State campus with a larger, homeless male German shepherd and our neighbor's small white dog. The little white dog made it home, but the beautiful larger dogs were shot and killed by campus police who claimed they were a dangerous pack. We and our kids were devastated, but we were also at fault. Odd that this incident would return to haunt Al's dream at this time almost forty years later.

TUESDAY, SEPTEMBER 18, 2012. Doc grants Al permission to travel abroad for the first time in almost three years. "Paris is fine; but avoid Timbuktu," he advises. "Yes, Sir," Al replies.

But the Paris we craved to visit last summer is no longer alluring. Betty's six-week Paris exhibit is over so we missed it. Carrie has died. We are bereft, disbelieving. We cry often, sometimes uncontrollably. Al has lost a beloved cousin. I have lost a sister figure. The world has lost an extraordinary human being.

FRIDAY, SEPTEMBER 28, 2012. For the first time since Transplant, Al rides his bike to work and back. In his understated style, he says,

After all the procedures, restrictions, therapies, and drugs, it is so liberating to get on a bike.

OCTOBER 2012

A l's work returns to center stage. The Global Reporting Initiative, his co-creation with Bob Massie, is now an eight-million-Euro organization with offices in New York City, Saul Paulo, New Delhi, Beijing, and Johannesburg. With seventy employees worldwide, GRI is changing the face of corporate sustainability reporting, moving a concept from the extraordinary to the exceptional to the expected business practice in little more than a decade.

Al now applies his restored energy and focus to a new initiative, Corporation 20/20, which he co-founded in 2004. A visionary, forum, and advocate for redesigning corporations (www. Corporation2020.org). And he births yet another new initiative, Global Initiative for Sustainability Ratings (www.rate-sustainability.org) aimed at "redefining the definition of corporate value and value creation."

I am researching and writing sequels to my debut novel, *The Seventh Etching*, the first book of my *Amsterdam Trilogy* series. Book two, *The New Worlds of Isabela Calderón*, follows an *Etching* character many readers seemed to love as she leaves Amsterdam behind and returns to her native Spain. It's exhilarating having the time to work steadily again on developing characters and placing them in context in the seventeenth century and to continue the life of my darling Isabela.

WINTER 2012–FALL 2013
Eli
No More Dreams Deferred

T he year of required anonymity between donor and recipient has passed. It is a system Al respects for its prudent protection of both parties. Early communication in the case of a failed Transplant may occasion profound distress to one or both sides. Some anecdotes regarding premature contacts tell stories of demands and conflicts. With a year elapsed, however, timing seems right. Al is ready—more than ready. Never far from his mind is the anonymous donor, the source of his revitalization, rebirth, and restoration. Impatience to meet his donor stalks Al virtually every day. He fervently hopes to visit the mystery man in Germany someday.

Al sent the donor a message via the proper Dana contact and is disappointed that several months have gone by and he's not received a replay. After contacting Dana again he receives this email from the Search Coordinator:

Dear Dr. White–

Thank you so much for contacting me re: having direct contact with your stem cell donor. The short answer is—we haven't heard back from the donor yet, but are still working on it. I will let you know as soon as I hear anything, one way or the other. At this point, no news is still good news!

I would be happy to give you more details; do let me know if you want the long version.

Kind regards–Jane

Thursday, December 13, 2012. Al, irritated, but still hopeful, emails me:

I talked with Jane. A breakdown (which no one can explain) occurred after Jane transmitted my disclosure form months ago. The central registry, which connects with the German clinic, has no record of receiving it. They now have the form after Jane resent it. Maddening . . . but at least the glitch has been corrected. I'll reconnect with Jane in a month if I hear nothing. Fingers crossed.

Thursday, December 27, 2012. The Call. We're in our Florida apartment sharing meals with our daughter's family downstairs and taking granddaughters to the beach. My "study" is in the bedroom. Al has a separate room—"Zayde's office"—off the bedroom, where he can close the door, close out child noise and other distractions, and concentrate on his work. I hear him answer his cell phone. I hear his excitement build as he reacts to information from the caller. I hear his goodbye: *"Thank you, Jane. This is wonderful news."* I hear him weeping.

I enter his office where he sits at his desk facing a window, his head bent. I put my arms around him and hold him until he's ready to share with me whatever he's learned that has so moved him. Then I notice a notepad on his desk where he has written a name I hadn't seen before. A decidedly Jewish name; no longer "Abram," but the name of a real person. Next to the name are other bits of information. A phone number. An email address. A town in New Jersey. An age—twenty-one. I know instantly who this is. I know now the source of Al's new black hair. All over again we marvel at the miracle of perfectly matched blood—those twelve markers—"Abram's" gift of life.

I return to my study. Within a minute, Al calls me back. *"Jude, here's a photo."* Alone in front of a large blue/green expanse of water, our "Abram" wears a sweet expression. He's so handsome, with slender, swarthy, youthful looks and dark tight curly locks. We love him instantly. We try to absorb all at once the information on his Linked-In page, on his Facebook page. We want to know everything. Who are those people in the photos? Where is that body of water? The Dead Sea, maybe? Because he seems to have Israeli heritage. We learn that a favorite film is about Prime Minister Netanyahu. We see some Hebrew writing. It will take a few days for Allen to gather his emotions before emailing our young donor. Stay tuned.

SUNDAY, JANUARY 6, 2013. **Allen emails Eli.**

Dear Eli:

Two weeks ago, a caller from Dana Farber Cancer Institute in Boston informed me that you have agreed to share personal contact information with me, the recipient of your stem cell donation in August 2011. With heartfelt gratitude, I write today to open a line of communication, a follow-up to your gracious, anonymous note I received in June 2011.

Since my stem cell Transplant, my health has steadily improved with only a few minor setbacks along the way. Your gift has allowed me to pursue my personal and professional life in ways unthinkable two years ago as my health, energy, and optimism were slipping away. After months of dietary, socializing, and travel restrictions during the post-Transplant year, all have been lifted.

In the Transplant business, you may know that the day of the procedure is often referred to as the recipient's "new birthday." I prefer to think of August 9 as my second birthday, marking the beginning of a new chapter of my life at age sixty-six.

I would love to chat with you by phone if you are interested in doing so. The next two weeks work well for me as my wife Judith and I continue a working holiday here in Florida with our three grandchildren. Let me know if and when we might connect.

With profound and eternal thanks, Allen White

A mere thirty minutes later, Al's cell phone rings. Eli's name lights up the screen. With emotions barely in check, Al receives the call. At last, the long-awaited voice—warm, youthful, energetic.

Eli is at a cousin's wedding in Miami, flying back to Baltimore tomorrow. When Eli learned that Al was also in Florida, he asked where, hoping they might have dinner together that very night. Alas, we are at the opposite end of this long state—in Jacksonville near Georgia. But Eli's readiness to connect signals the same warmth evident in his Internet photo.

Eli is a second-semester college junior studying economics. He has older siblings, a brother thirty-two and a sister twenty-eight. He's an uncle.

Al learns that the donation procedure took six hours—about three hours longer than normal. He was recruited by Gift of Life while visiting Israel. The results of his saliva swab were entered in the international donor registry that Al's medical team contacted in their search for a match. There is no German connection. Eli has never been to Germany. Eli said that he understands the first donor chosen backed out and he was second in line. That first donor may have been from Germany or donated in Germany. We remember that we had a definite July 2011 date for Transplant, but were told that date was not convenient for the donor.

Al shakes his head with tears in his eyes, *"He sounds like such a sweetie."*

Eli is off for a semester in Prague in early February, so there may not be a chance to meet before that. He'll send his parents' New Jersey contact information in case we can get together with them before he returns. They would like to meet Allen. The family is Orthodox.

AL EMAILS HIS CHILDREN AND SISTERS:

Today I spoke with my stem cell donor Eli, age twenty-one, from New Jersey, youngest of three children of an Orthodox Jewish family. He's a sweetheart. Asked lots of questions about my kids, grandkids, and, of course, my health. Shared with me the details of his donation, beginning with a cheek swab sponsored by the Gift of Life organization while he was visiting Israel. A junior in college studying economics, off to Prague next month for a semester abroad. He called from Miami attending a cousin's wedding, hoping I was nearby so we could have dinner! Unfortunately, Miami is a seven-hour drive. But we agreed to find a time to meet in the coming months.

I'm thrilled to connect with my life saver. A deeply moving moment in time I wanted to share with you. Love to all, Dad

Daughter, Kate responds:

Thank you for sharing this, Dad, I hope you can relay to Eli how eternally grateful we are to him!! Lots of love xoxo

SUNDAY, JANUARY 20, 2013. Al emails Eli.

Hi Eli:

It was a great pleasure to talk with you a few weeks ago. Hearing your voice and your donation story, and bits and pieces about your family was deeply moving for me.

I hope your plans for travel to Prague are in good shape. Did you say you leave on Feb. 2? I depart for Boston tomorrow after a month here in Florida with my daughter and grandchildren. The next two weeks are very busy, though I was hoping I might find time for a quick trip to either NYC or NJ to meet you before your departure. January 27th and February 1 are still

possibilities. Do either of those work for you?
   Wishing you well. Allen.
MONDAY, JANUARY 21, 2013. Eli emails Allen.
Hey, Allen,
   Sorry for the late reply. I was traveling most of today. I also very much
look forward to meeting you and I would greatly appreciate your coming to
the New York area before I leave. I am still on track to leave for Prague on
February 2nd. I will probably not return home until late at night on January
27. Thursday night the 31st would be a possibility for me or, if you would like
to come for a Shabbat dinner in my parents' home, Friday the 1st would also
work just as well.
   Great hearing from you. Eli
   FRIDAY, FEBRUARY 1, 2013. FACE TO FACE AT LAST. Al flew back to Boston a week ago. I stayed in Florida that sixth week in order to continue research for my Isabela novel part of which takes place in nearby St. Augustine.
The morning after my return to Massachusetts, we drive to a hotel in New
Jersey to rest before our engagement. We are both somewhat nervous about
spending the evening with an Orthodox family. We know nothing of their
rituals or expectations. Apart from occasional encounters during Al's childhood, our only experience with Orthodox Jews is on the sidewalks of our
community, Coolidge Corner. They're known for being insular. They never
smile or acknowledge us in any way. The women are usually occupied with
a slew of children a year apart. The men are dressed in black and wear wide-
brimmed black hats. If they glance at us at all, it is with an expression that we
experience as arrogance, even scorn.
   I swim whenever and wherever I can and enjoy a half hour in the hotel
pool. Usually a hotel pool is a short elevator ride away from the room. In this
New Jersey hotel, the pool is under the same roof, but at a distance of about
two city blocks. Returning to the room takes me longer than I expected. Al is
anxious about an evening he has looked forward to since he learned he had
a match. He is uncharacteristically angry that I still need to shower and get
dressed before we can leave.
   I assumed he had the directions to Eli's family's home, but he doesn't seem
to. He just has an address. He's darting around the lobby, trying to get his
bearings, approaching various people for information. The only two people
manning the tiny reception desk in the enormous foyer under construction
seem like they're about fifteen years old. They know nothing. We run around
the parking lot asking a bus driver, whose accent we cannot understand, and

other drivers who are tourists. No one even seems to know the names of any of those highways surrounding us.

I do not know how far away Eli's home is, but I realize that we cannot possibly drive. Al is becoming more unnerved by the moment. I fear we would get hopelessly lost or even have an accident. I see no taxis in this isolated spot surrounded by whizzing autos and trucks just off I-95. I approach someone who looks like he might be a chauffeur of some kind. His private car is available. Relief.

Forty-five minutes later he deposits us at the correct address. The street is filled with parked cars because the Orthodox do not drive on Fridays. We ring the doorbell. When a young man opens the door, we are momentarily confused because, although he resembles the photos we've seen of Eli, he's holding a two-year-old. We know Eli is not a father. But the handsome young man IS Eli. The child in his arms is his beautiful niece, Rosie, who is just two months younger than our youngest granddaughter. (Several years later, he tells us that he had not wanted to go to the door all alone, so he scooped up Rosie on his way to answer the doorbell.)

We've hardly stepped inside when Eli's mother, Susan, rushes from the kitchen to greet us. Our first impressions are reinforced throughout the evening. She's the very best of Jewish mothers. Warm, affectionate, utterly devoted to her family . . . and a fabulous cook. She's dressed normally. Unlike those Brookline neighbors we pass, she wears no long dress, no head covering. We begin to relax, especially when we meet the other members of this family with whom we will spend the next three emotional hours. Seated around the table are Rosie at one end and Eli's father, Danny, at the other. Across from us are Susan; Eli; Eli's four-year-old nephew, Victor; and Eli's brother-in-law, Uri.

Allen and I sit on the other side of the table with Allen facing Eli, me next to Tamar, Eli's older sister, who is Uri's wife and the mother of Victor and Rosie. With thick black hair and a lovely smile, Tamar looks like she could be an Israeli film star. She also has her mother's warmth and sparkle and is expecting a third child.

Danny explains that the family is MODERN Orthodox—a term that is new to us. Later I research it. According to Wikipedia, Modern Orthodox Judaism is a movement within Orthodox Judaism that attempts to synthesize Jewish values and the observance of Jewish law, with the secular, modern world. Rabbi Saul Berman describes it this way: "Orthodox Judaism can 'be enriched' by its intersection with modernity; further, modern society creates opportunities to be productive citizens engaged in the Divine work of transforming the world to benefit humanity."[1] Modern Orthodoxy assigns a central role to the "People of Israel." Here two characteristics are manifest: in general, Modern Orthodoxy places a high national, as well as religious, significance on the State of Israel, and institutions and individuals are, typically, Zionist in orientation; furthermore, other "core beliefs" are a recognition of the value and importance of secular studies, a commitment to equality of education for both men and women, and a full acceptance of the importance of being able to financially support oneself and one's family.[2] I see all of the above values reflected in the lives of Eli's family:

TRADITION. Before the meal is served, Danny leads us in a short Shabbat service which includes readings and prayers. We then all leave the table for a hand-washing ritual in the kitchen. By a small sink we use a delicate, probably silver, two-handled bowl to pour water over each palm.

SIGNIFICANCE OF THE STATE OF ISRAEL. Susan has been to Israel sixteen times. It was in Israel that Eli was introduced to the Gift of Life and where he agreed to have his cheek swabbed. When we answered, "No, we haven't" to Susan's inquiry, "Have you visited Israel?" I could see she was disappointed, possibly even disbelieving.

IMPORTANCE OF A SECULAR EDUCATION FOR BOTH SEXES. From pre-school through high school, all of the children attend Hebrew schools. But they are not reading Torah all day. The varied curricula prepares them for success in today's complex world.

EMPHASIS ON SUPPORTING ONESELF AND ONE'S FAMILY. Danny has his own, prosperous Manhattan-based business where both Susan and Tamar also work.

INTERSECTION WITH MODERNITY TO CREATE OPPORTUNITIES TO BE PRODUCTIVE CITIZENS ENGAGED IN THE DIVINE WORK OF *TRANSFORMING THE WORLD TO BENEFIT HUMANITY*: Eli's gift to Al and his family's strong support for his donation is just one example.

During the service and the hand washing, Allen and I savor the delicious aromas wafting toward us from the kitchen. First a loaf of golden, perfect-ly braided *challah* is proudly displayed—baked by a neighbor who wanted to contribute to tonight's celebratory meeting. A bowl of hearty chicken soup with Matzo balls based on a family recipe would probably have been satisfy-ing enough for us. But one scrumptious dish after another appears: chicken,

---

[1] Rabbi Saul J. Berman, *The Ideology of Modern Orthodoxy*.
[2] http://en.wikipedia.org/wiki/Modern_Orthodox_Judaism.

brisket, roasted butternut squash, salads, potatoes. And for dessert, fresh fruit and apple cobbler.

Ten months later when I ask Susan to refresh my memory—"What wonderful dishes did you serve when we first met?"—she lists them for me and adds "Of course the food served during that Friday night's memorable meal was secondary as it was a perfect evening and everyone's emotions were so high."

Yes, tears are shed tonight, as Al looks with moist eyes across the table to the engaging young man whose life-giving cells now circulate through every organ and bit of tissue in Al's body. Both of us tear up as we listen and absorb the details of Eli's experience.

About a year after Eli was swabbed in Israel, Gift of Life contacted him. "We have matched you with a recipient. You will soon receive further details."

The next time they contacted him, though, they said they had found another donor for the recipient. This was apparently the donor in Germany we had been told about. We'll never know exactly what happened to that potential donor. We hope he eventually made a life-saving match in Europe or elsewhere.

A few weeks later after the initial call, Eli was driving alone from New York City to New Jersey, crossing the George Washington Bridge, high above the majestic Hudson River in rush-hour traffic, when his cell phone rang.

"Hello. Gift of Life calling. We have found a recipient who is a perfect match for you. His situation is urgent. We're asking that you give us a verbal agreement right now. During this phone call. There is something you need to know. If you do commit and later change your mind, you may be responsible for this recipient's death."

We were riveted, imagining our young man—nineteen years old at the time—being forced to make a major commitment under precarious driving circumstances. We groaned when Eli said those last words, "You may be responsible for this recipient's death." How dare they pressure him that way?

Later, we re-evaluate this blunt message. In anticipation of Eli's donation, Al had spent a week in the hospital suppressing his immune system via various chemotherapies in preparation for the new stem cells. On the seventh day—the day the fresh stem cells were expected—only hours after Eli's donation process was completed—Al was at far more risk than at any time since his diagnosis twelve years earlier. Thus, Gift of Life was being truthful. The situation required absolute clarity and commitment. They needed to extract a promise from Eli who was, after all, still a teenager who might be prone to changes of heart and mind.

Over dinner now, one and a half years after the procedure, Eli jokes with us that the most difficult part of the process was that he could not drink beer for an entire month before donating. Alcohol does not mix well with the drugs used to accelerate stem cell production in the weeks prior to a donation. This process usually leaves the donor with a sore, "packed" feeling as the abundance of cells clog the marrow and tissue. Eli was no exception. "Drink water," he was told, "Lots of it."

For over six hours at a local clinic, they drew blood from Eli's left arm, twirled the blood in a centrifuge extraction machine, and returned the remaining blood components to his right arm in a nearly continuous flow. The bag of pinkish, bubbly liquid into which the treasured cells flowed was the exact bag Nurse Tracey held out to us at midnight on the same day of Eli's donation.

Eli had been told the procedure would take only three or four hours. Owing to his slow heart rate, however, it took nearly twice as long. All that while, Eli could not get up. Connected to so many devices, he was immobilized, comforted only by his loving mother, Susan, at his side.

During dinner, it soon becomes apparent to us that the family feels ALLEN is the giver in this exchange, that because of HIM, Eli experienced the joy of giving—a Mitzvah.

As the meal progresses, the talk moves on to amusing family stories. "Tell about that time, Dad . . . No, let Mom tell it, she tells it better." We feel completely accepted, involved, and embraced as new family members.

After some photo-taking, Eli presents Al with a gift: *Out of the Depths: The Story of a Child of Buchenwald Who Returns Home at Last,* by Israel Meir Lau, former Ashkenazi Chief Rabbi of Israel. This autobiography recounts the miraculous survival of an eight-year-old boy rescued from the Buchenwald death camp who later became one of the most beloved spiritual leaders in the world. Eli's inscription reads: "This book is about personal survival. You are an inspiration to me and I wish you a continued recovery. All the best, Eli." Beholding the innocent face of young Lau on the book jacket and absorbing Eli's gracious message of humility and gratitude, Al again is overwhelmed by this unforgettable moment with this precious donor and his family.

Months earlier when we asked nurse Toni, "Does ethnicity make a difference?" she answered, "No." But we later learned that it does, both biologically and, in Eli's case, emotionally. Three of Eli's grandparents are Russian Jews. Al's are Russian and Lithuanian. All share the genetic characteristics of Eastern European, Ashkenazi Jews. Lineage, continuity, and connection—bonds forever between two human beings who were strangers until this momentous evening. When we say our goodbye's, I embrace Danny and Susan and say, "Thank you for creating Eli. And thank you for being Russian Jews."

I can sense Al's reluctance to end the evening, to separate himself from Eli. Susan follows us out into the frosty February night. "I just want to tell you," she whispers through tears, "how much Eli has matured through this experience. I've been worried about him being away on his own in Europe, but I feel less anxious now, seeing how he has interacted with you tonight. Thank you SO much for making the effort to visit us."

Within hours, her youngest child—her baby—will fly to The Czech Republic. We are having trouble parting from him. I can only imagine how difficult it is for her.

The next morning over breakfast at the hotel with local friends, we struggle to find labels to define our relationship with Eli. Our initial feeling is parental. But he has two strong parents and we have three children. That doesn't fit. We certainly feel related, though. If we were Latinos, he would be like a godchild. We and Eli's parents would be considered *compadres*. But there is no English equivalent. The closest is uncle and aunt. But the connection feels far more complex.

CARING BRIDGE: FEBRUARY 3, 2013, 9:30 P.M. FINAL *CARING BRIDGE* ENTRY–BY ALLEN: "MY DONOR, MY LIFE"

Family, Friends, Colleagues:

Many months have passed since I last communicated regarding my stem cell Transplant that occurred on August 9, 2011. At that time I reported a steady recovery with only minor, temporary setbacks. The good news continues, with all restrictions on travel, socializing, and food now lifted and the return to normalcy, thankfully, complete.

I write today hours after a seminal moment in this miraculous journey—a face-to-face meeting with my stem cell donor, Eli, age twenty-one, and his family in New Jersey. You may recall that rules of communication between donor and recipient require anonymity for a year after the procedure, followed by direct contact if both parties consent. On December 28, while visiting daughter Lena and family in Florida, my cell rang indicating "Private Caller" (aka, normally, Dana Farber Institute) on the screen. Such calls always trigger anxiety. This call turned out to be the one I had long awaited. "I have the name, email and cell phone of your donor, and he has yours. The relationship is now in your hands; we are bowing out."

After three days of contemplation during which I behold (thanks to Goo-

gle) a photo of a tall, dark, soulful young man, I email Eli with an invitation to open communication. Half an hour after hitting the send button, while chatting with granddaughter Zoey, my cell rings with Eli's name on the monitor. My shaking finger barely able to slide over the screen to answer the call, Eli greets me with a voice rich in warmth and generosity. We talk and talk. It all feels so natural—the young man whose cells now inhabit my body, sharing with me his life as a college student, a Modern Orthodox Jew, and a donor to a no-longer-anonymous recipient.

Fast forward to February 1. Judith and I sit at the Sabbath dinner table with Eli, his parents, his older sister and brother-in-law and their beautiful four- and two-year-old children. For three hours, we hear details of Eli's donation, beginning with a mouth swab in Israel and culminating in a grueling six-hour (twice the usual time required) procedure at a New Jersey hospital to extract his life-giving stem cells. Family stories and mountains of delicious food amidst a heartfelt embrace that welcomed us as new "family members." A thrilling, emotional roller coaster for me, punctuated by long glances across the table at this handsome young Ashkenazi Jew whose donation he regards as much a gift to himself as to me.

And so we have reached another milestone in this fourteen-year journey that began with my diagnosis in 1999. Eli and his family are now part of the community that has enabled me, in so many different ways, to stare down the demon that threatened my life. To each and every one of you, my eternal gratitude.

As always, Allen

RESPONSES:

- As I sit here reading Zohar, I received your wonderful posting. We know so little about why things happen the way they do. Maybe we are not supposed to know. All I know is that we have to recognize in our scientific lives that there is a mystery that perhaps needs to remain a mystery. I do believe however, for whatever reason, that Eli was meant to be there for you (along with all the rest of us). We are indeed a world unto ourselves. Eli's blessing to you is also a blessing to him, for he is now a spiritually 'more evolved' person who will go on to make this a better world, as will you, with his gift of life. Love you much Allen. Love to the family. We hope to see you and the family soon. Richard

- What a wonderful end to a wondrous journey, Allen. Looking forward to celebrating further in Amsterdam. Paul H.
- This is incredibly wonderful. I am so-o-o happy for you. God has truly blessed you . . . and Eli! Love, Rickie
- "Have we reached the end?" asked Pooh." Yes, I suppose it seems so . . . and yet . . . "
  "Yes, Piglet?" "It is also the beginning." Allen, thanks so much for sharing the heart-warming story of your meeting with this remarkable young man. A fitting conclusion to an amazing journey—and also a beginning! Love, Faye
- Another amazing chapter in a wonderful, beautiful story. . . . thank you so much for sharing with us the latest part of this journey, Allen. Makes me remember that all seven billion of us on this planet in many lands are of one extended family, joined in ways we scarcely understand but for which we must be thankful. Reading your latest posting causes me to pause for a moment and reflect on my own blessings like the fact that our paths somehow crossed along the way. I thank you deeply for being who you are in my life—I never know how you will surprise and engage me next, but it's always for the best! Every good wish for the future to you and Judith, and to Eli too. Alan
- Allen, dear heart, The circle is completed, your journey now has a denouement, and Judith has a glorious ending for her book-in-progress about your travails and triumphs together during the years since your story began. Can't imagine how joyous and poignant your meeting with Eli and family must've been. What a noble soul he must be. Will we get to learn more about him in a subsequent, illustrated CB posting? We love happy endings, but not as much as we love you and Judith. Nina and Nathan
- Allen, we are so moved by your story! And meeting with the donor who meant life itself. I could not help crying as I read your story to Marvin. We remember how you have talked for so long about yearning to meet your donor, and now it has happened, even with a Shabbat dinner, and his whole family. The fact that Eli considers his donation a gift to himself as well as to you is very powerful. How wonderful that you carry in your body the cells of such a fine, idealistic young man. What a good match! Charlene and Marvin

And this posting from a new friend, Danny, Eli's father:

- To Allen, family, and friends, "To know even one life has breathed easier because you have lived this is to have succeeded." Ralph Waldo Emerson. As the parents of Eli, Allen's donor, we consider our family blessed to have been included in Allen's circle. Not many donors are lucky enough to have a recipient that is so caring and wants to include his donor so closely in his next stage of life. For a twenty-one-year-old to know that his small act has saved another—is a priceless gift that he can carry with him with pride and maturity for the future. Our meeting last Friday night was wonderful. It was emotional, exciting, and rewarding. We now consider Allen and Judith to be connected to our family by "blood." Eli and Allen's connection has just started and we hope that the feelings we experienced Friday night will continue for many years to come. We truly consider ourselves blessed—that the encouragement of our children to be donors has led us to such wonderful and unique people who have entered our lives. Danny.

AUGUST 2013
Congenial Rivals and a Thrilling Surprise.

During our memorable evening with Eli and his family, Allen and Eli discovered a mutual interest in professional baseball. They also discovered a conflict. Eli and Danny are Yankee fans. Allen, of course, avidly follows the Red Sox.

THURSDAY, AUGUST 9, 2013. Al emails our three children, son-in-law, and daughter-in-law.

Kids: August 9 marks the two-year anniversary of my stem cell Transplant. My "new birthday," as my docs say. At 12:30 a.m. the new cells started flowing into my veins. Ninety minutes later, I stood up and walked into my new life.

All of you have been immense sources of strength and inspiration throughout this journey. Which in large measure accounts for why I'm sitting here counting my blessings, in good health and strong spirit, thinking about all the caring and tenderness you've brought to me over the past two years of uncertainty and restoration.

Next weekend, I'll celebrate again in the company of my donor Eli, together with his Dad, brother-in-law, and nephew at a Red Sox-Yankees game at

Fenway. Now that's worth living for. Much love, Dad

Yes, Eli's family is coming to Boston, explicitly apparently to enjoy a Red Sox/Yankees game with Al. He's thrilled.

I'm disappointed that it seems to be a male-only outing. I invite Susan to join me for lunch or walk or museum visit, but with two new grandchildren and Tamar's family of five living with her temporarily, there are too many demands on her time. I do get to visit with the men-folk at their hotel and during the walk to Fenway Park—a lovely treat since each of them is so personable.

The week before, I again find myself grappling with Modern Orthodox etiquette. I'm haunted by the experience of our dear nephew, Simon, after a week-long visit in the home of an Orthodox family several years ago in Israel. As Simon said goodbye and thanked the mother for her gracious hospitality, he quite naturally reached out to hug her. She seemed shocked and took a big step backward. He felt terrible—both because his gesture was apparently forbidden, but also because it felt like a scolding and a rejection—just as he was leaving.

I knew I would be very glad to see Eli, Danny, Uri, and Victor and wanted to do the right thing. Since meeting them eight months ago, I've discovered that several of my gym buddies are Modern Orthodox. I ask their advice, but get no consensus. One says, "My grandson refuses to hug anyone but ME, his grandmother." Another says, "Just ASK them if you can hug them." That seemed like it would be awkward, though, asking each of the four in turn. "May I hug you? And you? And you? And you?" Too formal. Too silly. Making too big a deal of a simple so-glad-to-see-you greeting.

Then I realized exactly what to do. Ask Eli's mother, Susan. We communicate regularly and have become good email friends. Susan's immediate reply is totally reassuring: "Definitely! We are family! Everyone is so excited about the trip to Boston."

They've timed their trip to fit perfectly into their Sabbath rules. They will arrive before sundown on Friday and park their car at the hotel garage. Saturday, they will walk all over Boston and take a Duck Boat tour through the city and into the Charles River. By the end of the game, it will be dark, the Sabbath will be over, and they will drive back to New Jersey.

Now, late afternoon, we all walk down the Commonwealth Avenue Mall to the ballpark and take photos along the way. I hug them goodbye and walk home, leaving the four men and one boy as they head for Fenway Park.

One of many Red Sox traditions is to honor a hero during a break after the sixth inning. It may be a teacher who dedicated extra hours to help a troubled and struggling student; a firefighter who risked his life to save a family;

a stranger who dove into a river to save a drowning child. Since the Boston Marathon bombing, many heroes have been recognized in this way.

It's the end of the sixth inning with the Red Sox ahead 5-2. Suddenly, a booming voice on the public address system blares to the crowd: "Today we have with us Stem Cell Donor Hero Eli from New York and his Boston Recipient, Allen. Welcome Eli and Allen." Thirty-eight thousand people stand and applaud. Danny points to Eli and Allen, just returning from a refreshment break. The fans close by reach out, shout, point to Eli and Allen, and pat them on the back.

The right-field billboard lights up with the same message. In huge letters, between ads for Dunkin Donuts and Ford Motor Company: "Today we have with us Stem Cell Donor Hero Eli from New Jersey and his Boston Recipient, Allen. Welcome Eli and Allen."

Al and Eli embrace, astonished by the attention, both utterly surprised by the recognition. Turning to Eli's father, Danny, who is grinning, they soon learn that the entire episode was orchestrated by Eli's sister, Tamar, who contacted the Red Sox, urging recognition for her brother, a true hero, and Allen, the recipient of Eli's wondrous act of giving.

Al comments on what that surprise meant to him: *"Another magical moment in this magical relationship."*

NOVEMBER 2013

S UNDAY, NOVEMBER 17, 2013. Remembering two years ago and the coincidence of that healing marker—DAY 100—falling on our anniversary, I post our wedding photos on Facebook with the words, "Forty-five years ago today and I love the guy more than ever." Thirty friends respond with congratulatory greetings.

We've just returned from Washington, D.C. where we always walk by the 21st Street NW apartment I was living in when we met. We are looking forward to a Thanksgiving trip to Ohio plus a New York City business/pleasure trip, followed by five weeks in Florida. We're also planning a trip in 2014 to Asturias in Spain—the setting of my second novel, *The New Worlds of Isabela Calderón*. I'm pushing to publish it by then, so that I can introduce Isabela's story to her modern countrymen.

Even in the darkest days of his illness, whether in the hospital room or quarantined at home, Al found solace in pursuing his passion for transforming corporations in pursuit of a just and sustainable future. This passion remains undiminished two years after Transplant.

So how are we celebrating today? Quietly. Domestically. Gratefully. Sipping home-made chicken soup from new red-and-white china bowls. Walking through our neighborhood. Enjoying the crisp fall. Napping. Reading. Talking to our kids. Being together when not long ago that possibility seemed to be slipping away forever.

To Al I leave the final words:

As the saying goes, who needs fiction when life itself is the greatest story of all? Forty-five years of an extraordinary partnership recounted in this tale of romance, resilience, and rebirth has been a gift. The continuous flow of trials, adaptation, and renewal—most poignantly expressed in my near-death experience—is now on record, thanks to Judith's determination to share it with friends, family, and beyond. The unbounded strength and love she brought to our shared journey was, and continues to be, my sustenance. My greatest wish is that every reader of this story be blessed with a life of equal beauty and fulfillment.

All things appear and disappear because of the
concurrence of causes and conditions.
Nothing ever exists entirely alone;
everything is in relation to everything else.

Buddha (B.C. 568-488)

Appendix

A small example of the nearly 3,000 responses
we received to our Caring Bridge postings.

Loving, clever, insightful, these responses
buoyed our spirits, comforted us, and made us laugh.
We're convinced they also contributed to the outstanding
success of the procedure.

July 11, 2011 – by Allen. "Background Story"

- Hey my dearest cousin – You know how much I am always with you in heart and spirit. You and Judith exemplify what a supportive and loving partnership truly is. Can't wait to hear how those new little stem cells are making their way into you! Thanks so much to you both for this great way to communicate with you and all your great family and friends. With all love, Carrie

- Allen – I received your formal message about this today—on the second anniversary of my own liver Transplant. You know how it completely changed my life. I wish you every ounce of peace and courage that you need—you are surrounded by people who love and respect you and we all offer our support and affection. Having travelled with you around the world and participated with you in what must be hundreds of meetings and gatherings, I know what an extraordinary contribution you have made to the planet and its people. This phase will pass and we will be celebrating our lasting friendship and continuing to make trouble (and progress) for many years to come. Love to you also, Judith, in this additional step in your wonderful and inspiring partnership with Allen. With my deepest friendship. Bob Massie

- Hey compadre – You have been in our thoughts frequently, and Theta and I are, in Quaker parlance, "holding you in the light." We look forward to seeing you both asap after a successful recovery. Love from Jim and Theta

---

Friday, July, 15, 2011 – by Judith. "Our Dear Donor"

- What a disappointment! That's so hard just when you're all geared up for such a critical date. The donor selection process is fascinating, amazing to be able to sift through hundreds of thousands for the perfect match. And then there's the whole drama of getting the stem cells to Al. We'll be eager to hear the new date, and Al— we'll be rooting for you during that long recovery period. Love, Charlene and Marvin

- We are each of us a world unto ourselves. The beautiful and heartfelt tributes to you prove that to be true. As you proceed forward, know that there is a world-stretched collection of arms embracing and holding you. See you soon! Richard

- Dearest Al and Judith –I can only imagine the disappointment in learning of the delay. I really appreciated the explanation of the procedure. When I looked it up online, there were too many questions. Now it's clearer. You're both strong and courageous people, and I know this fortitude will carry you through this difficult time. You're in our hearts. (and happy 65th, Al!). All our love, Kina and John

- Dear Al and Judy – Some of the greatest times of my life were spent next to you all in Columbus, Ohio. I remember the applesauce, the laughs, and babysitting Kate and Lena. It goes without saying you will be in my thoughts and prayers. When you get home and can accept visitors, expect a visit . . . without Chunga!!!!! Love, Rickie, Rachel, Caroline

- Dear Allen and Judith –I've known you two for over twenty years, so I can attest, Allen, that yours is a life well lived and that you have received many gifts in all the ways you mention in your story. I'll be checking in both in this forum and by phone, post, and email as the saga continues. With fond memories of Newton, Amsterdam, and Brookline. Love, Roberto

- Uncle Al and Aunt Judith – Sorry to hear about the setback, sending lots of love! When those stem cells get into you they will be soooo happy they will just dance and sing; they are waiting for the right time. Thinking about you tons and sending love and positive energy! Your loving niece, Anna

- Hi Father! – Sending you the warmest greetings from Hollywood! Glad the appointment is finally set and you are ready to regain new strength in your life. It's like a rebirth! Keep up the positive energy. And let my music constantly be a source of inspiration! Love you! Your son, Doug

---

SUNDAY, JULY 23, 2011 – BY JUDITH. "THE WONDER OF STEM CELLS"
- They also might be corporate cleansers, like Al, who march right in, clean up the body's act, creating a more wholesome organism. Sarah
- Al so excited about the date. They couldn't be entering a better body. Lisa
- Dearest Al – Besides knowing that you are one of the few people I know in the world whose body will flourish with new stem cells, I wish only that it could have been me or Lisa who had the proper blood type and could have been the donors. There would have been no delays then! It is clear to me from all these wonderful notes of love

that everyone has sent, that you continue to touch people in the same way that I always remember being touched by you . . . I cannot imagine that anyone has felt closer to their brother than I to you . . . you are one of those special people who one never forgets . . . your logic, humor and warmth are unforgettable. I love you and am always thinking about you. Betty

---

Tuesday, July 26, 2011 – by Allen. "Metaphors and Root Beer"

- Hi Al – Do you know the "Fantastic Voyage" movie/book? A group of people get miniaturized and travel by some aquatic vessel through a person's blood stream. Well, we're all in there on this adventure and fantastic voyage with you—coursing the seas of your circulatory system until the tide of new stem cells flows into your full health and recovery. Then you and Judith will have decades of time to continue your adventures on the outer skin of our planet. And if there's need of any potion/prescription for Magic Cookie Bars, Molly will fill the order and send it out with a dose of love to make the "pills" go down easy. All the best, Al. Keith, and the rest of the family.

- Allen – Will and I had a lovely weekend away in Southern Virginia this weekend. We walked through a meditative labyrinth where I spent time picturing you at home after your surgery this week, comfortable, and peaceful with the love of your life, Judith, beside you. I will continue to create that image with both of you in mind in the coming days. Richard

- Know that I admire so much the way you adore Judith and those who are closest to you, Allen. You have always made me feel so loved, and I hope I can return even just a tad bit of that to you now . . . and always. Big hugs! After all the waiting, surely putting even your tremendous patience to a test, tomorrow is the day that this remarkable process will begin. All of us, from our assorted corners of the globe, will be rooting for you, cheering for you, and sending you positive energy . . . so we might feel a little shift in gravitational pull, a tilt of the earth's axis, perhaps a small nudge to line things up the way they should be . . . very much the way you have worked to fix the world for the rest of us. Go, little stem cells! Go! Hans

Tuesday, August 2, 2011 – by Judith. "To the Hospital Today"
- Uncle Al – Sending lots of love and positive energy your way and thinking about you tons, those stem cells are seriously going to do the jig in your body, I can feel it!! Lots and lots of love. Your loving niece, Anna
- I am inspired by the number of poets and visionaries in my parents' circle and so appreciate all the metaphors. Thank you Hans for the gravitational pull, Jody for the peaceful healing image, Keith's "fantastic voyage," Marjorie's living plants, Sarah's corporate cleansers, and Anna's dancing, singing stem cells! I have appreciated reading and integrating all these images—along with your outpouring of love and support. It really means so much. Thank you, dear ones! Kate

Thursday, August 4, 2011 – by Judith.
"Brief Update From the Hospital Room"
- Thinking of you today (and every day), especially after reading today's journal update. It's hard to imagine you tied down to essential hospital devices like drips! Your unquenchable sense of humor must be a great asset in the whole process. Be strong, my friend—I'm there for you all the way! Alan. PS. GISR = Getting Infused (with) Stem cells Reinvigoration!
- Good Morning Allen! We are all sending our various forms of spiritual and cosmic positive ions; sorry to hear about the medical tether, but if this is the way to fight the battle, hang in there! Dave and Gloria
- Allen and Judith – Great to be able to follow the process and your progress through this site. I can't help but make the analogy of the stem cell process to Allen's Corporation 20/20 efforts—a systematic re-purposing of the system. James & Nancy

Saturday, August 6, 2011 – by Judith. "Losing It – A Little"
- Dear Allen –The analogy that came to mind when I read your journal was giving birth to my children—the terror when you realize you are pregnant and there is no turning back, the pain of actually giving birth, and then the immense joy when the child is finally in your arms and you get to go home with a new life. It seems to me that this is what you are going through—the fear, the pain, and then the joy next week when Abram is literally in your arm and then you get to go home with a new life. *L'Chaim!* Love, Faye

- Almost, Dad—we are with you EVERY second! Love, Lena

August 8, 2011 – by Allen. "Day Zero"
- Dear Al and Judith – How wonderful to read the breadth of support and love you are receiving from your community. I've had you on my mind constantly, especially tonight as those beautiful little guys enter your body. It's all terribly surreal. And wonderful. I'm feeling very hopeful in my gut, and will be sending all the positive energy I can your way. Yes, laughter is the supreme healer, and TG you've got humor in spades to help carry you through. Big love to you both, Kina
- Such eloquence in describing your body and soul's marshaling of forces for the new arrivals! And there's a whole phalanx of supporters right behind you, huzzahing and bearing flags of welcome. Love, Sarah
- *Compadre – Estamos contigo.* Jim
- Dear Zayde – I hope that everything goes as planned tonight and that I hear from you tomorrow that everything went well!!! I can't wait to see you and Gramma ASAP! Maybe we can visit you in Boston again soon. I love you, Coley
- Hi, Allen – This is all very strange to me and it sounds grueling. I am hoping all WILL go as planned—EXCEPT that you will have a quicker and smoother recovery than expected. I'm sure you will find many ways to fill the time. You are usually so busy it will seem odd at first. Think of it like going to the beach for 100 days. First, you are restless, bored, don't know what to do with yourself. Then that pulsing of the surf gets into your bones and your sense of time and priorities shift. Relaxation. One day at a time, each with its own weather. Being and taking care of your own basic welfare is all there is. Could be kinda nice. I so hope it will be. Much love, TC

Tuesday, August 9, 2011 – by Allen. "New Cells, New Chapter"
- Allen – your last two entries have been so powerful and moving—must confess to crying upon reading both. The one before last--written at 2:30 a.m.—created a strong sense of your presence and your place—I felt as though I was right there with you!! And am so glad and relieved to read the Transplant is now a reality!! I hope you get to go home tomorrow and all will proceed with health and new life beckoning from there. Love, Martha

- Whew! *Enfin!* Like everyone else, we have been sitting by our computer and waiting for the news. And like Martha, I, too, cried on reading your last entry. Let the healing begin, *mon cher cousin*. We wrap you in a blanket of comfort and love to both protect those cells from escaping and to keep you from infection. And kudos to dear Judith whose endurance, fortitude, and strength have kept us all going! Thanks so very much for the great communication throughout. We all await the next chapter. With all our love, Carrie
- Yes, what an important day of celebration, Dad! I would think those cells would have some sense of how anticipated they are by you and your huge circle of loving friends and family. May you continue to adapt beautifully and strongly to Abram—and get lots of new help now beating those damn bad ones OUT! I love you dearly. Kate
- Stem Cell Blessing –

    God, today we witnessed the gift of new life. Please bless these stem cells. We thank you for the donor who so graciously gave them; to give another a new chance at life.

    As these stem cells flowed into Allen, we trust in your care and blessing this day. We pray that Allen's body be fully receptive to this new day of birth and as we go forward. Strengthen and bring comfort to Allen, as each day will hold its own challenges. We beg for peace in body, mind and spirit, so that good energy will flow at the dawn of each day

    Bless all those in Allen's circle of love and support. Nurture their compassionate hearts and illumine their lives so that your light be ever present to Allen.

    Walk us into the future and we pray in gratitude for your blessing this day. Amen.

    Richard Backer
- Abram. Bless Abram! It is indeed awesome. All of us are privileged that you share these feelings and moments with us. We're glad the suspense and waiting is behind you, and now the best of luck with the next step of avoiding infection and rejection of the cells. I feel confident you will succeed, especially with Judith by your side all the way. Love, Charlene and Marvin
- Dear brother, congratulations. Your miraculous body is working wonders yet again, a testament to a life lived well. You have given so much for so long. Now is your time to reap. See you soon. Love, Johnny

Wednesday, August 10, 2011 – by Judith. "Home Today"

- Sounds like a miracle waiting to be completed—hard to believe that he is home already and beginning this next leg of the journey. Sending love and kisses. Mindy and Norman
- Amazing! So happy to hear you're home already, and that recovery's going well so far. Thinking about you a ton, and sending all kinds of positive thoughts. Much love, Nephew Simon (and Niece Babs)

Tuesday, August 16, 2011 – by Kate. "Day Seven"

- Hello and much love to all of you. With the good food from Sarah in Kate's capable, loving hands, the healing will go so much faster. We are thinking of you each day and cannot be thankful enough that the care in Boston is so wonderful. Please know that I am available to do errands or whatever. Just ask! Xx Babsie
- We were both sooooo appreciative of Kate's great entry . . . it gave us more insight into the daily routine you are both going through. I, too, was reminded of Aunt Sarah's wonderful cooking . . . that meat loaf with mashed potatoes on top, made with such love for us all. So wish we lived closer to be of some help, but know that we continue to be with you every day with our continued love and support. Hugs to all THREE of you! Carrie and Hans
- Dear Family – Thanks for the portrait of daily life in this early phase, Kate. Sending you all love and good cooking karma. And since another reader asked for Allen's thoughts on a *New York Times* article, I'd like to know what Allen thought about the piece in Sunday's paper on CSR, "First, Make Money. Also, Do Good." After all, we know that so much of what drives Allen is his passion for ideas around social change so this kind of thinking and reading will surely help his new cells acclimate! Love, Maureen
- Al: – I recently heard about your situation—what a shit-eating world, but what else shall I call it?—through the back door of the path by which information flows. But flow it did. I take encouragement that your attitude is strong, positive, and rational. I have loved you from close-up and also from afar for about sixty years; I will not be so immodest as to request another sixty for both of us, but a significant chunk of that, in good health, will do just fine. Arnold

Saturday, August 20, 2011 – by Allen. "Downs and Ups"

- Hi Allen. We are very happy to read about your progress and your time with the "masked and gowned family members who have arrived." I picture a new Harry Potter look! :) We'll continue to send *"root-in you little Abram critters,"* vibes with no questions asked at the border crossing! Gretchen and Jack

- Allen and Judith –I've been thinking about you as I embark on my European trip. This practicing Jewish man is lighting candles for you (really) in some pretty incredible churches. The cathedral in Munich. The village church in Hall, Austria. More to come, no doubt. Keep up with the postings. News is important way over here. Len

- Dearest Cousins –This delicate balance that you so eloquently describe makes the miracle that is going on in your body even more incredible. I am jealous of those who get to visit you, so let me know when you feel up to a Skype conversation. No germs will be involved, I promise. *Avec mille bises,* Carrie

- Hi You Two!! Glad to read your latest! Peter is looking forward to seeing you soon!!! Oceans of love, Peter and Claudia

Saturday, August 27, 2011 – by Judith. "Mr. White, You're Engrafting. Congratulations!"

- What a welcome, welcome report! We shall be eager for word from the Wizard of Oz on Sept. 8! And yea for the shower! Yea for a whole week without a clinic visit! Much Love, Charlene and Marvin

Sunday, September 4, 2011 – by Allen. "Rough Patch"

- Hi Allen – Kien and I have been following your progress from Amsterdam. We are greatly encouraged by the positive news and join your many friends and family in sending our love and best wishes. Let us know when it's good to send over a care package of raw herring, Gouda cheese and some Dutch *speculaas* cookies. Warmly, Paul and Kien

- Keep the faith, Father. You are doing great and you're always in the thoughts of your children and friends. What a lucky guy to have so much love and support! This can be a very lonely world for many people out there. It's inspiring that you have found all these amazing people in your life and have maintained such incredibly profound relationships! Did you find my music page? www.youtube.com/douglaswhitemusic. I hope it's a source of inspiration to you in these trying times. Always remain positive, thankful, and realize that there are many who care about you! Love you Pop! Your son, Doug

- My dearest cousin – I can't begin to tell you how much we all appreciate your updates . . . even with all the gory details. It makes us feel closer, more in touch, and more able to cheer you and Abram along this path. I do so hope that the days ahead will be less *désagreable (en français)*. And what a testament to your great relationship that it was YOU who felt better when Judith finally got her night out! Please know that we are saving up all the goodies you will finally be able to eat when you come to visit! With love, as always, Carrie

- So sorry about the rough patch, Dad, you are the last person in the world who deserves such challenges. Nausea is the worst! But so thrilled with the blood levels news. Patience. And very glad to hear Mom is getting some well-deserved girlfriend time out. Sad to not have you and Mom at my 40@40 exhibit August 26th but as you have heard, you were well represented with Levensons (Nat and Nina), Klines (Betty and Bobby), and Peace Corps 1968 (John and Kina)! Everyone wanted to hear all the latest about you. Yesterday, Maureen and I took CityCarShare out of foggy SF and got some sunshine and stunning vistas in Point Reyes. And even got a look at the once-endangered 800-lb. Tule Elk with their massive antlers. Thought of you and how, with some protective love, these beautiful creatures are now roaming, running, mating, chomping on shrubs, healthy, safe, and free. Soon, Dad, so you will be. Kate

---

Thursday, September 15, 2011 – by Judith. "Balance"

- So beautifully written, Judith!! I'm sure it makes us all join the struggle for the straight line on the teeter-totter (my word, too), legs hanging but perfectly balanced. That's what I wish for Al and Abram, the two A's coming to a perfect point at the top. Love, Sarah

- Hi to Judith and Allen from Wilcox, AZ – Stopped into this little one-horse town to check the *Caring Bridge* and our emails. Thanks, Judith for your great post on balance. We visited a few days ago Biosphere 2—balance is what it's all about there—as it is on Biosphere 1 (earth itself!!)? Allen, congratulations on reaching the thirty-day mark with no infections and no hospitalizations. Love, from Martha

- Dear Allen and Judith – what a wonderful posting today. The analogy of the see-saw (a Worcester term) and Allen and Abram's struggle for balance was perfect. But, I thought of playgrounds with swings when sometimes we need a push. The two of you are the perfect duo for swinging as high as one can go with the love and help of another. Thinking of you each day. Love - Babsie and Howard

- Dearest Al and Judith – The word teeter-totter brought me back to Fairmount Park in Wichita, Kansas where I spent most of my childhood! Your description was poetic, Judith, and the perfect analogy. Balance. *Equilibre* in French . . . which is so apt because it also refers to the state of mind. Which you two clearly have. We are all with you, counting the days until we know how Abram is faring inside you, and hoping that his cells remain as strong as you. Tough competition. With love, love, love, Cousin Carrie

- Dear Allen and Judith – "He cautiously, but joyfully, rode his bike to the clinic." What courage, perseverance—and hope—shine through with those few, simple words—words that brought tears to my eyes and joy to my heart. Judith's analogy of the see-saw was amazingly appropriate (since I grew up within twenty-five miles of Worcester I, too, played on a see-saw as a child). According to Wikipedia both see-saw and teeter-totter demonstrate a morphological process called reduplication—a term also used to describe a cell's ability to multiply. A remarkable coincidence or an encouraging sign from a higher being as we wait for more good news next week? I prefer to think the latter. With love, Faye

---

THURSDAY, SEPTEMBER 22, 2011 – BY ALLEN.
"CHIMERA, ABRAM, AND ME"

- Kien and I welcome this amazing grace news, Allen, and send our continued good vibrations to you and the family. We are all well this end, enjoying our two granddaughters on a regular basis, doing some rowing, and continuing to bang on the "It's the Planet, Stupid" drum. Paul H.

- Hello there, dear neighbors! I am breathing one huge sigh of relief right now! This is glorious news, and we are just hoping that your progress continues, gradually but surely. Your missives are wonderful, informational, humorous, and inspiring . . . oh, yes . . . and just downright enjoyable! Wait a minute . . . can you guys do lunch in the next week or so? Enough of this computer stuff . . . We could meet at the park and celebrate. Sibyl

- Once again, excellent news! I hope you'll forgive me, but it inspired the following limerick:

  The cells of Abram chimerical
  Were asked to perform quite the miracle;
  And they've managed to quench
  In Allen (THE MENSCH)
  Bad cells right down to a trickle.
  Jim T.

- Mazel TOUGH! Jeff L.
- Hi, Allen and Judith!! Yayyy! Wow, who would've thought the news would be this good, this soon? I'm so glad you're in the hot-bed of some of the greatest medical care in the world! I love the audio image of Lena singing "Amazing Grace." We might not have heard it all the way out here on the west coast, but I believe we certainly felt it. Love, hugs and kisses, Maureen
- Great news, Allen and Judith! Cheers for the marathon, the jittery screen visit and the song *Amazing Grace*—if ever a tune could heal, that's it! Love from Kate (Taylor Mighty) and me and see you soon. Roberto
- Dearest Allen and Judith – I write this through a veil of tears. Your story is as heart-warming as a bowl of soup. The way you tell it is pure poetry. Please know that from here in the depths of *la France profonde* we send you our love and our admiration and our healing wishes. Jane and Marc

---

WEDNESDAY, OCTOBER 5, 2011 – BY JUDITH.
"A BLACK EYE YET LOOKING GREAT!"

- KEEP IT UP FATHER!!!! :) SUCCESS!!!! :) Doug
- Here's the title of your new comic book series: "The Adventures of Black-Eyed Al and Nurse Judith." Follow our intrepid heroes as they storm the bastions of medical totalitarianism with their Abrams Tank. Seriously . . . what a rollercoaster. Love the images of Judith reading the *New York Times* for hours and Al thrilling the local kids. Yikes, Roberto

- Can't wait to check out this intrepid black-eyed lad and his funny, faithful servant lass for ourselves on the 18th, by which time the eye will have turned to greenish yellow. He'll be back on his exercise routine, though, so expect some of that glorious ruddiness to shine through. Love to both. Kina
- You guys are such troopers; seeing the upside after so many physical assaults and right on for questioning the nurses (says Nurse Andy). One needs to see the whole person not the little piece of the body you're working on. We are still in limbo, awaiting the scan which will tell us if the Transplant is "a go." So far lab values show good tumor re-trenchment but there have been other challenges as a result of the latest treatment, such as GI pain and low white cells. All improving but very tough as you well know. Yes, it's a marathon and not a sprint. Love to you both and glad you're doing so well. Andy and Paul
- Hi, Judith and Allen – Each year, a few weeks after the summer ends here on the Vineyard, I take a deep breath, think hard, and wonder what I failed to do in recent months. I'm embarrassed to say that I usually find more than I wish I would. This process led me here and suddenly I found myself wound up in the extraordinary web of your ordeal. An hour later, after reading your entries from mid-July to now, I sat back and exhaled. I was trying to think how to describe you. Miracle workers, that's what you are. Kind of a trite phrase, but when I think about it I like the juxtaposition of those two seemingly incompatible words. Miracle workers. Miracle workers surrounded by miracle workers. Chris and I are so grateful to know you and to be able to share—in some small way—this remarkable journey. Our hearts are with you and we send lots of love your way. John A.
- Judith – You say you leave your writing to care for Al, but we all think your writing continues to impress us while you are being a superb nurse Judith! Thank you for these images, vivid scenes of your daily life, and clear descriptions woven with humor. They help us, more than you might realize, stay close to you both. Allen: Through Quasimodo, Frankenstein, and Scarman scenarios, your beauty will always shine through. Cousin Carrie

FRIDAY, OCTOBER 14, 2011 – BY ALLEN. "WEEP, EAT, SLEEP"

- Beautiful, Allen, just beautiful! I was particularly moved by your "weep" section. My sense is that post-steroid you'll be as moved by life's blessings as you are now. There's a Hebrew blessing I recite frequently, the "*shehecheyanu*," that gives thanks for any particular moment. Sarah

- Dear Energizer Bunny – Getting by on five hours a night of sleep sounds like Nirvana to us. That fertile brain of yours has undoubtedly laid plans for saving the planet, curing all of humanity's ills and cracking the Enigma Code. Please send us a year's supply of those steroids you're taking, Allen. Seriously, your account of frequent and unbidden weeps moved *us* to tears. How sweet that you are so vulnerable and so emotionally buzzed. We're delighted to hear that your appetite is roaring back and want to hear in your next communiqué that you've gained back all of those twenty pounds and a few extra for good measure. You and Judith set the standard for loving and healing in your remarkable life partnership. Excelsior . . . and love, Nina and Nat

- Dear Al – I remember when they took my spleen back in '87 they tapered me off 120 mg of Prednisone. Same deal—sobbing in the supermarket checkout! Hang in there my hero! L, Jeff

- Dear Uncle Al (and Aunt Judith of course!) – I love reading these updates. I find the image of you weeping during basketball quite beautiful actually. Therapeutically weeping, eating, and sleeping sounds like my perfect type of day. :) Prayers of continued healing and strength are coming your way. My mom is looking forward to visiting. Love, Niece Jeanna

- Hi! "Tangerine" playing on VPR . . . Peter en route from Marlboro (after long day giving his 200 percent plus) and such good news from you!! Weep . . . yes, dear ones, as I glance at your picture on the left of the screen. Both so beautiful!!! Your careful care-taking is just such happy precious news . . . a little bit of salty tear here and there is good! (Interesting . . . tear (as in tear up) and tear (torn up . . .) (((and how about tear drop))). Thanks for your updates and thoughts this week. Anyway, wish my little teardrop could salt your dinner in person. xoxo Claudia

- Not surprised that all those basketball shots—combined with everything else going on —would make you weep, Dad! We all know how much you love the game, even though "your feets too big." Mom's menus made my mouth water, so glad there's some more flexibility in diet now. You sure look gorgeous and healthy in that new photo! I just arrived at my hotel room in D.C., the city where I know you and Mom were part of the sixties revolutions. Now I'm attending RailVolution, and can't wait to have you back up to 100 percent to continue your critical leadership in transforming the world. Love you ferociously xoxo, Kate

---

FRIDAY, OCTOBER 28, 2011 – BY ALLEN.
"THE MANY FLAVORS OF CARING"

- Some life-affirming Bach from Mr. Milstein! http://www.youtube.com/watch?v=waxat-_tRH8 Jeff

- Such wonderful news! Your entries just keep getting better and better. I have been thinking so much about you this past week . . . Sasha and I are in Israel for the first time . . . a mother and daughter voyage in every sense of the word. Hesitant to make this trip, I now understand why this land is so coveted. Magnificent vistas of desert mountains, lush oases of waterfalls and greenery, history that goes back millenniums, and a people more welcoming than I had imagined. At the Wailing Wall, I had an exceptional experience that brought me kaleidescoping backwards in time, beyond our grandparents and touching the core of our ancestors. I gave thanks at that Wall for Abram, his cells filling yours with the strength of generations. Your openness to receiving them and to their life-giving source has been what has made this all possible. The words *Shalom* and *L'haim* have taken on a deeper meaning for me now . . . and I send them to you with everlasting love and awe, dearest cousin. Carrie

---

TUESDAY, NOVEMBER 8, 2011 – BY JUDITH. "SIGNS AND SCIENCE"

- I had heard, but forgotten about, the Jeep story. Thank goodness he jumped out! xo, offspring from your forty-three years of love, Kate

- God bless the laugh lines! They're contagious. And wow, why don't I remember the Jeep incident? Of course, being a passenger in any kind of conveyance in up-country Nicaragua was a religious undertaking, an exercise in faith, in those days. Probably still is. You are a lucky pair, and we're lucky to know you. Jim and Theta

- Thanks, Judith, for this very moving post and portrait of your many years together. And thanks for your wise and lovely posts, Al. I am filled with gratitude and hope by the good news. May your progress continue and those trips get booked. Jim and I celebrated our twentieth anniversary in September. We're right behind you two! We recalled Al saying at our wedding, "Lost a tenant, gained a cousin-in-law." (Thanks to the yenta supreme, Judith.) Your love and caring for each other, and your sharing of this present stage of your journey, are truly an inspiration. Hugs to you both, Katie

---

THURSDAY, NOVEMBER 17, 2011 – BY ALLEN. "DAY 100"

- WOO-HOO! Allen and Judith – That's the news we've been waiting for and we couldn't be happier. Also, may your experience with donor Abram be all that you want it to be. At the same time, the news about your friend Paul is sobering. It brings reflections on notions of randomness vs. a grand plan. Our condolences to his family and friends, and yourselves. Love to you both – Roberto, Kathryn, and Kate.

- HOOOORAAAAAAH! I can't imagine a better anniversary gift, for my super-social, uber-active parents: restrictions lifted. Happy forty-third, folks!!! Sending piles of love, gratefulness, and awe from SanFran, Kate

- Oh, Allen, Oh, Judith – We celebrate this remarkable milestone with you. Could there be any better news awaiting you at the finish line of your heroic 100-day endurance test? As lifelong atheists, we are beginning to suspect there IS a God. The grace and dignity, the humor and candor that shine through all of your *Caring Bridge* updates say it all about why we love you and what makes you both such extraordinary people. AND, Happy Anniversary! We remember your wedding day fondly and are so pleased that we were there for the official launch of a marriage that is the envy of everyone who knows you. Nina and Nat

- Hurahhhhhhhhhhhhhh! We are over the moon. Much love, The Strauss's

- Dear Judith and Al – I felt tingling in my head as I read your wonderful news! The interconnectedness of all life is so poignantly evident—from Abram's cells to yours and, as well—in the life of your friend Paul. I am sharing with you both in the many blessings. Love from *ta cousine*, Marie

- The nuclear winter of radiated cells is over!! Humankind—especially the Allen and Judith kind—can come out of their bunker and breathe directly the wonderfully, mildly polluted air of Boston. We've so enjoyed the pithy sharing of your journey here, and not one of pathos and despair, but of radiant and grateful optimism. The world continues to spin on its axis of everyday miracles that we so often take for granted. This occasion calls for many festivities, one of which could be a family game of hoops in Ohio, replete with magic cookie bars and fresh lemonade at the break. Does your new blood help you jump higher? I'll bet now you can dunk your joy and your magic cookie bars over the rim and into a new game. You're standing on Holy Ground folks, and we can feel the drumbeat of your blood pumping and thumping through the souls of your feet all the way to and through the good earth to us, here, knowing we are ALL bloody cellmates (as the English might say . . .) in this glorious body of humanity. *Namaste* – Keith and Mol

---

THURSDAY, DECEMBER 1, 2011 – BY JUDITH.
"FAREWELL *CARING BRIDGE* . . . FOR NOW"

- Dear Judith and Allen – Reminds me of that wonderful song by Roberta Flack— http://www.youtube.com/watch?v=5JWAmF-Z4r4. See you soon! Lots of love, Maureen
- Judith, what you have written so beautifully makes us appreciate anew the gift of life and the gift of friendship. We copied down the line, ". . . the intricate human body is not a robot and always subject to setbacks." This is something we both need to keep in mind, especially as we are fast approaching our 84th and 82nd birthdays. Much love, Charlene and Marvin

---

TUESDAY, FEBRUARY 28, 2012 – BY ALLEN.
"SIX MONTHS OF BLESSINGS"

- It's great to have you back, Allen. You are a light in so many lives. Here's to 100 more six-month anniversaries. Warmly, Marjorie
- Thank you for the wonderful update, Dad, I know many of your "followers" appreciate hearing from you directly, as some of them have been asking me how you are doing. I wanted to take this opportunity to again thank your phenomenal medical team at Dana and your and

Mom's wide circle of friends and family who have made this swift recovery from stem cell replacement possible. Your entire community, with your kids and grandkids at the top of the list, are so so blessed to have you healthy and strong and in our lives with your wise, intelligent warmth and nurturing. We are so lucky to have your love and to be able to continue to love you. Xoxo. Kate

- Dear Allen and Judith – Hurrah!! Seems miraculous, really, like something out of a screenplay your son might write. Thank you for continuing to check in on *Caring Bridge* with these updates because I also love to hear what everyone else in your Caring Community has to say. Lots of love, Maureen

---

DAY 365, THURSDAY, AUGUST 9, 2012, 5:50 A.M. – BY ALLEN. "DAY 365!"

- Yay, what great news. And new hair, what could be better, where do I sign up! Best wishes, Joel
- Dear brother Allen, I, personally, am reassured to know that your great mind, good heart, great sense of humor, and outstanding contributions to the world through your work, will live on and on. With tears in all our eyes, we drink a toast to Abram and Allen! Betty
- I am so thankful!!!!! I am tearful with joy right now! Yeah!!!!!! Anna
- Allen and Judith – We could not say it better! . . . the tremendous journey that you have run, the generosity of a stranger, the almost unthinkable results of the treatment, the loss of others among our friends and family members in recent times, and thus, the further work to be accomplished in terms of cancer prevention and cure . . . but this is a moment in time for gratitude and celebration! David and Gloria
- Dearest Brother-in-Law – I am so, so grateful for your humble and productive life. Love, Mol

---

FEB. 3, 2013, 9:30 P.M., FINAL *CARING BRIDGE* ENTRY – BY ALLEN. "MY DONOR, MY LIFE"

We kept the responses to our final *Caring Bridge* post in the main text, pages 268-270.

ACKNOWLEDGEMENTS

We wish to thank early readers—Marion Freedman-Gurspan, Barbara Gorney, and Dr. Deborah Spitz—whose thoroughness and wise suggestions helped shape this work; Faye Camardo for her skilled, sensitive editing; András Rátonyi for preparing 46 years of photos for submission; Carlyle Carter for lending her publishing expertise to the project and agreeing to coordinate all publishing tasks; plus Sylvia Frost and Erika Nygaard for their clever and pleasing designs. We will be forever grateful to the staffs of Dana-Farber Cancer Institute and Brigham and Women's Hospital for their expert care of the highest caliber delivered with humor, compassion, and grace. We are indebted to Eli and his entire family for their generosity and warmth. Our lives will be forever entwined.

ABOUT THE AUTHORS

Judith K. White is the author of *Phrase-a-Day Series for Children in French, Spanish, and English;* and of *Amsterdam Trilogy: The Seventh Etching (2012); The New Worlds of Isabela Calderón* (2014) and *The Rise of Dirck Becker* (forthcoming, 2016). Her careers span linguist, educator, entrepreneur, and non-profit fundraiser. She is the co-founder and former president of Global Child, Inc. Judith can be reached through her website: http://www.judithkwhite.com/

Allen L. White is Vice President and Senior Fellow at Boston-based Tellus Institute. He is an author, educator, and social entrepreneur in the field of global corporate sustainability, while serving as advisor to multi-lateral organizations, foundations, non-profits, and business associations. He is a former Fulbright Scholar in Peru and co-author of *Corporate Environmentalisms in a Global Economy.*

The couple, who live in the Boston area and Jacksonville, Florida, travel and speak frequently in both the United States and abroad.

Made in the USA
Charleston, SC
12 September 2015